Words of praise for *Get Hired Now!*

"I was in the staffing industry for over 18 years in San Francisco, and I wish this book had been in print then. Securing an ideal position is the most difficult of all work, whether jobs are plentiful or scarce. The 28-day program Hayden and Traditi have created is a sure-fire way to find that ideal job. Job hunters, my best advice to you is to read, believe and follow the program; you will be well rewarded with the job you deserve!" **Judy Litteer**, Former owner, ProServ Temporary Placement

"*Get Hired Now!* is the perfect companion for every new college graduate. It forges the necessary link between getting an education and getting a job. Traditi and Hayden have performed a remarkable service for all job-seekers by making the often confusing and obscure job search process transparent."
David Figuli, President, Higher Education Group

"*Get Hired Now!* is the ultimate example of using power thinking plus positive action to create your ideal career. If you're ready to stop dreaming about a new job and start doing something about it, this book will make it happen."
Caterina Rando, Author, *Learn to Power Think*

"For job seekers everywhere, this book is pure gold. *Get Hired Now!* shares a wealth of secrets for getting the job you really want with the talent you already have. If you want to find the right job in the most effective and efficient way possible, this is the best book for you." **Susan Harrow**, Author, *Sell Yourself Without Selling Your Soul*

"Lucky you! If you're looking for work, you have found the treasure map to quickly discover the perfect job for the 'authentic you' rather than just settling for what shows up. I have used C.J.'s book *Get Clients Now!* with great success, and if I were looking for work, I'd be using *Get Hired Now!* No question."
Ric Giardina, President, The Spirit Employed Company,
Author, *Your Authentic Self: Be Yourself at Work*

"Searching for a job can be an overwhelming and often daunting task. Where do you start? How do you find that great new job without the search consuming you? How do you stay motivated when you feel so frustrated? The thorough and practical set of job search strategies offered by *Get Hired Now!* will help you plan and manage your time, give yourself permission to rest and regroup, and ultimately land the job you want."
Leslie Salyer, Vice President, Knowledge Management & Communications, Express Scripts, Inc.

"Losing your job can be a frightening and lonely experience. Isn't the best recovery plan to move yourself through this life experience as quickly as possible? Why not grab your new-job-getting task by its figurative collar and take it on with full vigor and passion? *Get Hired Now!* offers you a robust plan to land on your feet in only 28 days. It's a sprint, a dash and there you are! So, be sure to reach out to people who are a positive influence, tell yourself each and every day that you can and will do this, take the authors up on their offer to 'get hired now' and then look forward with gusto to celebrating your success, your new job."

Laura Halpin, CSP, Vice President, McCall Staffing Services

"Successful people achieve in life because they take responsibility for their careers, decide what they want, and make a game plan to get there. *Get Hired Now!* is a blueprint for doing exactly that. It's a step-by-step guide for breaking through barriers to get the job you want, despite the odds."

Pamela Boucher Gilberd, Author,
The Eleven Commandments of Wildly Successful Women

"Finally! A book that not only tells it like it is in the job-hunting world, but lays out a road map of exactly how to uncover that elusive job opening. It's written in a very 'coach-like' manner, providing plenty of opportunity for a coach to help a client work through any roadblocks they might have or for a job seeker to do plenty of self-reflection. I would recommend this book to anyone seeking a new position or to any coach serious about helping clients succeed in their job hunting effort!"

Michael J. Beck, President & Executive Coach, Exceptional Leadership, Inc.

"C. J. Hayden is the unquestioned master when it comes to tricky issues like job hunting and client-finding. Yes, you can live your dream and with C. J.'s work in *Get Hired Now!* you can turn that dream into a lucrative, paying job."

Suzanne Falter-Barns, Author, *How Much Joy Can You Stand?* and *Living Your Joy*

"In a world where a 'job for life' is a thing of the past, you could wish for no better guides than Hayden and Traditi. In this groundbreaking and highly practical book they provide the intelligent reader with a superior game plan for winning the perfect job. *Get Hired Now!* is filled with clear, reliable advice and proven techniques for succeeding in a tough market. Buy this book today, read it at once, and put its wisdom into practice as soon as you can."

Professor **Tom Lambert**, CEO, International Centre for
Consulting Excellence, Author, *High Income Consulting*

"There are key concepts to know when you are ready to find the ideal job. *Get Hired Now!* will give you the principles to start your job search off on the right foot, stay organized, and sustain a positive attitude. If you are ready to explode your life, then I recommend you purchase this book immediately."

Ken D. Foster, CEO, Shared Vision Network, Author, *Ask and You Will Succeed*

"Employment experts C. J. Hayden and Frank Traditi have written a gem of a book which aids the job-seeker in finding their dream job. *Get Hired Now!* is a very specific and focused 28-day program. The goals laid out in the text of *Get Hired Now!* will help you to make great progress in finding and getting that dream job that you've always wanted."

Ward Johnson, VP Sales, Assessment.com

"*Get Hired Now!* distills the advice and experience of career coach Frank Traditi into a practical guide to landing that next job. Most importantly Traditi reveals strategy and tactics to help guide the job seeker through the maze of wrong turns to a job that is rewarding—from all perspectives."

Owen Jones, President and Owner, Colorado Careers

"You need only two things in life to succeed—the desire and a plan to get there. Desire comes from within you. The plan lies within the pages of *Get Hired Now!*"

Robin Wise, President and CEO, Junior Achievement Rocky Mountain, Inc.

"This reader-friendly book provides motivational tools for establishing the kind of authentic personal connections that flow naturally into career success. It's like having your own intelligent and wise cheering section."

Lee Glickstein, Author, *Be Heard Now!*
Tap Into Your Inner Speaker and Communicate with Ease

"I have always been a great fan of C.J. Hayden's *Get Clients Now!* and am delighted to see the same principles brought to the challenge of finding a new job. The great strength of *Get Hired Now!* is that it gives any job-seeker a clear framework for taking consistent focused action, and that is the best way to achieve any goal. What's more, the plan of action will be tailor-made for the individual's temperament and preferences."

Mark Forster, Author, *Get Everything Done and Still Have Time to Play*

"*Get Hired Now!* is packed with powerful and uplifting strategies to help you take action and stay focused on landing that ideal job. You do have a choice—you can invest thousands of hours and dollars searching for answers or you can buy this book Now!"

Rich Fettke, MCC, Author of *Extreme Success*

"C.J. Hayden always amazes me with her contributions to the working world. She knows how to succeed and makes certain others will too. For career coaches, *Get Hired Now!* is a must. As the founder of CertifiedCareerCoaches.com and a certified career coach myself, I see this book as an essential tool for every coach who works with job-seeking clients.

In *Get Hired Now!,* Hayden and Traditi have created a valuable resource for job seekers and career coaches alike. The book focuses in detail on each stage of the job searching process and provides step-by-step instructions on how to develop and implement a 28-day program that delivers results. Serious job seekers will find great value in this book just by reading the table of contents! If you're a career coach, I highly recommend adding *Get Hired Now!* to your resource library."

Maria E. Hebda, Founder, CertifiedCareerCoaches.com

GET HIRED NOW!™

GET HIRED NOW!™

A 28-Day Program for Landing the Job You Want

C.J. Hayden and Frank Traditi

Bay Tree Publishing
Berkeley, CA

Bay Tree books may be purchased for business or promotional use or for special sales. Please call 510.526.2916 or e-mail: orders@baytreepublish.com.

Design by Twin Engine
Composition by BookMatters, Berkeley
Copyedited by TypoSuction (Jim Norrena)

Library of Congress Cataloging-in-Publication Data

Hayden, C. J.
   Get hired now! : a 28-day program for landing the job you want / by C. J. Hayden and Frank Traditi.—1st ed.
      p.   cm.
   ISBN 0-9720021-3-8
   1. Job hunting—Handbooks, manuals, etc.   2. Career development—Handbooks, manuals, etc.   I. Traditi, Frank.
   II. Title.
HF5382.7.H396 2005
650.14—dc22   2004023528

First Edition

Contents

To all the gracious people who went out of their way
to help us with our careers.

Foreword

For more than twenty years I've worked with people in career transition—professionals, managers, executives, and others. Throughout this time, if I've learned anything at all, it's that people need a plan and a process by which to manage their job search. If they can find a plan that works for them, and if they can keep themselves motivated during their search, the results can be phenomenal! I've worked with clients who have landed new jobs—the kind never imagined, not even in their wildest dreams—largely because of their newfound ability to effectively plan and manage their search campaigns.

At no time in our past has the need for a plan and a process been more critical than it is today. The employment market we're faced with is unbelievably complex, jobs can be difficult to find, the competition is fierce, and it can be extremely difficult to keep oneself on-track when it's so easy to get frustrated and lost in the process. Should you spend your time networking, posting your résumé to job search sites, responding to online and/or print advertisements, contacting recruiters, or some other approach taken from this list of seemingly endless possibilities? How do you know how and where to proceed in your search campaign when today's options are virtually unlimited?

Well, C. J. Hayden and Frank Traditi have taken the mystery and uncertainty out of the job search process, eliminated the confusion, and created the path to job search success with their one-of-a-kind job search system that truly can work for you! Using a step-by-step plan with prescribed daily activities, their 28-day program for conducting a successful job search is like none I've ever seen. The comprehensiveness of the program is phenomenal, yet it's easy to understand and follow. No longer do you have to muddle through your search alone; rather, you can now follow their program to identify your goals, develop your search competencies, create an effective search program, and launch your successful search campaign. What's more, the tools, exercises, and activities included in the book are all extremely valuable in helping you chart your course for effective forward movement.

Whether you're a job-seeker looking for your next opportunity or a career coach or counselor looking for new tools to help you help your clients, this book will be of great value to you. In particular, job-seekers can benefit in so many ways. You'll:

- Accelerate your job search, get more interviews, and find a new position faster and easier.
- Better understand your career goals and objectives, as well as the necessary strategies to achieve them.
- Identify the appropriate job search channels that will yield the most opportunities and save valuable time by eliminating unproductive leads.
- Master the intricacies of truly effective networking and discover how to make use of your contacts to open new doors.
- Learn how to take charge of your search campaign, stay in control, and achieve your desired results.
- Stay focused, motivated, and on-track throughout your entire search.

In short, you will succeed!

Wendy S. Enelow, CCM, MRW, JCTC, CPRW
Founder and past president, Career Masters Institute
Author of more than twenty books on résumé writing,
interviewing, job search, and career marketing

Acknowledgments

We wish to extend our heartfelt thanks to everyone who made this book possible:

Our spouses, Lisa Traditi and "Friendly Dave" Herninko, whose unconditional support and love sustained us through all difficulties.

Our animal companions, Corky, KimChee, and Seabiscuit, who soothed our overworked brains with their affection, playfulness, and loud snoring.

Our clients who teach us new tricks every day.

Our licensees who helped to test and refine this program, particularly Bev Lutz and Nona Haller, whose early contributions got this project off the ground.

Our virtual assistant Angee Robertson and C. J.'s assistant Annelise Zamula, without whose aid we would never have found the time to write.

All the job seekers who bravely contributed their job search stories, and the coaches and consultants who gave generously of their time and ideas.

Our publisher, David Cole, who became a true partner in bringing this book to life.

Our graphic designer Barbara McDonald for her superb illustrations and unfailing humor.

Steven Van Yoder, author of *Get Slightly Famous,* for his expert assistance in helping us get the word out.

Frank's parents, and in-laws Peggy and Paul, for their positive thoughts and encouraging words.

The special people (and places) who supported us in countless ways: Michael

Beck, Breeze Carlile, Wendy Enelow, Lyn Farrugia, Kathy Hagenbuch, Hilton Johnson, Steve Luther, Bill McGee, Gordon Miller, Caterina Rando, Becca Robinson, Leslie Salyer, Laura Whitworth, Mike Wood and the Professional Network Group, the Tuesday evening Weight Watchers group, the staff at Barotz Dental, Frank's cycling buddies, the gang at Come 'n' Get It, the Sunset Girls, and the majestic campgrounds of Colorado and quiet paths of Golden Gate Park, which provided each of us the perfect setting for writing much of this book.

Introduction

Change is the law of life. And those who look
only to the past or the present are certain to
miss the future.

— JOHN F. KENNEDY

The average working adult will change jobs ten times over his or her lifetime.
Given that average, you can expect to be looking for work about once every
four years. Isn't it time you had a system for finding a job?

Get Hired Now! is a complete job search system for the job-seeker in any field.
This book contains a 28-day program for coaching yourself to job search success. It has everything you need to get your job search unstuck, make the best
use of your time and energy, stay motivated in the face of rejection, and land
the job you want.

Who Should Use This Book

If you were recently laid off, fired, or had your contract terminated, the 28-day
program will help you immediately get on the fast track to finding a new job.

If you have been looking for work too long and you're feeling lost or stuck,
our unique system will help you find where your job search is blocked and determine exactly what to do about it.

Or perhaps you are planning a major life transition, such as graduating from
college, returning to the workforce after an absence, or contemplating a career

change. Our program will help you get into action now while you still have time to explore your options when under less pressure.

It doesn't matter if you are an entry-level worker or a top executive, an administrative assistant, an engineer, or a sales manager. This program will work for anyone seeking a job because each person will use the program differently.

Get Hired Now! is for anyone actively seeking a new job or a career change. If you are ready to do something about your job search tomorrow morning, this book is for you.

When to Use This Book

Alert: if you are in a contemplative phase of exploring your career goals and desires through self-examination, inner dialogue, and other solo exercises, our program will not be a good choice for you—yet. This is a program of action and it will only be valuable if you act. Once you are ready to begin interacting with the outside world to make your transition, come back to us. Our program will help you then.

Also, if you are choosing a career from scratch, whether it's your first or your fourth, you'll need help outside this book to do so. *Get Hired Now!* is a program for job-seeking rather than a guide to choosing a career. But if you have at least a general idea of the type of work you want to do and in which industry, we think our program will help you find it, even if you don't yet know what that job is called.

How to Use This Book

Get Hired Now! uses a cookbook model to help you create a job-search action plan. First you will discover where on the Job Search Pyramid your current diet of activities may be out of balance. Next we will help you identify the Success Ingredients that may be missing from your job search efforts. Then you will choose from our Action Plan Menu the specific courses of action you will take. We provide detailed "recipes" for the job search techniques we suggest to help you successfully implement your plan. This road-tested system for marketing yourself as a job-seeker is based on the *Get Clients Now!*™ program first introduced by C. J. Hayden in 1995.

You will get the most value from this book if you commit from the outset to completing the exercises as you go. Just reading the information we've presented here will be helpful, but where job search is concerned, more learning is rarely enough to do the trick. You need to choose a direction, take action, and keep moving forward in order to succeed.

Once your job search action plan is designed, the 28-day program will put your strategy into action immediately. You can use the program quite successfully by yourself, or to make it even more powerful, team up with a job search buddy, job club, or career coach.

For additional resources on any of the topics discussed in the book, or to find a buddy, club, or coach to help you work the program, please visit our web site at www.gethirednow.com. Our free newsletter and online message board will connect you with other job-seekers and keep you up to date on the latest job search techniques.

C. J. Hayden, MCC
San Francisco, California

Frank Traditi
Highlands Ranch, Colorado

Whenever you are asked if you can do a job, tell 'em, "Certainly I can!" Then get busy and find out how to do it.

—THEODORE ROOSEVELT

PART ONE

THE SYSTEM

CHAPTER 1

What Really Works?

Effective Job Search Approaches

To know the road ahead,
ask those coming back.

— CHINESE PROVERB

How People Find Jobs

Finding a job is all about people. It's the people you know, people you meet, and people you locate who have information, who will inevitably help you get a job. Sending out your résumé to hundreds of companies won't work; neither will it work to sit by the phone waiting for it to ring. You have to find and connect with the people who will ultimately pave your way to getting hired.

There are literally millions of résumés sitting on managers' desks right now that are headed for the reject pile or the wastebasket. Many companies receive from 200 to as many as 10,000 résumés a month. How will you and what you have to offer stand out in that sea of paper and e-mail?

Surveys estimate that seventy-four to eighty-five percent of available jobs are never even advertised. If you limit your job search activities to finding and applying for advertised positions, you're missing many more possibilities than you are finding. How can you find these unadvertised jobs?

Internet job boards are rarely much help. Whether you use them to seek out job postings or to post your résumé, only two to four percent of job-seekers find a job using one of these services.

Finding the right opportunities, getting a company to invite you in for an interview, and then having to compete with so many other candidates for the same job appears to be a daunting task. So how do job-seekers find open positions and eventually get hired? Ask any successful job-seeker that question and here is what you'll hear: "my network," "referrals," "a lead from someone inside the company," "word of mouth," and "contacting people."

Perhaps you already knew those answers. So why don't you have a job yet? If you're like most first-time users of the *Get Hired Now!* system, one or all of the reasons below will sound familiar:

- **You don't know where to start.** Finding the right job seems like an overwhelming task. There are either too many job listings to sort through, or you can't find any opportunities that seem to fit. You make a few stabs at job-hunting but you get nowhere. Interviews aren't coming your way; nobody is calling you back, so you end up feeling frustrated and do little else.

- **There are too many things to do.** You realize that you need to increase your network, but you think your résumé isn't quite good enough, so you work on that. You know that contacting potential hiring managers is important, but it's easier to look at the help wanted ads in the paper. You question whether all of your time spent in informational interviews will ever be worth it. You don't have a way to prioritize your job search activities and manage your time.

- **It's difficult to stay motivated.** You may know exactly what you need to do, but you avoid doing it. It's much easier to surf the Internet or watch television than go to an association meeting where you might meet the right person who can lead you to a great job opportunity. You've gone weeks or months with few interviews and no job offers. When you get a rejection letter or no response from companies you've contacted, you take it personally. It's easy to blame the economy, lack of job openings, or the time of year.

If any or all of these obstacles have stopped you in your tracks, then you are in good company. Job-seekers rarely fail because there are no job opportunities.

They fail because they don't effectively contact and follow up with the people who can lead them to jobs. This is why the *Get Hired Now!* system works; it provides both a structure and tool kit for taking action to find the people who know about job opportunities—and it helps eliminate the roadblocks.

How Our Program Works

Get Hired Now! breaks down the job search process into a series of simple steps so you will know exactly where and how to start finding a job today. It organizes the steps into a proven system built around three powerful elements: effective job search approaches, an action-oriented, 28-day program, and suggestions for managing the fear, resistance, and procrastination that may hinder your job search. The program shows you how all the pieces of the job search puzzle fit together: what to do, when to do it, and how to measure your results.

Cooking Up Your Own Job Search Program

We think that designing and implementing a successful job search campaign is a lot like cooking a nutritious meal. When you are cooking, you need to decide what's on the menu, shop for ingredients, and make sure your food choices combine to make a healthful diet. In the first five chapters of this book, we are going to guide you to select a regular menu of job search activities, prepare the essential ingredients for job search success, and evaluate your choices to create a balanced job-seeking approach.

When your personal job search action plan is ready for consumption, you'll begin the 28-day program. We'll help you start each day with a specific list of things to do and provide plenty of daily advice for working through internal and external barriers to effective action.

We recommend reading Chapters 1 through 5 in sequence, completing the exercises as you go. When you are ready to begin the 28-day program, start reading Chapter 6, one section per day. Two rest days per week are built into the

Always Looking for the Next Job

Some people say I've been lucky and been in the right place at the right time, but you have to be able to recognize opportunities and be willing to take advantage of them. I worked for an environmental disposal firm straight out of college, picking up hazardous waste throughout a ten-state territory. I was sent to Missouri to clean out a manufacturing facility that was shutting down. There I met the divisional Environmental Health and Safety manager. I strove to do my best for him, and when I left, I gave him my card.

Two weeks later he called and offered me an EHS manager job at a plant in Arkansas. I worked at that plant for three years before they sent me to a smoke school seminar at a power plant where I met several of the plant operators. My husband was looking for a new job, so I asked them if they had any job openings that might fit his desire to be a lineman.

They said no, but they did have an opening for an environmental specialist. I read the job posting and thought I didn't have enough experience to get the job, but that an interview practice session wouldn't hurt. It didn't hurt at all. Two weeks after the interview, I came to work for them at one of their largest coal-fired power plants.

In less than six years from graduating with my bachelor's degree, I've tripled my salary, gotten my master's degree, and am working for one of the largest utilities in the country in a job that I love. Success is a choice, and I continually choose to succeed. Don't ever make assumptions. You may miss a golden opportunity.

Kellee Cook
BATESVILLE, ARKANSAS

program. Chapters 7 through 11 contain our job search recipes. You can use these for reference while you are designing your action plan, or for help in implementing your plan as you go. Each of these chapters covers one stage of the Job Search Pyramid that you will learn about in Chapter 2. You will choose a single stage to focus on during the program and will need to read only the chapter that pertains to the stage you select.

By making this a 28-day program, do we mean you will find a job in twenty-eight days? In some cases, yes. Since 2003, when this program first became available, we have seen many *Get Hired Now!* participants find a job in less than twenty-eight days. But because everyone's situation and starting place will be different, there are no guarantees. You may need to repeat the program for a second twenty-eight days, or a third. That's okay; the program is designed with this intention.

After completing the program, you may choose to repeat the program using the same action plan for another twenty-eight days or begin again starting in Chapter 2 to design a revised plan. Either way, you will continue to benefit from the strategy, focus, and motivation that the system provides.

KEY COMPONENTS OF THE PROGRAM

The *Get Hired Now!* Action Worksheet is the principal planning tool for designing your personal 28-day program. (See the "Completed Action Worksheet" below.) Here are the six key components of the program included on the worksheet:

1. *Job Search Approaches.* The two or three overall strategies you will be using to look for a job during the month of the program. You will choose these later in this chapter.
2. *Pyramid Stage.* The stage of the Job Search Pyramid where you are stuck or need the most work. You will discover this in Chapter 2.
3. *Program Goal.* The specific result you plan to achieve during the 28-day program. You will set this goal in Chapter 3.
4. *Success Ingredients.* The missing ingredients you require to be successful

GET HIRED NOW!™ Action Worksheet

What approaches will you use?

1. NETWORKING & REFERRAL-BUILDING	2. CONTACTING POTENTIAL EMPLOYERS	3. INFORMATIONAL INTERVIEWING	4. EMPLOYING RECRUITERS & AGENCIES	5. SEARCHING SPECIALIZED JOB LISTINGS	6. USING HELP-WANTED ADS
☑	☑	☐	☐	☐	☐

Where are you stuck or lost?

☐ Knowing what you want   ☑ Finding opportunities and contacts

☐ Applying to employers   ☐ Getting interviews   ☐ Landing the job

What is the job you really want? **project manager in the telecommunications industry**

What would that get you? **buy a new car**

What is your goal for this month? **contacts at 10 potential companies**

What will be your reward? **take a long weekend and forget about job hunting**

Success Ingredients	Target Date
1. Ten-second introduction	5/6
2. Networking skills (at 75%)	5/13
3. Target company list (20 companies)	5/20

Daily Actions

1. Appetizer: Complete 1 item each day from my Success Ingredient project list
2. Main Course: Attend 2 networking events each week
3. Main Course: Schedule 2 lunch or coffee meetings each week
4. Main Course: Meet 3 new people from my target companies each week
5. Main Course: Ask for a referral once per day
6. Main Course: Volunteer in my industry once per week
7. Main Course: Research companies in print or on the Internet 1 hour per day
8. Main Course: Review 1 trade publication daily
9. Main Course: Write to 1 person at a target company every day
10. Dessert: Exercise 3 times per week

Special Permission I can stay positive no matter what happens in your job search, which you will create during the program. You will choose these in Chapter 4.

5. *Daily Actions.* Ten specific steps you plan to take on a daily or weekly basis over the next twenty-eight days. You will design these in Chapter 5.

6. *Special Permission.* The permission you will grant yourself to assure success in areas where you failed in the past. You will learn about this in Chapter 5.

Getting Help to Make It Happen

By using this program, you are going to add a new level of focus, strategy, and structure to your job search that will substantially increase your likelihood of success. But you can stack the odds more in your favor by adding some outside help. Here are some of the additional aids that can make your job search more effective and less stressful:

- *Accountability.* Find someone (other than you) to whom you can be accountable. Have that person ask you once or twice a week what you have done so far, and what's next.

- *Perspective.* Get a different point of view on your progress or your challenges. Just hearing your problem restated by another person can give you insight that will help you find a solution. When you are feeling low because you haven't yet reached your goal, it's also great to have someone point out that you are more than halfway there.

- *Support.* It's helpful to have someone else to complain to or celebrate out loud with; someone who cares about your progress. If you are up against a roadblock, grousing about it for a few minutes may be all you need to get back into action. And having someone with whom to share your success can make it much sweeter.

You could use your spouse, partner, best friend, or a co-worker to provide this extra help, but the individuals closest to you may not be the best choice.

You Gotta Have a System

The aspect I like most about the *Get Hired Now!* program is that it is an organized system. The system allowed me to focus on the specific tools I needed to be successful and the actions that would lead me to eventual success. Fear of doing the wrong thing caused me to fail to act in the past. The systematic approach of the program gave me the confidence that my actions were the right actions — no more fear.

I think one of the biggest problems most job-seekers have is working in a start-and-stop mode. They try a few things and when they don't get immediate results, they try something else or put their job search on hold. But you really sabotage yourself that way. Many job search approaches take time and repeated contacts to pay off. If you lose your momentum, leads get cold, people forget about you, and you end up having to start over from scratch.

Using *Get Hired Now!* to decide what I should be doing was as easy as ordering from a menu at my favorite restaurant. It helped me decide on the best actions and most important success ingredients to keep moving forward. When I needed to continue on for a second month, the system allowed me to make simple changes to refocus my efforts. My fear was replaced with confidence and my inactivity was replaced with results because I stayed in action.

Scott Martin
HUNTSVILLE, ALABAMA

The people in your personal life will not always be thrilled to learn you plan to spend more time on your job search, and co-workers may tend to sidetrack you with immediate problems or day-to-day tasks. You may find it more beneficial to look for accountability, perspective, and support from someone with more detachment, yet who clearly understands the importance you are placing on achieving your job search goals. The best way to get this extra advantage is from a job search buddy, job club, or personal coach.

SUPPORT FOR YOUR JOB SEARCH

A job search buddy is a friend or colleague who also wants help to get into action and stay on track with his or her job search. The two of you assist each other in reaching your goals by setting up a regular check-in, with each of you reporting on progress, announcing successes, and stating challenges. The buddy's job is to listen, celebrate, commiserate, and be a brainstorming partner.

Job clubs serve the same function for a group of people who wish to work together. You may be able to find an existing support group for job-seekers through career centers, schools, industry associations, or online communities. You may also discover other support groups with a career focus (sometimes called success teams or action groups) through local periodicals, community organizations, or resource web sites. If you would like to be part of a group in which all members are using the *Get Hired Now!* program, you can connect with a group on our web site www.gethirednow.com. Some groups have a professional leader, while others have each member take turns leading.

You can also hire your own personal coach or life coach—a professional who is trained in assisting people to set and achieve goals. Some coaches specialize in career transition and working with job-seekers. They may call themselves career coaches, job coaches, or career consultants. Ask your friends and colleagues if they have worked with a coach to whom they could refer you, or get a list of coaches who are familiar with this program from the *Get Hired Now!* web site.

Keep in mind that support from a buddy, group, or coach does not have to involve in-person meetings and travel time. Many groups meet via telephone conference lines or live online chats; and your buddy or coach can work with you by phone or e-mail.

What Works and What Doesn't

You've learned that the first secret to finding job opportunities and eventually getting hired is to connect with the people who will help you find the job you want.

Here's the second secret: a successful job search is more like a marketing campaign than it is an actual search. The traditional picture of job-seeking is that you look for open positions that have been posted somewhere and follow a formal application procedure to be considered for them. But if seventy-four to eighty-five percent of positions are never advertised, how effective can this be? And with thousands of job-seekers applying for only those positions that are advertised, the competition can be overwhelming.

While a portion of your job search may be devoted to locating posted positions, the only way to beat the odds and the competition is to actively market yourself and locate positions before they are advertised.

Marketing yourself as a job-seeker means locating the people who can offer or lead you to opportunities and telling them what you are capable of, over and over. You do have to seek them out—you can't wait for them to find you. There are many ways of telling them what you can do—in person, in writing, by phone—but you must tell them. And you have to tell them over and over. No one will remember you if they hear from you only once.

Just as any company selling a product or service works from a strategic marketing plan with proper tactics to put the plan into action, so should you. In this case, you are the product. Finding job opportunities takes a disciplined approach using strategies that are proven to work. "Effective Job Search Approaches" (below)

Effective Job Search Approaches

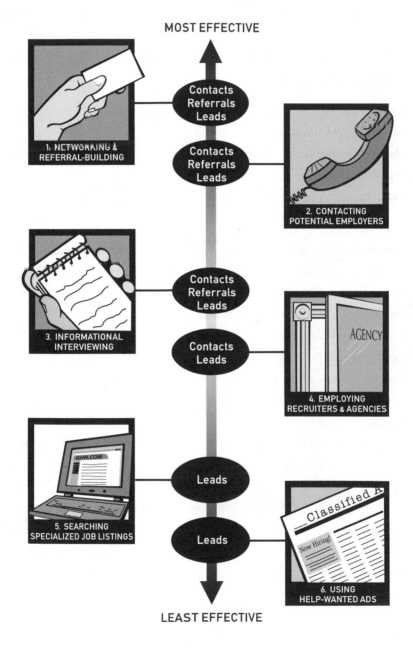

MOST EFFECTIVE

Contacts
Referrals
Leads

1. NETWORKING &
REFERRAL-BUILDING

Contacts
Referrals
Leads

2. CONTACTING
POTENTIAL EMPLOYERS

Contacts
Referrals
Leads

3. INFORMATIONAL
INTERVIEWING

Contacts
Leads

AGENCY

4. EMPLOYING
RECRUITERS & AGENCIES

Leads

GHN.COM

5. SEARCHING
SPECIALIZED JOB LISTINGS

Leads

Classified A

Now Hiring!

6. USING
HELP-WANTED ADS

LEAST EFFECTIVE

illustrates the six approaches from which you can choose to design your job search campaign. All six approaches can work, but the approaches listed at the top are more effective than those at the bottom because of their increased payoff. The payoff for each approach is indicated on the diagram's middle line. Each of the top three approaches can produce:

- **Contacts.** An increased number of people in your network helping you seek out opportunities.
- **Referrals.** Introductions to new people for your network or people with the power to hire you.
- **Leads.** Information about open positions or companies that might have opportunities for you.

Networking and referral-building will provide you with the maximum number of all three payoffs, so that approach is ranked as the most effective. Contacting prospective employers and informational interviewing are about equal in terms of their potential payoff, but contacting employers (once you are ready) is more likely to lead directly to a job.

Employing recruiters and agencies will give you more contacts looking out for you and more leads to pursue, but they are unlikely to refer you to others. Using job listings and want ads can provide you with leads, but no new contacts or referrals.

In any effective job search, you will most likely employ a combination of several approaches, used in varying degrees. In this book, we're going to tell you exactly how to use each approach, including ways to make the less effective approaches work better. The following section defines each of the six job search approaches and gives some examples of how you can use them. The activities listed are samples of what would appear on your daily job-search action menu if you chose that approach. In Chapters 7 through 11, you will find detailed recipes for each one.

APPROACH:
Networking and Referral-Building

Networking is the process of developing relationships with people who can help lead you to job opportunities. When you attend an event of any kind, you may meet hiring managers, job lead sources, and other valuable contacts. When you follow up with the people you meet, you begin building relationships. Your network is a community from which you find out about open positions, companies needing your expertise, and influential people who can facilitate your job search.

Referrals from people who have insight into job opportunities can flow directly from your network. You are creating a word-of-mouth system that will constantly feed you information.

SAMPLE ACTIVITIES FOR NETWORKING AND REFERRAL-BUILDING

- Attending networking events, classes, or workshops
- Lunch or coffee meetings
- Personal calls and letters
- Working as a volunteer or serving on committees
- Participating in an online community
- Attending sporting or cultural events
- Participating in job clubs
- Contacting alumni of your school
- Contacting professional associations
- Reading the trade press
- Writing articles in your field
- Public speaking in your industry or community

The Network Always Works

I had a great job in an empowering environment, making more money than I'd ever made. My branch office revenues were ahead of plan, our office was profitable, and the bonuses were excellent. Then I returned from a two-week vacation in Costa Rica and found out the company had decided to close my branch office. It was a huge shock for all of us.

I've always tried to keep in touch with a network of key people in my field. That very day, I picked up the phone and called several influential contacts in my industry. Within days, potential job opportunities started to come out of the woodwork. Within a week, I had three interviews set up. One position required that I come in to take an assessment prior to any interview. I took the test on a Wednesday, flew to Chicago for an interview on Friday, and had an offer Monday morning for an even better job that the one I was losing.

I can't stress enough the importance of building relationships within your industry. In my twenty-five-year corporate career, I never once secured a job from a newspaper ad, job board, or even a recruiter. A commitment to life-long learning, knowing my strengths, and a strong network were the keys to my corporate success.

Christy Donner
BLUE SPRINGS, MISSOURI

APPROACH:
Contacting Potential Employers

The best way to make contact with potential employers is to place a phone call or send an e-mail, letter, or fax directly to a specific person at a place you wish to work. This approach helps you locate unadvertised job openings you would otherwise not find.

You need to direct your message to an individual, not a company, department, or job title. In your communication, you must demonstrate your ability to solve problems or create opportunities for the organization. The best contacts are executives or individual department managers. Much less effective is contacting an organization's human resources department because someone will typically only respond to you if the company already has an advertised position.

SAMPLE ACTIVITIES FOR CONTACTING POTENTIAL EMPLOYERS

- Warm calls to people you've met or to whom you've been referred
- Cold calls to people you don't know
- Sending personal letters
- Informational interviews
- Sending job proposals that describe how you can help the organization
- Researching potential employers to tailor your approach
- Follow-up calls and letters

Informational Interview Led to a Job

I quit a job I'd had for twenty years as CFO for various entities of a Fortune 500 company. I spent two months trying to decide what career I wanted, exploring work environments, types of work, and what mattered to me personally. One step I took was to interview people who held the jobs I was considering to find out if they were really what I was looking for.

First I spoke to a training manager at a real estate firm who told me the hours wouldn't suit a mother of young children, and that the job prestige wouldn't be nearly what I was accustomed to. Next I interviewed three financial advisors with very different practices from each other. I asked each for half an hour of their time and honored that by sticking to a uniform list of questions I had developed.

By the time I'd interviewed the third one, the first advisor, who was with an independent firm, called and asked to have lunch, saying he might need somebody. I've been working with the independent advisor's firm for two years now and think this may be what I want to do for the rest of my professional working life.

Amy H. Maley, CPA, CFPR
MACON, GEORGIA

APPROACH:
Informational Interviewing

Informational interviewing is like what journalists do to get information for articles they are writing. You learn more about a company or industry in a nonthreatening setting. You set up meetings like these not to interview for a job, but rather to explore your interview subject's industry, company, and opinions on the marketplace while mapping out your next career move.

A word of caution about informational interviewing: don't bait and switch the person with whom you are meeting and try to turn the encounter into a job interview. However, if your interview subject expresses interest in your qualifications and abilities, the door will be open for future discussions about working in the organization.

SAMPLE ACTIVITIES FOR INFORMATIONAL INTERVIEWING

- Researching industries, jobs, and employers
- Warm calls, cold calls, and personal letters to set up meetings
- Meetings with people in any of these categories:
  — top executives
  — line managers
  — salespeople
  — clients and vendors of potential employers
  — recruiters and employment agencies
  — alumni of your school
- Contacting professional associations
- Follow-up calls and letters

APPROACH:
Employing Recruiters and Agencies

The key fact to know about working with recruiters and agencies is that they work for the hiring company, not you. They make their money by filling positions at the organizations that hire them, not by placing you somewhere.

Recruiters for executive, professional, and technical positions tend to work with the upper end of job responsibilities and salaries and can be quite selective of whom they present to their client companies. There are typically one to three other candidates the recruiter recommends who are interviewing for the same job.

Employment agencies work with a wider range of positions and salary levels. They are not as selective about who they present to their clients because they spend less time on any one search, but they still insist on candidates possessing the specific skills the employer specifies for the position. Many agencies use a temporary-to-permanent model wherein an employee is first placed with their client company as a temporary employee at an hourly rate with little or no benefits. Then if the employee performs at or above expectations, an offer for permanent employment might be extended.

SAMPLE ACTIVITIES FOR EMPLOYING RECRUITERS AND AGENCIES

- Registering with selected agencies
- Contacting specialized recruiters
- Sending letters that describe your specific qualifications
- Educating recruiters about your skills
- Consistent follow-up

APPROACH:
Searching Specialized Job Listings

Job listing services and Internet job boards offer a wide array of information about open positions. You'll find positions listed with individual employers, state, county, or provincial employment departments, professional associations and networking groups, job fairs, career centers, and many other resources that serve specific communities.

The Internet is bursting with job listings and your time spent here needs to be managed appropriately. Most postings have a short shelf life and may attract hundreds of applicants. We recommend avoiding the big job boards and only frequenting sites that specialize in your industry, job field, or local community.

SAMPLE ACTIVITIES FOR SEARCHING SPECIALIZED JOB LISTINGS

- Reviewing postings of advertised jobs
- Posting résumé on job boards
- Registering with government-sponsored services
- Visiting career centers, association offices, and other community resources
- Attending job fairs
- Applying for advertised positions
- Using listings as a data source for researching industries or companies

Forget the Net

After twenty years of great performance, I found myself laid off and without a job. I moved across the country to be with family, thinking that the major metropolitan area I was moving to would offer lots of employment opportunities. But I didn't know anyone in this new area. No problem, I thought. I'll just look at those great job search sites on the Internet.

There were lots of listings out there that fit me. I researched the companies, wrote terrific cover letters, and made sure my extensive résumé highlighted what each job description said they needed. The ratio of responses was about ten to one—for every ten résumés, I got one answer. But the answer was always, "Thanks, but no thanks" and "We'll keep your résumé on file." The few times I got a response from a headhunter or company, I found that the job was at a much lower level than the advertisement implied and wouldn't begin to match my skill level.

After I started networking in this area—joined the local chapter of my professional association, became part of a social group, and joined a group of people with the same hobbies as I have—I finally started to get job interviews.

I never once got an interview from a job posting on the Internet.

Cookie Burkhalter
WILMINGTON, DELAWARE

APPROACH:
Using Help-Wanted Ads

This is usually the first place job-seekers look for opportunities in their field of expertise. Unfortunately, many people stop there. Discouraged by the lack of ads that meet their requirements, they start thinking finding a job will be impossible. But the help-wanted ads don't tell the whole story behind the job market. Many companies never advertise open positions because they get plenty of applicants referred by people who already work at the company as well as through the managers' personal networks.

Instead of applying for the positions you see advertised, you will have more success using the classified sections of newspapers and trade publications as research tools to help guide you to organizations and industries that might be hiring but aren't advertising the job you want.

As a general rule, we don't recommend applying for any positions listed in major metropolitan newspapers. However, it is possible to find positions worth your time to apply for advertised in the want ads of smaller or more targeted publications.

SAMPLE ACTIVITIES FOR USING HELP-WANTED ADS

- Reviewing help-wanted ads in selected publications
- Applying for advertised positions
- Proposing a position which isn't advertised
- Approaching similar companies who aren't advertising

Making Your First Selection

After reading this overview of the six possible job search approaches, you probably have some idea of which ones you would like to employ in your *Get Hired Now!* program. Consider which two or three of the approaches you might like to use. Any more than three would be too many to focus on in a twenty-eight-day period, and less than two won't give you enough flexibility.

If you're unsure which approaches might be best for you, keep reading. You'll find more guidance on selecting approaches in Chapter 2.

What If You Want to Start Now?

If you follow the instructions in Chapters 1 through 5 carefully, completing the Action Worksheet as you go, you will end up with a well-considered action plan for your 28-day job search program. This is our suggested approach. Yet we've worked with enough job-seekers to know that you may be eager to get started immediately and may not wish to take the time to follow all the steps. If so, skip forward to the blank Action Worksheet at the end of Chapter 2 and begin completing it now, using the sample completed worksheet in this chapter as a guide.

If you feel comfortable proceeding with the plan created by that simple method, jump directly to Chapter 6 and begin your 28-day program. Will it be as effective as following the steps in the remaining chapters? Probably not. Will it get you into action immediately and produce some results? We think it will. Just by filling out the worksheet, you will have made some specific choices about how to conduct your job search and set up a structure to keep it in motion. This by itself is a move in the right direction.

CHAPTER 2

Where Do You Start?

The Job Search Pyramid

You've got to be careful if you don't know
where you're going because you might not
get there.

— YOGI BERRA

Climbing the Job Search Pyramid

Imagine you were planning to climb a mountain. Before you set out, you would probably study a map of the terrain and talk to other climbers about the best route. The information you gathered would help you decide what climbing techniques you might need to use and what equipment to take along. As you began your climb, you would encounter different conditions at each stage of the journey. In one stretch, you might be able to make good time hiking a well-marked trail on a moderate incline. In another, you might need ropes, a harness, and pitons to inch your way up an unmarked rock face. You would probably spend much more time planning your ascent for the trickiest parts of the climb. While you were on the mountain, most of your climbing effort would be expended on the segments that were the most difficult.

Your job search journey may already feel a lot like climbing a mountain. Yet you may not have realized that some pre-planning could help make it easier. There are some stages of your climb when you won't need a lot of help; in others, you could really use a better map, advice from other climbers, and improved equipment. If you choose one specific stage of your job-seeking climb to focus on, you'll be able to put the extra effort exactly where it is needed.

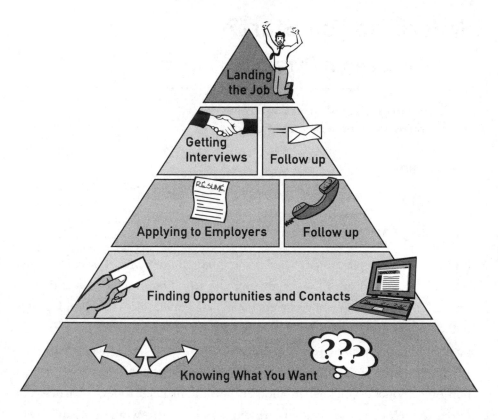

The Job Search Pyramid

While each person's job search is unique, you may be surprised to learn that the general route every job-seeker follows is the same. "The Job Search Pyramid" above provides a map of the journey ahead. The Job Search Pyramid is made up of five separate stages:

1. *Knowing what you want*
2. *Finding opportunities and contacts*
3. *Applying to employers*
4. *Getting interviews*
5. *Landing the job*

There is a series of typical activities that takes place in each stage and these activities can change from person to person or job to job. You'll learn more about these action steps in Chapters 4 and 5. Knowing more about how the Pyramid works will enable you to determine exactly where to focus more time and energy in your job search.

In the *Knowing what you want* stage, you define the type of job for which you are looking. In creating that definition, you are determining which positions, organizations, and industries match your unique and marketable skills and fit with your personal vision for your career. Just like a company targets the market that is best suited for its products, you also must make choices about where your skills, abilities, and desires will fit best.

Once you know what type of job you are seeking, you enter the *Finding opportunities and contacts* stage. In this stage, you look for people who can help your job search and for specific job opportunities—advertised or not. Advertised positions are found through newspapers, trade journals, the Internet, recruiters, agencies, and your personal network. Unadvertised positions are those you discover through networking, referrals, research, and contacting employers directly.

In the *Applying to employers* stage, you make contact with companies regarding the opportunities you have uncovered. The word "apply" isn't meant to suggest you are necessarily filling out applications or sending résumés to human resource departments, although you might be. You also apply for advertised and unadvertised jobs by placing phone calls, writing letters, and scheduling meetings with people who are in a position to hire you. These people may be individual managers, not human resources staff.

In the next stage, *Getting interviews,* you convince organizations to interview you. The interview may be formal or informal; it may take place in person or over the phone. During an interview, you discover an organization's needs and desires for a position and demonstrate how you can meet them. You may have multiple interviews with a number of people from the same organization.

In the Pyramid, you will notice that areas labeled "Follow up" appear in both the applying and interviewing stages. Following up with contacts and opportunities is important at any stage of the job search process, but it is in these two stages that follow-up becomes critical. You'll need to follow up with your referral sources, hiring managers, recruiters, human resources staff, and any other key players. This is how you will keep your job search in constant motion and avoid getting stuck.

In the final *Landing the job* stage you successfully manage your job search from the point of being interviewed to receiving a job offer. When you get an offer, you may need to do some negotiating. When you don't get an offer, you'll want to follow up to find out how you compared to the other candidates and what held the organization back from hiring you.

How Does the Job Search Pyramid Work?

Let's first look at how to use the Pyramid to manage your entire job search from beginning to end. We'll walk through it step by step, just as you might in looking for a job.

Before starting your job search, you need to know what type of job you want to pursue. So you decide to explore several areas, both inside and outside of the industry you've been working in. You research a number of industry trends using the Internet, newspapers, and trade journal articles. You look at job listings to help you understand what challenges these industries currently have and who is hiring.

The word "industry" here and throughout the book could be used to refer to an industry, a job field, or both. You may define the type of work you are looking for by naming an industry such as health care or food service. Or it may make more sense to describe it by naming a job field that exists in multiple industries, such as information technology or accounting. In some cases, you will be able to narrow your definition to include both industry and job field; for example, health care accounting. Think of your industry as being the phrase you use to complete the sentence, "I'm looking for a job in . . ."

You make contact with professional associations that support the industries you are exploring and arrange for some informational interviews with people experienced in those fields. Conversations with people in your current industry point you toward an area where they need people with your experience. But you also discover through researching some specialized job listings that your skills would easily transfer to a completely different industry, which interests you more. You decide to pursue this new career change when looking for your next job. You are ready to graduate from *Knowing what you want* to *Finding contacts and opportunities*.

Now that you've chosen the type of job you want to look for, you begin building a network of people who can help you find specific opportunities. You decide to get involved in one of the associations that serve the industry you are interested in and begin attending their meetings. You start to get acquainted with people employed in the industry.

In your earlier research, you noticed several companies that seem to be excellent job targets. You also identified four or five key people you already know who may be familiar with the industry that interests you. You set up coffee or lunch meetings with these people and ask them about the industry in general, the companies you have some interest in, and where your expertise could fit. You begin to contact the companies that interest you to find out what opportunities exist there. (Note that the word "company" here and elsewhere in the book is meant to indicate any organization that could hire you, including nonprofits, government agencies, universities, neighborhood businesses, and so forth.)

The network you are building also leads you to a couple of recruiters or employment agencies that might be able to connect you with some opportunities. You set up interviews with them to see if their clients have any possibilities for you.

Eventually your persistence in developing your network and making contacts pays off. You begin getting referrals to companies, hiring managers, and other influential people who have information about job opportunities in your field. Through phone calls, e-mails, and letters, you set up meetings or phone appoint-

A Healthful Job Search Diet

Keeping track of all the things you need to do while you are looking for a job can be overwhelming. It feels like what I went through when I was trying to lose weight. I was counting calories, measuring portions, limiting sugar and fat, and recording everything I ate. But then one day I was looking at the USDA Food Guide Pyramid and realized that all I really needed to do was eat five servings of fruits and vegetables every day. If I did only that, I would automatically be eating a more healthful diet and wouldn't be so hungry for all the foods I didn't need.

By applying the same principle to job-seeking, what happens is that you don't have to worry so much about doing everything in the right proportions. You just choose one area where you need to make a change in what you are doing and concentrate on that. As a result, you find yourself doing more of the right things without having to think so much about it. Because you're so busy doing what's right, there's much less opportunity to do something wrong.

Barb Little
MINNEAPOLIS, MINNESOTA

ments to discuss what these people know about the opportunities. While you will continue to expand your network and stay in touch with your contacts as your job search progresses, you are ready to switch your primary focus from *Finding opportunities and contacts* to *Applying to employers*.

Armed with a strong cover letter, a skillfully written résumé, and a telephone script, you begin contacting companies where you believe opportunities exist. In some cases, you apply for open positions that a company has already posted or advertised. These applications may go through a human resources department. Other times, you contact directly the manager of a department or branch about an opportunity you heard about (or guessed at) that may not have been publicized in any way. Sometimes you may be suggesting a position that does not yet exist. Your approach in this case may look much more like a proposal than it does an application.

Some of these contacts take more than one attempt to make a connection, but you don't give up. One of your applications results in scheduling an interview. You realize that you can't disregard other opportunities while pursuing this one interview, so you continue applying for other jobs and following up. At some point, you will probably begin to feel that you are getting pretty good at applying for positions and will have many applications in progress, so you will turn your attention to *Getting interviews*.

To turn your applications into interviews, you consistently follow up. If you first try a phone call and don't get a response, you send an e-mail. You follow up your letters by placing more phone calls. You ask people in your network who they know on the inside of the companies you are applying to and then request personal introductions. Your efforts begin to produce the rewards you seek—more interviews.

In your interviews, you try to uncover the specific challenges your target companies are facing. You describe how your skills and expertise can help them meet those challenges and how you've handled similar problems in the past. You share success stories that demonstrate how you are the right person for the job. You try your best to make a good enough impression to be called back for a second interview or elicit a job offer.

Following up is also important in this stage. After each interview, you write a powerful letter outlining what you discussed and recapping how you can help the company solve its problems. At some point, you notice that you are successfully getting interviews fairly often, but you still haven't gotten the job you want. So you then direct your energy toward *Landing the job.*

In addition to continuing your follow-up on all the possibilities in the works, you investigate how you might be able to improve your chances of getting hired. You rehearse interview scenarios with a friend, learn more about what's happening in your chosen industry, and talk to your network about the companies where you are interviewing.

Your extra effort results in a second interview at your favorite company, and then a job offer, but the salary isn't quite what you had hoped. You respond by reiterating the benefits of hiring you rather than another candidate and request a higher salary. The company makes a counter offer that you accept. You have landed the job you wanted.

One last thing to do before leaving the Job Search Pyramid is to reconnect with anyone who helped you along the way. You thank them for their time and let them know you've landed a great job. You tell them that any time they need assistance they should feel free to call you. These people are still quite important to you; they're in your network. It's almost certain that you'll need to call on them again in the future.

Do I Really Have to Do All That?

The above description of managing your job search from beginning to end may seem familiar to you because you have done this before. If that's the case, we think our system is going to help make your job-seeking journey easier, less stressful, and more effective than it may have been in the past.

Yet if you have never conducted a directed job search before, you may be thinking right now, "This sounds way too hard! I can't do all those things. I don't even know how. Can't I just find a job on the Internet?" Well maybe you can. Perhaps you will be one of the lucky two-to-four percent of job-seekers who actually land a job from a posting on the web—but wouldn't it be better to join the vast majority of seekers who find a job in some other way? And keep in mind, too, that our goal is to help you find not just any job, but the job you really want. That kind of opportunity doesn't often fall into your lap; you have to go looking for it.

The good news is that you don't have to take all the steps the Pyramid illustrates at the same time. In fact, what the *Get Hired Now!* system will teach you is that trying to do everything at once is a sure path to failure. Instead, we're going to show you how to tackle your job search one segment at a time. By focusing your efforts on just one stage of the Pyramid at any particular moment, you'll be able to make your job search manageable and avoid getting overwhelmed.

The Pyramid in a Microscope

Before we guide you to choose a stage of the Pyramid where you will begin (or pick up) your job search, we'd like to show you another function of the Pyramid. We described earlier how to use the Pyramid to manage all your job search activities at once, but you can also use the Pyramid to aid you in landing a particular job opportunity.

Let's say you are a project manager whose specialty is working in small-to-medium software development companies and you have decided to pursue another job in the same field. You begin climbing the Pyramid with the *Knowing what you want* stage already complete, starting with *Finding opportunities and contacts*.

You attend an association meeting and meet a director of software development for a growing software-application company. You spend some time talking with the director about how difficult it is to get project team members to work together, and then exchange business cards with him. The director is now one of your contacts and his company may hold an opportunity.

When you get home, you enter his information into your contact management system and set up an auto-reminder for a follow-up call the next day. (You

His Network Dropped a Job in His Lap

Much of my career has been in sales, so networking is a critical part of my success. In my last job, I networked with my counterpart at a sister company. He and I worked together to develop leads and to service our mutual customers. Then his position was eliminated and he was looking for work in my company, but the opportunity was pulled due to position consolidations. Shortly thereafter, my position was also eliminated.

He and I maintained contact and periodically lunched to exchange ideas and contacts. Eventually he found a position as a general manager. About three months into his new job, he was looking for an experienced operations manager and contacted me to see if I knew anyone for the position. What he didn't know was that I had an extensive operations management background myself. I provided him with my résumé and was immediately in the running.

While I still had to go through the screening and interview process with his company, I landed the job. It goes to show you that networking is a very strong tool for your job search. You need to stay connected with people in your industry because you never know from whom or where an opportunity may arise.

Ken Rosenkrans
LITTLETON, COLORADO

are still in the *Finding opportunities and contacts* stage for this opportunity.) The following day, your reminder to call the director pops up on your computer. You leave a message on his voice mail referring to your conversation at the meeting and reminding him that you are a project management specialist in software development. In your message you suggest the two of you should discuss how you can help his team. You then schedule in your calendar to follow up with a call in two days.

You don't hear back from the director so when your follow-up reminder appears two days later, you call again. This time you reach him, but he is pressed for time. You let him know how interested you are in working for his company. He asks you to send a résumé and says he will get back to you. You have just moved into the *Applying to employers* stage for this opportunity.

You prepare a résumé customized for the specific opportunity you suspect exists at the director's company. You highlight accomplishments that demonstrate your capabilities in handling difficult project teams. You also craft a personal cover letter referring to your discussion at the networking event. In your letter, you summarize your previous experience related to what his organization is going through. You close your letter suggesting that the two of you meet to explore how you can help solve his current project-management challenges. Your letter states that you will call him on a certain day and time, one week from the day you mail it.

A week later, your contact management system alerts you to follow up with the director. This time you reach an executive assistant who screens his calls. You haven't spoken with his assistant before so you try to establish a relationship with her. You ask what role she plays in the company and discover that she has participated on some of the software development teams. You suggest to her that your capabilities would be helpful with some of the challenges with which she is familiar. The assistant is now another contact for you at this company. She takes your number and says the director will call you back.

Your approach and timely follow-up have completed the *Applying to employers* stage for this opportunity, and now it's time to focus on *Getting interviews*.

Three more days go by and still you haven't heard from the director. Once again you call his office. You reach his assistant, and she puts you right through to him. You speak briefly about his challenges and your background and suggest that you meet. He agrees, and you set a date and time for an interview.

During your interview you spend about half the time talking about your qualifications and give specific examples of how you can help the director's organization get a handle on project management. You answer his questions about your ability to handle dysfunctional and non-productive teams. You use the other half of the interview to find out more about the company, his team, and the challenges they are facing. The director appears quite interested in you.

At the end of the interview, you ask what the next step will be. The director tells you he will speak with his boss the vice president about you, and that if the vice president agrees, you will meet him for a second interview. The director says his assistant will call to let you know.

When you get home from the interview, you compose a detailed follow-up letter. Your letter outlines five key points discussed in your interview. For each point, you briefly explain how you would handle that particular challenge or opportunity. Your letter closes with your conviction that you are the right person for the job. You e-mail your letter to the director. This completes the *Getting interviews* stage for this opportunity. Now it's time to work on *Landing the job*.

Over the next week you have several conversations with the assistant. You find out that the director has spoken with the vice president and he has agreed to interview you. But the vice president is a very busy individual and hard to pin down for even a short meeting. After several rounds of exchanging possible times, you finally set a date for a thirty-minute interview.

Your interview with the vice president is quick and to the point. He asks specific questions to determine how well you would work with the group and fit in with the company culture. You are prepared with solid, succinct answers. At

They Said They Weren't Hiring

I found a part-time job while I was looking for new clients for my freelance writing and editing business. I contacted an advertising agency because I liked its *Yellow Pages* ad. It said, "If you're picking an ad agency from the Yellow Pages, we need to talk." The head of writers and producers told me the agency did not hire freelancers, but he added, "Come in anyway and I'll take a look at your portfolio."

I had no agency experience, but the department head mentioned that the agency was thinking of adding a part-time person to help write newsletter articles. I had no desire to take on a full-time job, but I liked the idea of working part-time at the agency to supplement my freelance income. After the interview, I called the department head to ask if the partners had made a decision about adding a part-time copywriter. He told me they had not yet made a decision, "But call me back in two weeks."

After six months of calling him back and getting the same response, I began to feel discouraged and wanted to give up. Then I decided that he would have to give me an outright "No" before I would let him off the hook. I almost dropped the phone when I called again and he told me, "The partners have made a decision to add a part-time copywriter, and we'd like you to come in next week and apply for the job." I applied and was hired. Persistence paid off!

Janet Tilden
OMAHA, NEBRASKA

the end of the interview, you ask his opinion about how your expertise might fit with their needs. He seems positive, but says he'll have to discuss the situation with the director. He promises you will hear back soon.

When you arrive home, you write a personalized follow-up letter to the vice president, recapping the important points of the meeting and stating briefly how you can benefit the company's bottom line. You conclude your letter by expressing your strong desire to work for the company.

After a week with no news, you place a follow-up call to the director. When you don't reach him, you leave a message and when he doesn't call back, you call again. Finally he picks up the phone. He apologizes for the delay in getting back to you and says the company is prepared to make you an offer. He tells you an offer letter is coming in the mail.

A few days later, you get the letter. Nearly everything the company offers is to your satisfaction. However, the salary is lower than what you were expecting. In a follow-up call to the director, you talk over the issue and ask for a five thousand dollar annual increase. Your justification is your confidence that you can hit the ground running in managing the project teams with no upfront training. The director agrees and you settle on a start date. Your next move is to celebrate your new job.

The entire process of landing this job took about six weeks from the time you first met the director to your receipt of the offer letter. This timeframe is not unusual and it could take even longer. You can see from this example that persistent follow-up was crucial to keeping the opportunity alive and your name in front of them at every stage. Often it's persistent and creative follow-up that can set you apart from other job-seekers.

Another important point is that this opportunity was not posted or advertised anywhere. You were able to create a position for yourself at a company that had a particular problem you could solve. Because you took the time to inquire about the company's needs, you were able to uncover a great opportunity that resulted in a new job.

Choosing Where to Focus

The purpose of the Job Search Pyramid is to keep you focused during your job search. When you have a particular opportunity you want to pursue, the Pyramid will let you know what to do next at each step of the way. But if you use the Pyramid to organize your entire job search, you will be able to pursue many opportunities simultaneously. This will vastly increase your chances of finding the job you want more quickly and with less stress. The key to success is narrowing your job-seeking focus to work with just one stage of the Pyramid at a time, even when you are following up on many possibilities.

As you consider your own job search situation, look at each of the five stages of the Pyramid carefully. Then consider these two questions:

Where might you be stuck?

Where might you be lost?

You may have been trying your hand at the job search game for a while. All your efforts to find opportunities, get interviews, and land a job seem to fall flat. Nobody is calling you back. Every interview results in a rejection letter. You look in the paper or on the Internet and jobs in your field are few and far between. Maybe you're not even sure what you want any more. It feels like you're not getting anywhere—you're stuck.

Or maybe you have never had to be proactive about finding work before. Opportunities may have come your way without too much effort on your part. Your field may have had many openings in the past that now seem to have dried up. You may have just graduated from college or a training program and are entering a new and unfamiliar field. Or perhaps you have looked for jobs many times before, but always ended up taking a position that wasn't right for you.

The process of finding the job you really want may have you confused. You're not sure where to start, who to talk to, what your résumé should look like, or which position to pursue. In essence, you're lost. Time passes by and you remain unemployed, underemployed, or unhappy.

In which stage of the Job Search Pyramid do you feel the most stuck or lost? Or to put it another way, where do think your job search needs the most work?

1. *Knowing what you want.* Determining the industry, field, and type of job you are going to pursue.
2. *Finding opportunities and contacts.* Seeking out new people to contact, companies to approach, and positions for which to apply.
3. *Applying to employers.* Applying for the openings you already know about; approaching the people and companies you have already found.
4. *Getting interviews.* Turning your applications and approaches into interviews.
5. *Landing the job.* Converting your interviews into job offers.

Do you already know where you are stuck or lost? If so, skip ahead to the next section, "What Approaches Should You Use?" If not, try asking yourself the following questions:

- Are you newly entering the job market or re-entering after a long absence?
- Are you uncertain what you want to do next?
- Have you been applying for a wide variety of jobs?
- Do you find yourself constantly revising your résumé?
- Are the job opportunities in your field extremely limited?
- Are you thinking of changing careers?

If you answered Yes to the questions above, you probably need to focus on *Knowing what you want.*

Or:

- Are you just beginning your job search?
- Does none of the opportunities you are finding seem right for you?
- Is your personal network very small or nonexistent?
- Are you relying on want ads and the Internet to find open positions?

- If you sat down to contact every lead you currently have, would you be done before it was time for a coffee break?
- Have you already followed up with every one of your contacts or leads within the past thirty days?

If you answered Yes to the questions above, you probably need to focus on *Finding opportunities and contacts*.

Or:

- Do you have a stack of leads and opportunities on which you haven't followed up?
- Have you been in the habit of applying only for posted positions or only by contacting human resource departments?
- Have you applied for positions for which you did not receive a response?
- Are you wondering how to go about pursuing opportunities you've uncovered?
- Do you struggle with composing cover letters or what to say when you phone a prospective employer?
- Do you give up when an employer doesn't respond to your first letter or call?

If you answered Yes to the questions above, you probably need to focus on *Applying to employers*.

Or:

- Have you applied for a number of positions for which you felt well qualified, but didn't get an interview?
- Are you following up consistently on your applications and approaches, but interviews do not result?
- Are you relying on your qualifications alone to get you in the door?
- Do employers refuse to take your call or brush you off when you do get through?

- Are the companies you're approaching telling you they don't have any openings?
- Are you approaching only companies in which you have no contacts?

If you answered Yes to the questions above, you probably need to focus on *Getting interviews.*

Or:

- Are you getting preliminary interviews but neither second interviews nor job offers as a result?
- Do the jobs for which you're being interviewed seem off target or too low level?
- Do you feel awkward or wonder what to say during an interview?
- Do you walk into interviews knowing little or nothing about the company?
- Do you get the feeling your interviews aren't going well?
- Have you gotten job offers that you couldn't take because the salary was too low or there wasn't much opportunity to advance?
- Do you feel your only option is to "do nothing but wait" once an interview is over?

If you answered Yes to the questions above, you probably need to focus on *Landing the job.*

Once you know where you are stuck or lost, it's time to choose where and how to focus your job search efforts for the next twenty-eight days. If you think you need work in more than one stage, start with the first in the sequence. For example, if you feel lost or stuck on both *Getting interviews* and *Landing the job,* choose *Getting interviews.*

If you aren't sure where to start, begin with *Knowing what you want.* If that's not truly where the problem is, you will find out soon enough and move forward to the right stage anyway. Just be sure at this point to pick only one.

What Approaches Should You Use?

Once you have chosen a stage of the Pyramid upon which to focus, the next step toward designing your own personal *Get Hired Now!* program is to determine which of the job search approaches discussed in Chapter 1 you are going to use for your action plan. The following chart illustrates which approaches are most appropriate to use during each stage.

If you chose . . .	You should use the approaches
Knowing what you want	1. Networking and referral-building 2. Informational interviewing 3. Searching specialized job listings 4. Using help-wanted ads
Finding opportunities and contacts	1. Networking and referral-building 2. Contacting potential employers 3. Informational interviewing 4. Employing recruiters and agencies 5. Searching specialized job listings 6. Using help-wanted ads
Applying to employers	1. Networking and referral building 2. Contacting potential employers 3. Informational interviewing
Getting interviews	1. Networking and referral-building 2. Contacting potential employers 3. Informational interviewing 4. Employing recruiters and agencies
Landing the job	1. Networking and referral-building 2. Contacting potential employers 3. Informational interviewing 4. Employing recruiters and agencies

Just Tell Everybody

I had been a stay-at-home mom and decided to return to work outside the home. To prepare, I took a job search course at the local university. The bottom line, they told me, was to tell everyone I knew that I was looking for work, ask if they knew of anyone who would need my services, and if not, would they keep me in mind and keep an ear open for possibilities for me.

The job market at the time was very depressed. But the second person I talked to referred me to a friend who he thought was looking for a secretary. I knew I was no secretary, but this was a way to get into one of the best employers in town. My contact willingly called, gave me a good reference, and I got an appointment to meet with his friend.

I got a wonderful job as a dispatcher of truck drivers in a large national trucking company. Who knew that geography class I thought was so useless in high school would pay off!

Judy Granius
GREEN BAY, WISCONSIN

The approaches recommended for each stage are listed from most to least effective. Networking and referral-building is considered to be the most effective approach overall, regardless of which stage you are in. While any of the approaches listed for your stage will work, the ones listed first in each case are most likely to produce the desired result with the least struggle. It's a good idea to employ the most effective approaches unless there is a specific reason to doubt a particular approach will work for you.

The way each approach is used will differ depending upon the stage you are in. For example, informational interviewing in the *Knowing what you want* stage could help you find out what type of jobs are available in an industry that interests you. In the *Landing the job* stage, informational interviewing could be used to discover more about the current issues of a company to which you're applying. You will find out all about how to use the appropriate approaches for each stage later in Part Two of this book.

Your task now, though, is to choose which two or three job search approaches are the best ones for your situation. Review the approaches you thought about choosing in Chapter 1 and compare them to the appropriate approaches for the stage of the Pyramid on which you're working. Choosing specific approaches to use consistently is one of the most important ways the program will help you to focus your efforts.

For most stages you should be able to fairly easily limit your choice of approaches to two or three. But if you're working on *Finding opportunities and contacts,* you have six different approaches from which to choose. You could simply pick the first three approaches—all of which help you find contacts and referrals, as well as leads to specific opportunities—and that would be just fine. But you may also wish to include one of the last three approaches. These approaches emphasize generating job leads rather than making personal contacts. They can be particularly useful in several situations:

- You are conducting a long-distance job search
- Your job search must be highly confidential
- You are entering a new industry or field in which you have almost no contacts
- The time you have available to conduct your job search is limited to outside normal business hours

- You are so uncomfortable when speaking with strangers that you find it quite difficult to call people you do not know

If you need to use one of the lead-generating approaches to make your job search more effective, our suggestion is to pick just one of the last three approaches and combine it with two of the first three listed. For example, you might choose Networking and Referral-Building, Contacting Potential Employers, and Employing Recruiters and Agencies.

Don't worry that you will miss opportunities if you don't use all six job search approaches at once. The fact is that you can't use all six at once—at least not effectively. By concentrating your efforts on a carefully chosen set of activities for the next twenty-eight days, you are going to dramatically increase your chances of successfully landing a job.

Filling Out the Action Worksheet

With your two or three job search approaches chosen, you are ready to begin filling out your Action Worksheet. A blank worksheet is provided below. Because you may wish to make changes to your worksheet later or repeat the program after the initial twenty-eight days, make an enlarged photocopy of the blank worksheet, or download a copy from our web site at www.gethirednow .com.

Make your first entries on the worksheet now. Check the boxes that correspond to the job search approaches you will be using and the stage of the Pyramid where you need the most work. Now let's go onto the next step: setting your job search program goal.

Are You Looking for a Shortcut?

In the next three chapters, we'll help you choose a specific goal for the twenty-eight days of your job search program, identify what are the missing ingredients you need for success, and select daily activities to carry forward your job search.

GET HIRED NOW!™ Action Worksheet

What approaches will you use?

1. NETWORKING & REFERRAL-BUILDING	2. CONTACTING POTENTIAL EMPLOYERS	3. INFORMATIONAL INTERVIEWING	4. EMPLOYING RECRUITERS & AGENCIES	5. SEARCHING SPECIALIZED JOB LISTINGS	6. USING HELP-WANTED ADS
☐	☐	☐	☐	☐	☐

Where are you stuck or lost?

☐ Knowing what you want   ☐ Finding opportunities and contacts

☐ Applying to employers   ☐ Getting interviews   ☐ Landing the job

What is the job you really want? _____

What would that get you? _____

What is your goal for this month? _____

What will be your reward? _____

Success Ingredients   Target Date

1. _____   _____

2. _____   _____

3. _____   _____

Daily Actions

1. _____

2. _____

3. _____

4. _____

5. _____

6. _____

7. _____

8. _____

9. _____

10. _____

Special Permission _____

If you want to get started with the 28-day program sooner and feel you don't need all the help those chapters would provide, you can from here take a short-cut up the Job Search Pyramid. As with most shortcuts, there is a possibility you might get lost if you don't follow the main trail. But if saving time now is more important to you than following the safest route, read the sections "Setting Your Goal for the Program" in Chapter 3, "Shopping for Success Ingredients" in Chapter 4, and "How to Make the Best Selections" in Chapter 5. These sections will quickly give you the essence of what you need to begin the 28-day program in Chapter 6.

CHAPTER 3

Where Are You Headed?

Setting Your Immediate Job Search Goal

The greater danger for most of us is not that
our aim is too high and we miss it, but that it
is too low . . . and we reach it.

— MICHELANGELO

How Having a Goal Will Help You

In this chapter, you are going to set your job search goal for the twenty-eight days of the *Get Hired Now!* program. We will be using goal-setting techniques many times throughout this program, so let's take a moment to examine our core philosophy about goals:

1. Set a goal that will stretch you, but that you believe is realistic.
2. Try your best to meet it.
3. When your goal becomes unrealistic, change it.
4. Reward yourself for effort, not just results.

The reward is a key element of the process. Job-seeking is unpredictable. Sometimes you do everything exactly right and still don't get the results you want when you want them. If you reward yourself only when you get results, all the challenging work that led up to the result often gets discounted. And in the meantime, you feel as though you aren't getting anywhere.

Get into the habit of rewarding yourself for effort, regardless of your results. To do this consistently, you will always need a goal. If you decide, for example, that you will make ten follow-up calls on Monday, and you make them, you deserve some acknowledgment even if none of those people agrees to interview you. If you hadn't set a goal for the day, you would have nothing to reward yourself for, and no cushion for the disappointment you may feel.

Setting goals for your job search on a monthly, weekly, and even daily basis can provide you with a number of significant benefits. The first one is an improved focus. Looking at your goals each day will keep them in the forefront of your mind. Knowing that you have only twenty-eight days to achieve the results you want will tighten your focus on job-seeking and help you ignore distractions.

Second, your goals will produce evidence. By regularly measuring your level of effort and comparing it to the results you create, you will get a constant reality check on your progress. You will discover right away if you are not working hard enough or are spending precious job search time on activities like cleaning out your desk drawer. You will also be able to tell when you have done enough and can take a day off without feeling guilty.

Your goals will also provide you with direction. For the next twenty-eight days, you won't need to worry as much about what you should do next to find a job. Your completed Action Worksheet will indicate exactly what to do. Whenever you feel uncertain about your next move, ask yourself, "Which choice (action, decision, and so forth) is more likely to lead me in the direction of my goals?" Often that reminder is all you will need to stay on the right track.

Finally, your goals can help you with motivation. Post your Action Worksheet on the wall where you will constantly see it. Run a contest with yourself to see how early in the day you can complete your job search activities, and then try to beat your own record. Set up a reward for finishing each job search project or reaching a certain percentage mark toward your program goal. Invent a job search game and make up your own rules. The more fun you can have, the easier the next twenty-eight days will be.

What Is a Goal, Anyway?

If you are planning to cook a meal, it's necessary to know if your intended dish is soup or pasta before you begin. A goal is your statement of intention. It is your own personal declaration of what you want, what you plan to focus on, and what you intend to accomplish. Having a goal gives you an immediate destination in your job-seeking journey. Only when you know where you are going can you choose the right path to get you there. And you have to be clear about your destination to know when you have arrived.

Many years ago, some unsung champion of goal-setting came up with the acronym SMART to describe the five important characteristics of a meaningful goal:

Specific. Your goal precisely spells out your desired result.
Measurable. The goal states your target in measurable terms so you will know
   when you have arrived, as well as where you are at any specific moment.
Achievable. A goal is physically possible to accomplish within any defined
   limitations.
Realistic. Your goal can be accomplished within the specified time and with
   available resources.
Timed. There is a calendar date by which you plan to achieve your goal.

Your desired goal for the twenty-eight days of the *Get Hired Now!* program may be to land a job, but it may be premature to set a goal to be hired in one month's time. Your entire job search may take longer than twenty-eight days. To have a realistic goal for the program, you may need to choose a more immediate result to achieve. Here are some examples of SMART goals you might choose to achieve by the end of the program:

- A written job offer in hand
- Clear definition of my desired industry and job
- Contacts at ten companies in my industry
- Four informational interviews
- Thirty new people added to my personal network
- Three job interviews
- Twenty opportunities for which to apply

Set Her Heart on What She Wanted

I was having problems at work and dreaded going back to the office after a great vacation. While I was on the plane back to Seattle, I wrote a list of ideal qualities that would describe my future workplace and job responsibilities. I looked at that list often in the weeks that followed to remind myself of future possibilities.

When I started looking for another position, my list of ideal workplace qualities was essential to finding a job. I applied only to jobs that met at least two of my qualifications. In interviews, I expressed my needs based on my list as opposed to saying only what the employer wanted to hear. In less than three months, I was offered a job—and am amazed that the job truly does reflect my list. Taking action with a clear purpose cut down on the frustration of applying and interviewing for jobs that I wouldn't really want . . . and reduced the amount of time I spent job hunting.

Heidi Hanson
SEATTLE, WASHINGTON

Your program goal will help get you into action. If you have a specific target that must be accomplished by a particular date, you will perform tasks that would otherwise languish on a to-do list. It will also help you measure your effectiveness. If you are moving toward your goal, your actions are effective; if you are not moving toward it, they are ineffective or not effective enough.

Now you're ready to set a goal. As you answer the questions in the next section, write your responses on your Action Worksheet. See "Beginning to Fill Out the Action Worksheet" below.

Setting Your Goal for the Program

The place to start in setting your program goal is to look at where you are ultimately headed. **What is the job you really want?** Answer this question as clearly as you currently can. If you have already completed the *Knowing what you want* stage of the Job Search Pyramid, you should be able to give as your answer the specific job type and industry you have chosen.

If you're still working with that first stage, answer what you do know. For example, you may know you want an accounting job, but not know what type of companies you'll be looking at or what position title you will be seeking. You might know you want to be in the hospitality industry yet remain uncertain which hospitality jobs would be right for you. Or you may want a job as a web designer, but are unclear which industries to pursue. Just start from where you are and write down as much as you can. However you answer, that is the direction in which you are headed.

If you had the job you really want, **what would that get you?** Would it give you something tangible you have always desired, like enough money to take a vacation cruise? Or something you urgently need, like being able to pay the bills on time? Or perhaps an intangible outcome is more important to you, such as peace of mind, or a feeling of success? There's no one correct response here so choose something that is personally exciting, inspiring, or fulfilling. This answer is your motivation.

Now in terms of job-seeking, **what is your goal for this month?** Four interviews? Six networking appointments? Twelve new industry contacts? The measurement of your goal is what will give you the evidence that your program is working (or not).

Remember the SMART goal-setting characteristics in designing your pro-

GET HIRED NOW!™ Action Worksheet

What approaches will you use?

    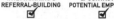

1. NETWORKING & REFERRAL-BUILDING	2. CONTACTING POTENTIAL EMPLOYERS	3. INFORMATIONAL INTERVIEWING	4. EMPLOYING RECRUITERS & AGENCIES	5. SEARCHING SPECIALIZED JOB LISTINGS	6. USING HELP-WANTED ADS
☑	☑	☐	☐	☐	☐

Where are you stuck or lost?

☐ Knowing what you want   ☑ Finding opportunities and contacts

☐ Applying to employers   ☐ Getting interviews   ☐ Landing the job

What is the job you really want? **project manager in the telecommunications industry**

What would that get you? **buy a new car**

What is your goal for this month? **contacts at 10 potential companies**

What will be your reward? **take a long weekend and forget about job hunting**

Success Ingredients   Target Date

1. _____   _____

2. _____   _____

3. _____   _____

Daily Actions

1. _____

2. _____

3. _____

4. _____

5. _____

6. _____

7. _____

8. _____

9. _____

10. _____

Special Permission _____

gram goal. The best goals are those that are measurable targets. "A better job" is not a goal; it is a wish. In order for your goal to help keep you on track it's useful for it to be numeric because we will ask you to measure your progress numerically as you move through the program. However, it will also work for your goal to be a concrete outcome that isn't numeric, such as "a written offer for the job I really want" or "knowing exactly what job and industry I'm looking for."

Your goal should also be a bit of a stretch. Be realistic, but challenge yourself to choose something slightly ambitious.

Finally, if you achieve your goal for the month, **what will be your reward?** Will you buy yourself a present; take some extra time off; have a special dinner? Choose something that will represent success to you and that you will look forward to having earned by the program's conclusion.

Merely by answering the questions above, you will already be on the path to success. It's part of the magic of goal-setting. When you set a specific goal and begin checking your progress against it on a regular basis, your day-to-day activities start to shift in the direction that supports your goal. This shift begins to happen without any conscious effort on your part. And, of course, additional effort in an informed direction can dramatically enhance the process, as you will see in Chapter 4.

Time for a Reality Check

Setting a realistic goal is important to your success. Choosing a target that is too easy to hit won't stretch you. You need to make an extra effort to produce your best results. Yet if you set a goal that is unreasonably high, you will become frustrated and discouraged. So how do you know if your goal is realistic? Here are four different ways of checking the reality of your goal. Choose whichever one you like best, or use all four:

1. *Straight-Face Test.* One way to use this method is to state your goal out loud to an audience in a strong, confident voice. If you can keep a straight

Goals Are the Key to Success

There was a study conducted on students in the 1979 Harvard MBA program. In that year, the students were asked, "Have you set clear, written goals for your future and made plans to accomplish them?" Only three percent of the graduates had written goals and plans; thirteen percent had goals, but they were not in writing; and a whopping eighty-four percent had no specific goals at all!

Ten years later, the members of the class were again interviewed, and the findings, while somewhat predictable, were nonetheless astonishing: The thirteen percent of the students who had goals were earning, on average, twice as much as the eighty-four percent of students who had no goals. And what of the three percent who had clear, written goals? They were earning, on average, ten times as much as the other ninety-seven percent put together.

Mark H. McCormack
AUTHOR, *WHAT THEY DON'T TEACH YOU
AT HARVARD BUSINESS SCHOOL*

face, it's probably realistic. Another way is to ask yourself the question, "Can I really do this?" If the most honest answer you can give yourself is a resounding, "Yes!" it is most likely a realistic goal.

2. *Prior Experience.* If the straight-face method seems too simplistic, review your prior experience with job-seeking. Have you ever had a month during which you reached the level of success implied by your goal? If you

have, no matter how improbable the set of circumstances was the last time, your goal is still realistic. If you did it before, you can do it again. And remembering that your goal is supposed to be a bit of a stretch, if you merely came close to your current goal previously, consider it realistic.

3. **Numerical Analysis.** If you received an inconclusive answer using the first method or are lacking sufficient experience to use the second, try looking at the numbers. Let's say you want to get four interviews this month. How many positions do you think you would need to apply for in order to get four interviews? Eight? Sixteen? Forty? Don't worry if you don't know for sure; just guess.

   However many you think it is, are you aware of so many existing opportunities, and do you have enough time to pursue them? Sit down with your calculator and crunch some numbers. Starting from where you are right now with your existing resources—can you deliver the level of effort needed to reach your stated goal in one month?

4. **Peer Comparison.** Have others you would consider peers accomplished in a month a similar goal in their careers? Ask friends and colleagues with similar career paths how long it took them to accomplish a goal like yours, starting from the same place you are. If someone you know has been able to do it, you have probably set a realistic goal, no matter how unattainable it may seem to you right now.

If any of these tests make you fear that the goal you have set is unrealistic, change it now. There's no fun—and even less value in struggling to meet an impossible goal.

One final hint: if you are just beginning your job search, consider setting a goal based on a certain number of contacts acquired, opportunities located, or meetings scheduled, rather than shooting for a job offer. Remember the six weeks it took our project manager to make his journey up the Job Search Pyramid in the previous chapter. If you are starting from scratch to find opportunities, landing a job in the next twenty-eight days might be out of reach for you.

A Goal That Fits

Looking for a new job can be like having to find the perfect outfit for an event: it seems there are tons of clothes available when you don't need any, but when you're actively looking, nothing is quite right.

I take my time in job searching, completing tasks with baby steps or small goals. Then I give myself rewards to help me continue to feel upbeat and positive about improving my career. I am deeply committed to instant gratification. Therefore I never wait for someone else to say they're impressed by me. I judge all my accomplishments based on my own personal bests and reward myself graciously when I achieve a milestone. For instance, there are few things more painful than having to update my résumé. I even had to take a deep breath after typing the word. Completing my résumé earns me a glass of wine and a take-out meal for the family. No way can I prepare a meal for four after the exhaustion of writing my résumé.

A killer interview affords me a bottle of champagne. Why wait to hear if you've got the job? You know you should get it after that interview, and it's their loss if they don't hire you. If not champagne, perhaps one of those outfits in abundance when you don't really need one.

My actual job goals are just as self-gratifying. I am a mother of two small children, and while I know that for me personally I would not want to be a full-time mom, I don't want to miss a thing my little bundles of joy do. Therefore my job has to allow me to work from home yet still make enough money to afford in-home child-care—and contribute to my obviously expensive shopping and drinking habits.

An important exercise for me has been to realize what things are not that important. One of the nice-to-haves that really isn't necessary for me is a fancy job title. I'm a sales rep and I've realized that I can make more money than my boss, have less responsibility, still work from home, and travel less. I may be giving up career advancement, but my kids are more important right now and I'm not willing to sacrifice my time with them. My biggest goal is to be a good mom and wife . . . and that goal is best served in the job role I have today.

So if you put my job in terms of clothes, I've found a nice fit, a good price tag, and something I can wear for a while. I'm sure my goals will change over time and I'll be out there again looking for that one perfect job. If only I could find it at Nordstrom's

Linda Sweeney
SCOTTSDALE, ARIZONA

Are You Resisting this Process?

Have you read this entire discussion of goal-setting without yet setting a goal? Or did you choose one but tell yourself, "I don't have to set a real goal. This is just an exercise?" Ask yourself why? Or better yet, what is in the way?

Are you afraid of something? What is it? Failing? Succeeding? Annoying someone? Looking silly? Do you have some past negative goal-setting experience that is causing you to avoid setting a goal? Whatever it is that is preventing you from choosing an honest-to-goodness, no kidding, I-can-do-this goal, get it out in the open now. This program will not work for you without a realistic goal.

Write down your fears and concerns; draw or paint them; talk them through with your job search buddy, job club, career/life coach, or a friend. Do whatever it takes to discover what is stopping you and get beyond it. Make a conscious choice to try goal-setting one more time or for the first time. Trust the process. It works.

Locking It In

Great work! Now that you have a goal, find someone to tell it to. If you are working with a buddy, group, or career/life coach, you already have a place to share your goal. If not, tell it to a friend or colleague. Stating goals out loud grants them more reality than just writing them down. And telling someone else what you plan to accomplish creates a sense of accountability on your part to give you an extra push toward that goal.

CHAPTER 4

What's Stopping You?

Selecting Your Success Ingredients

Be bold. If you're going to make an error,
make a doozy. And don't be afraid to hit
the ball.

— BILLIE JEAN KING

What Are the Missing Ingredients?

With a realistic goal in place, you are now ready to take the next step in design-ing the *Get Hired Now!* action plan you will follow for the next month. You will be selecting your Success Ingredients—the missing ingredients you need in order to be successful.

Success Ingredients are the tools, information, or skills needed to address the stuck or lost area you have discovered in your job search. Each stage of the Job Search Pyramid requires a different list of key ingredients for effective job-seeking. If you are working on the *Finding opportunities and contacts* stage, for example, you may need to find some sources for new job listings. But if your focus is on the *Landing the job* stage, this ingredient won't be helpful. You might instead need to work on your interviewing skills.

The place to begin in choosing Success Ingredients is to ask yourself why you are not making progress in your chosen stage of the Pyramid. "Why can't I find opportunities and contacts?" you might ask. Or "Why aren't I getting inter-views?" Your answer may point you to a needed Success Ingredient right away. Stop and think about this: what tools, information, or skills are you missing to

A Little Creativity Can't Hurt

I have been a career coach for several years, and the story I always tell to inspire my clients to do what's necessary to get the job they want comes from my older brother Jim. Jim was in college at a local state school. His career ambition was to follow in our dad's footsteps and become a successful salesman for an industry leader. In his senior year of college, my brother was disappointed to find out that the companies he wanted to work for were not included in his college's list of on-campus recruiters. A quick thinker, and a natural at sales, Jim tapped into his network of fellow students at another more prestigious college in the Boston area where these companies did recruit on campus.

That is how one fine day he found himself in front of a recruiter for the worldwide industry leader in consumer product sales. His interview went well until the recruiter stopped, looked at Jim's résumé a bit closer, then looked at my brother and looked at the résumé again. "Is there something wrong?" Jim asked. "Um, well . . . yes," the answer came. "I see here that you attend Salem State College?" the interviewer puzzled. My brother assured the recruiter that he did go to Salem State and that he would graduate in June.

"So how is it," the inquiry went on, "that I am interviewing you here at Boston College? Did you transfer?" "Oh no," Jim replied. "You see, your company does not recruit at Salem State College and because I want to work for you . . . here I am."

The recruiter was so impressed with my brother's tenacity and creativity that he offered him the job on the spot.

Mary B. Gallagher
HOPKINTON, MA

help you know what you want, find opportunities and contacts, apply to employers, get interviews, or land the job?

Shopping for Success Ingredients

In the design of your *Get Hired Now!* program, you should have at least one, and no more than three, Success Ingredients that you plan to work on over the next month. You may have already thought of some missing ingredients by asking yourself why you are lost or stuck in a particular stage. To help you select just the right ingredients for your plan, see the "Success Ingredient Shopping List" on pages 66–67.

In reviewing the shopping list, it is important that you look at only the section that applies to your chosen job-seeking stage. Don't overwhelm yourself by checking out all the other options. You have already determined exactly where you need to focus right now, so stay with it. If you are ready to move into another stage later in the month—or the next time you use the program—that will be time enough to look at the other possibilities.

Some of the items on the shopping list may be unfamiliar to you. To help you decide which are the best Success Ingredients for you, you may need to refer to the detailed job search recipes in Part Two of this book in which we've provided a chapter describing each stage of the Pyramid. However, don't rush to go there too quickly. You don't need to worry yet about the how-to's of acquiring and employing the ingredients. All you need to do now is choose those you would like to work on first.

USING THE "BLACK-BOX" PRINCIPLE

When an engineer needs to design a new process from scratch, many unknowns can surface. So many, in fact, that if the engineer were to try to answer every necessary question while creating the design, it might become hopelessly bogged down in detail, becoming almost impossible to complete. A handy solution to this obstacle is to enclose each unknown in a black box and design the rest of the process without knowing the details of what goes inside the boxes.

Adopting this idea to design your job search action plan can be a convenient solution to a common problem job-seekers experience. Let's say you are working on the *Knowing what you want stage* and you're pretty sure you will need some "industry networking venues" to help identify your job target. Yet you have no idea what those would be or where to find them. Your lack of information might cause you to say, "I can't choose that; I don't know enough about it," and ignore this important ingredient completely. Or you might go the other direction and try to fill in the gap in your knowledge by chasing after information about networking in your industry, delaying getting started on your action plan until you have some answers.

By using the black-box principle you can avoid both of these wrong turns. You can simply choose "industry networking venues" as something you need and put it on your Success Ingredient list, without knowing yet how you will acquire it. We suggest you do exactly this.

So refer to Part Two of this book only to find definitions for any Success Ingredients you don't recognize and gather just enough information to choose one to three with which you will start. You'll have plenty of opportunities to learn how to accomplish each one once you begin your action plan.

WHICH INGREDIENTS TO CHOOSE

You can choose any of the Success Ingredients listed under your stage of the Job Search Pyramid, but you should look most closely at those designated for the specific job search approaches you chose in Chapter 2.

Each ingredient listed in the "Success Ingredient Shopping List" on pages 66–67 displays an icon to the left that indicates for which of the six job search approaches that ingredient is typically used. (The icons are reviewed for your convenience below.) Some ingredients, such as "ideal job description" or "lead and referral sources" have all of the icons because they are tools that can be used

The Approach Icons

 Networking and Referral-Building

 Informational Interviewing

 Searching Specialized Job Listings

 Contacting Potential Employers

 Employing Recruiters and Agencies

 Using Help-Wanted Ads

with any of the approaches. The others are marked with only those icons representing the approaches that each specific ingredient supports.

For example, under the *Finding opportunities and contacts* stage you'll see "job listing sources" as a Success Ingredient that supports the approaches of Searching Specialized Job Listings and Using Help-Wanted Ads. The ingredient "business cards," on the other hand, is suggested for the approaches of Networking and Referral-Building and Informational Interviewing.

The best way to use the shopping list is as a source of ideas rather than as a prescription. You may already know exactly which ingredients your job search is missing. As you read through the list, keep asking yourself why you can't be or aren't being successful in your lost or stuck area. Place a check mark by each ingredient you suspect might be missing from your job search.

Editing Your Shopping List

If you chose three Success Ingredients or fewer, you can skip to the next section, "Setting Target Completion Dates." If you selected more than three, it's time to prioritize. To ensure you are choosing the most important ingredients,

Success Ingredient Shopping List

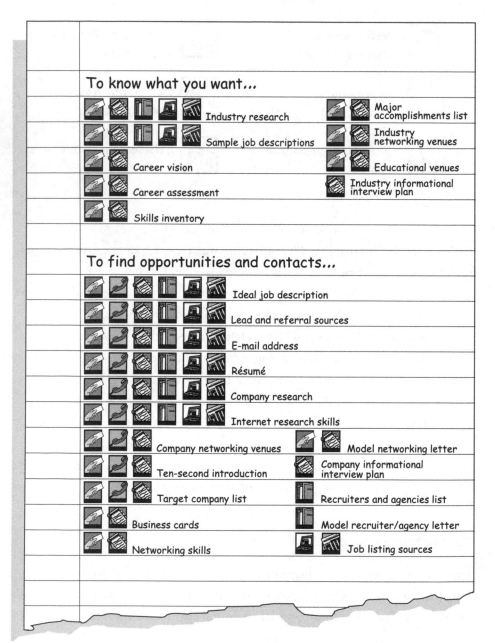

To know what you want...

Industry research   Major accomplishments list

Sample job descriptions   Industry networking venues

Career vision   Educational venues

Career assessment   Industry informational interview plan

Skills inventory

To find opportunities and contacts...

Ideal job description

Lead and referral sources

E-mail address

Résumé

Company research

Internet research skills

Company networking venues   Model networking letter

Ten-second introduction   Company informational interview plan

Target company list   Recruiters and agencies list

Business cards   Model recruiter/agency letter

Networking skills   Job listing sources

To apply to employers...

Hiring manager names

Contact management system

Career success stories

Thirty-second commercial

Electronic résumé

Model follow-up letters

Model cover letter

Job proposal

To get interviews...

Telephone script

Better résumé format

Telephone interview skills

Personal selling skills

Deeper company research

Public-speaking tools

Higher quality leads and referrals

Article-writing tools

To land the job...

Interviewing skills

Better-qualified prospects

Career portfolio

Model closing letter

Employer testimonials

Detailed job proposal

Narrower job target

Negotiating skills

A Pinch of Leads and a Dash of Referrals

Two years ago, I found myself unemployed for the first time in my adult life. I called on my friends, co-workers, and previous customers right away. I let them know that I was available and what I was hoping to find. In less than a month, one of my previous customers called me. He told me that he was now a vice president of software development and offered me the perfect job.

About eighteen months later, unfortunately, a round of re-organizations, project completions, and budget cuts left me unemployed again. I figured what worked once could work again, so I let my network of previous clients know again that I was available. Within a month, a previous client called to tell me that she was managing a consulting firm and offered me the position I have now.

With only one exception, every job I have ever held was found through networking. The last two have come from networking with satisfied clients from my past. I think that people forget to use past clients as lead and referral sources. They make excellent references and great contacts.

Neal Morgan
AURORA, COLORADO

first look at the job search approaches you have decided to use. Since you will be primarily using only those approaches, you can eliminate any ingredients you don't need immediately to implement the approaches you chose.

For example, if you are working on the *Finding opportunities and contacts* stage, but did not choose the approaches Searching Specialized Job Listings or Using Help-Wanted Ads, you should not be selecting "job listing sources" as a Success Ingredient no matter how attractive that sounds. You won't need that ingredient for approaches like Networking and Referral-Building or Informational Interviewing. You have spent quite a bit of effort already in diagnosing your lost or stuck area and picking the appropriate approaches to address it, so don't second-guess yourself now.

If you eliminate those distractions and still have more than three Success Ingredients, ask yourself which three you need first. During your *Get Hired Now!* program month, you will be acquiring or creating the one to three ingredients you choose. As you complete your first choices, you can cross them off the list and start work on others.

Let's say you are focusing on the *Applying to employers* stage and are considering the Success Ingredients "hiring manager names," "contact management system," "thirty-second commercial," and "model cover letter." It would make more sense to begin with the first three because the system will help you manage your list of names and the commercial will help you make the first contact. The cover letter would be more typically used once you have some names on your list and have begun contacting them. As soon as you complete any one of the first three ingredients, you can then start work on the cover letter.

The Success Ingredients you choose don't necessarily need to be completed within a month; you are just deciding to work on them during that time. A thirty-second commercial is something you might knock off in a couple of hours, but developing a career portfolio might take you six weeks from start to finish.

If which ingredients you should choose is still unclear, just pick any three to start. As long as the ingredients are appropriate for your stage of the Job Search

Pyramid and the job search approaches you chose, they will move your job search forward.

Setting Target Completion Dates

It's time to record your Success Ingredients on your Action Worksheet. Look at "Adding Success Ingredients to the Action Worksheet" on page 71. List your chosen ingredients on the corresponding section of your worksheet. Notice that the example shows target completion dates for each ingredient. To do this for your own ingredients, think about what would be a realistic amount of time to allow yourself to complete or acquire each item. It's okay to choose a completion date that is more than a month away as long as you will be working on that ingredient throughout the month.

In setting target dates for your Success Ingredients, use the guidelines introduced in Chapter 3 for realistic goal-setting. Review the "Time for a Reality Check" section if you need a refresher. You should consider both the actual time and the elapsed time needed for completion. If you choose to get business cards printed, it might take you only half an hour to decide how the copy should read. Yet then you will have to find time to go to the print shop and place the order and the shop will need time to print them. So estimate how much elapsed time will be required to get it all done.

If you are uncertain, avoid leaving the target date blank because you must check with the printer. Allowing others to determine your schedule may be a habit that has slowed you down in the past. Try this instead: decide when you would like to have the printed business cards in your hand; then call the print shop and say, "I need to have my business cards ready by the thirty-first. If I get you my copy for typesetting by the twenty-fifth, can you meet that date?" If your request is unreasonable, the printer will indicate so. Then you can negotiate for a new date and change the target date on your worksheet.

The function of having a target date for each Success Ingredient is to get you into action immediately. Once your business cards have a due date, you will make

Adding Success Ingredients to the Action Worksheet

GET HIRED NOW!™ Action Worksheet

What approaches will you use?

1. NETWORKING & REFERRAL-BUILDING	2. CONTACTING POTENTIAL EMPLOYERS	3. INFORMATIONAL INTERVIEWING	4. EMPLOYING RECRUITERS & AGENCIES	5. SEARCHING SPECIALIZED JOB LISTINGS	6. USING HELP-WANTED ADS
☑	☑	☐	☐	☐	☐

Where are you stuck or lost?

☐ Knowing what you want   ☑ Finding opportunities and contacts

☐ Applying to employers   ☐ Getting interviews   ☐ Landing the job

What is the job you really want? __project manager in the telecommunications industry__

What would that get you? __buy a new car__

What is your goal for this month? __contacts at 10 potential companies__

What will be your reward? __take a long weekend and forget about job hunting__

Success Ingredients	Target Date
1. Ten-second introduction	5/6
2. Networking skills (at 75%)	5/13
3. Target company list (20 companies)	5/20

Daily Actions

1. _____
2. _____
3. _____
4. _____
5. _____
6. _____
7. _____
8. _____
9. _____
10. _____

Special Permission _____

a call and say, "This is when I need them," instead of, "When can I have them?" You will immediately be in more control of your job search and much more likely to produce results quickly.

Changing the target date after establishing it is not cheating; it is being realistic. What is the point of beating yourself up because you failed to meet a target date that you had already discovered was impossible? It's preferable to keep your target dates realistic so you can reward yourself for reaching them. This goal-setting technique is particularly important regarding Success Ingredients. Having a good résumé may be crucial for the success of your job search, but the résumé alone will not get you a job. You will need to call, mail, and so forth, before that résumé turns into interviews, and ultimately a job offer. Therefore you need to reward yourself up front for all the effort that went into completing the résumé, before waiting to see its results.

Quantifying Your Success Ingredients

When setting target completion dates for your Success Ingredients, you may be puzzled about what to do if your Success Ingredient is a skill set instead of something tangible. Let's say that you want to improve your networking skills. Pick a target date by which you would like to have this ingredient completed and imagine that you are scoring yourself on a scale of zero to 100 percent. If zero percent means you can't network at all and 100 percent means you are a star networker, what would be your score today? Perhaps twenty-five or fifty percent? Now what would you like your score to be by the target date you chose? That's the answer you would write on your worksheet. For example, "networking skills at 75%—May 13."

You can use this same scoring technique to set targets for other intangible Success Ingredients, like "Internet research skills" or "deeper company research." Just pick your desired completion date and decide the score you would like to achieve by then. If this seems arbitrary, it is. Yet you are the only one who can accurately measure your own progress. The goal and your progress toward it

Small Wins on the Way to Big Rewards

I was looking for contract work in a new town, and really starting from scratch. I had no executive-level contacts, no local network, and no twelve months' salary tucked away in the bank. What I had was a mortgage, a car payment, two cats, and a relentless desire to succeed.

I spent most nights out at dinners, mixers, and networking functions. If there were places to meet people, I was there. On cold, snowy nights when everyone typically is at home in sweats, watching television, and sipping hot chocolate, I was "shaking hands and kissing babies." It was pretty discouraging at times.

I learned, however, that concentrating on how difficult things were didn't make them easier. Focusing on the negatives never made them positive. Instead I started focusing on all that I did have:

- A great house with an office, heat, and a place to sleep.
- My health — perhaps a cliché, but my outlook was brighter because I was healthy.
- Family members that fed me and gave me the leftovers.
- Friends who offered support and their shoulders on which to cry.
- A ski pass! Some days when the phone didn't ring, I headed to the mountains.

I am not a Pollyanna, but I know what works for me. Focusing on small wins helps me stay optimistic and gives me a feeling of accomplishment. Visualizing the big picture of my success provides daily motivation. By the way, my big picture of success is less about money than it is about helping my clients succeed and giving back to my community. That dream's tough to beat!

Susan Grattino
DENVER, COLORADO

have to make sense and feel good to you. That's the only way a goal can work its motivation magic.

Even tangible Success Ingredients might require some quantification in order to be specific enough to serve as a goal. If you chose "target company list," for example, how many companies are enough? Pick a number that would make you feel as though you had satisfied that need for at least a month's time and write it on your worksheet—for example, "target company list—20 companies."

Once you have chosen one to three Success Ingredients, written them on your Action Worksheet, assigned target dates to them, and quantified them in terms of number needed or scores you wish to achieve, you have completed four of the six steps in designing your *Get Hired Now!* program. In Chapter 5 you will be choosing the precise action steps you will take in your job search over the next twenty-eight days.

Here's What To Do:

Choosing from the Action Plan Menu

I find that the harder I work,
the more luck I seem to have.

— THOMAS JEFFERSON

What Is the Secret Formula?

The final and most important piece of designing your own personal *Get Hired Now!* program is to select the specific job-seeking action steps you plan to take on a regular basis over the next month. These are the actions that are going to land you the job you want.

At the beginning of this book, you learned two important secrets for a successful job search: find and connect with the people who can help you and conduct your job search like a marketing campaign. Now we're going to share a third secret with you: choose a set of simple, effective things to do; then do them consistently.

You are about to do exactly this. You are going to choose ten specific actions to take and perform them daily or weekly for the next twenty-eight days. What you choose will be based on the lost or stuck place you uncovered with the Job Search Pyramid, as well as the job search approaches you selected to address that lost or stuck area. These action steps are designed to enable you to connect with the people who can help you. But you need to actually do them in order to find a job.

There is an interesting phenomenon that occurs when you get serious about job-seeking in a focused, consistent way. You begin to get results in unexpected places. The telephone rings and it's a manager you spoke to six weeks ago now expressing a sudden interest in interviewing you. You go to a networking meeting that appears a complete waste of time and run into an important new contact in the elevator while on your way out. You get an exciting referral from someone whose name you don't even recognize. It's almost as if the universe is rewarding you for working so hard.

Don't make the mistake of thinking that these out-of-the-blue opportunities are accidents. There is a direct connection between the level of effort you put into your job search and the results that emerge, even when it seems as though the results are completely unrelated to your efforts.

This phenomenon is so common with people who use the *Get Hired Now!* program that it has a name: the Persistence Effect. If you persist in making ten calls every day, you will get interviews, but they won't all originate from the calls you made. If you consistently attend one networking event per week, job opportunities will appear, but not necessarily from the events you attended. Don't worry about why it works; just know that it works.

The existence of the Persistence Effect can help you enormously in choosing the daily actions for your program because there is one more secret to a successful job search: it doesn't matter so much what you choose as it does *that* you choose.

Picking ten things you can do about your job search—and actually doing them—will break you out of analysis paralysis, give you a plan, and get you into action. Even if you picked the "wrong" ten actions, the Persistence Effect would make this focused activity pay off for you in some way. Would it pay off as well as picking the "right" ten things? Probably not. That's why you are about to choose specific actions that represent the stage of the Pyramid where you are focusing and the job search approaches you already selected.

Ordering from the Action Plan Menu

There are two ways of going about selecting what Daily Actions to include in your *Get Hired Now!* program. One way is to choose from the selections already prepared for you that appear on the "Action Plan Menu" on pages 80–83). The other is to design your own unique actions. Let's look first at how to design your own.

Suppose you are focusing on the *Landing the job* stage and you have chosen Contacting Potential Employers as one of your approaches. How could you use this approach to move toward landing a job? Perhaps you could follow up better by re-contacting people with whom you have already interviewed, but who didn't call you back or make you an offer. The position you interviewed for may still be open or another position may have opened up in the meantime. To turn this into a specific, consistent action, give it a time frame and quantify it—for example, "Contact 2 employers each week who previously didn't hire me."

How do you know how often to do something and how much of it to do? You guess. How much activity do you think will be necessary to achieve the desired result? How much do you have time for? The answer is probably somewhere in the middle. Just know there is no right answer here; it doesn't matter so much what you choose as it does that you choose.

Remember the *Get Hired Now!* goal-setting philosophy:

1. Set a goal that will stretch you but that you believe is realistic.
2. Try your best to meet it.
3. When your goal becomes unrealistic, change it.
4. Reward yourself for effort, not just results.

You're going to use these same principles again in designing your Daily Actions. Pick a time frame and quantity that seem reasonable. Try it out—if it's not working, change it. And reward yourself for what you did, not what you got.

You can choose to perform an action daily, weekly, or several times per week. Daily typically means five days per week, which is the recommended schedule for the *Get Hired Now!* program. The only rule is that all actions must be performed at least weekly because you need to develop consistency in your job search in order for the Persistence Effect to work. While it's okay to change the frequency of your actions once you start the program, it's generally not a good idea

Luck Happens When Preparedness Meets Opportunity

The best jobs I ever had were the result of serendipitous connections and not from a laborious search of the want ads or mailing out lots of résumés.

One job in particular was the result of an impulse. I was on my way to an interview at a big company and stopped for breakfast. While waiting for my order, I looked across the street at another company and remembered that a friend worked there. After eating, I walked across the street and handed a résumé and letter of recommendation to the receptionist.

I didn't really expect any result from that action, but that very afternoon — after a not-so-stellar interview with the first company — a manager at the second company called me. He asked if I would be interested in a job as an hourly professional. I met with him and started immediately, making quite a bit of money.

After a few months, the manager offered me a full-time position at a salary that was beyond my dreams. It was a great job that was very good for my career and I stayed with the company for several years.

And I owe it all to a failed interview, an impulse, and taking time for breakfast.

Lee Hendrickson
SACRAMENTO, CALIFORNIA

to change the actions themselves until you are ready to move forward to the next stage of the Job Search Pyramid.

Now that you know how the process of designing a Daily Action works, take a look at the "Action Plan Menu" below. The menu is divided into three sections:

Appetizers. Actions that will help you to create or acquire Success Ingredients
Main Course. Actions focused directly on seeking a job
Dessert. Actions to help you be more effective and productive in general

You are going to choose a total of ten Daily Actions, either from the menu or of your own design. As with a meal, you will need to balance your selections. The best combination for a satisfying job search banquet is one or two actions from the Appetizer menu, seven or eight entrees from the Main Course section, and one Dessert. This design will create an effective balance between project work (e.g., improving your résumé), job search activities (e.g., calling potential employers), and self-management (e.g., getting enough sleep) in your *Get Hired Now!* action plan.

Start with the Fun Stuff

In a few pages, you will be choosing your Main Course selections—those actions that will directly lead you to the job you want. It's a good bet that the process of making those choices may bring up some fear and resistance for you, so let's start with the fun stuff—Appetizers and Dessert.

Appetizers are action items to move you forward in the process of creating or acquiring your chosen Success Ingredients. By putting one or two Appetizers on your list of Daily Actions, you are making a commitment to do what it takes to get those missing ingredients in place. If you chose only one Success Ingredient, you probably only need one Appetizer. But with two or three ingredients to create, you may want two Appetizers to help you along.

Appetizers: *Choose 1 or 2*

To create success ingredients...

Spend 1 hour each day on my Success Ingredient project
Complete 1 item each day from my Success Ingredient project list
Practice my skills or script once per day
Get feedback from 3 people per week
Read or write every day for 1 hour
Interview 1 person per week
Collect 3 new facts per day
Observe how it's done once per week

Main Course: *Choose 7 or 8*

To know what I want...

Research industries, jobs, or employers 1 hour per day

Review 3 trade publications every week

Meet 10 new people in a potential industry each week

Go to 1 industry networking event per week

Network online 2 hours per week

Schedule 1 lunch or coffee meeting every week

Spend 1 hour each day calling industry contacts

Write 2 new people in a potential industry each day

Contact 1 new industry organization each week

Schedule 1 informational interview each week

Volunteer 2 hours per week in a potential industry

Contact 2 alumni from my school weekly

Ask for a referral every day

Take 1 class or workshop each week

To find opportunities and contacts by networking & referral-building...

Review 1 trade publication daily

Attend 2 networking events each week

 Spend 2 hours per week networking online

Schedule 2 lunch or coffee meetings each week

Call or write 1 new contact per day

Connect with 1 new professional association each week

Volunteer in my industry once per week

Contact 3 alumni from my school weekly

Ask for a referral once per day

Give a referral twice per week

Take a class or workshop each week

Go to 1 community event weekly

Attend 1 job club meeting per week

To find opportunities and contacts by contacting potential employers & informational interviewing...

Research companies in print or on the Internet 1 hour per day

Meet 3 new people from my target companies each week

Spend 2 hours each day making cold or warm calls

Write to 1 person at a target company every day

Canvass for 3 hours per week in areas where I want to work

Schedule 2 informational interviews per week

Spend 1 hour per day surveying people in my industry

To find opportunities and contacts by employing recruiters & agencies...

Spend 2 hours per week researching recruiters or agencies

Register with 1 employment agency per week

Send résumé and cover letter to 2 recruiters each week

Schedule 1 meeting per week with a recruiter

Send a qualifications letter to a recruiter each week

Follow up with recruiters or agencies weekly

To find opportunities and contacts by searching specialized job listings & using help-wanted ads...

Spend 2 hours per week searching for specialized job listings

Visit a career center or job fair once weekly

Register each week with 1 new job listing service

Review help-wanted ads 1 hour per week

Review industry or company job postings 2 hours weekly

Contact 3 companies weekly about positions *not* advertised

To apply to employers...

Research target companies 2 hours per week

Place 3 cold or warm calls to employers daily

Make my follow-up calls first thing every day

E-mail everyone who didn't return my calls each week

Practice daily my 30-second commercial

Send 4 personal introduction letters weekly

Meet twice per week with target company contacts

Ask for referrals to target companies 3 times per week

Apply each day for 2 advertised positions

Propose an unadvertised position twice per week

Ask someone once per week to hand deliver my résumé

Follow up weekly on all applications and proposals

To get interviews...

Research companies where I'm applying for 2 hours weekly

Meet with employer contacts once per week

Ask for referrals to employers twice per week

Attend an industry event once per week

Network online 1 hour per week

Volunteer in a high-visibility position once per week

Speak or write for an industry audience once per week

Follow up on all applications and proposals once per week

Ask for an interview 3 times per week

Return all calls from prospective employers within 1 day

Practice daily my telephone script or phone interview skills

Send a follow-up letter each week to a recruiter

To land the job...

Research companies where I'm interviewing for 2 hours weekly

Meet with an employer contact weekly

Attend a high-visibility event once per week

Request referrals to employers twice weekly

Follow up on all interviews once per week

Get 2 rejections each week

Make 1 challenging phone call every day

Practice negotiating a job offer once per week

Role play a job interview twice per week

Send a detailed job proposal to an employer once per week

Contact 2 employers each week who previously didn't hire me

Talk with one successful job-seeker each week

Dessert: *Choose 1*

To be more effective in everything I do...

Plan my day each morning

Do all my "A-list" tasks first each day

Write in my success journal each evening

Exercise 3 times per week

Get 8 hours of sleep every night

Meditate for ½ hour per day

Schedule a day of fun each week

Review my personal finances each week

Spend ½ hour each day organizing my work space

Visualize daily my perfect job

The Appetizers on the Action Plan Menu are suggested actions from which you can choose, but you can also design your own. Remember that the time frame and quantity are up to you in either case. Here are some ways you can use the Appetizers on the menu:

- *Spend 1 hour each day on my Success Ingredient project.* Good for projects like "lead and referral sources" or "networking venues" that may take a while to ferret out.
- *Complete 1 item each day from my Success Ingredient project list.* Use this for projects such as "contact management system" or "career portfolio," when each project may have a list of many steps to complete.
- *Practice my skills or script once per day.* An excellent choice for ingredients like "telephone script" or "interviewing skills" that require practicing to make progress.
- *Get feedback from 3 people per week.* Appropriate for ingredients such as developing your "major accomplishments list" or improving your "personal selling skills."
- *Read or write for 1 hour every day.* Use this for information-gathering projects like finding "sample job descriptions" or creative work such as developing your "career vision."
- *Interview 1 person per week.* Good for projects such as "company research" or discovering how to find "better-qualified prospects."
- *Collect 3 new facts per day.* Another useful method of quantifying your progress in research or information gathering.
- *Observe how it's done once per week.* A great way to improve your skills in areas like networking or negotiating.

When you have chosen one or two Appetizers, write them down as the first two Daily Actions on your Action Worksheet (see "Adding Daily Actions to the Action Worksheet" on page 89).

Next look at the Dessert selections. The Daily Actions on the Dessert menu are suggested ways in which you can be more effective and productive in everything you do. Choose just one. To make the right choice, ask yourself what is likely to get in the way of your success this month. Have you identified any habits or behaviors that lead to self-sabotage? Is there something you need to do for yourself to perform at your best?

Use these descriptions of the Dessert selections on the Action Plan Menu to help you choose one or design your own:

- *Plan my day each morning.* If you often come to the end of the day and wonder where it went, this Dessert may be a good choice for you. Planning your day in advance will take only five or ten minutes. You could also make your plan the night before.
- *Do all my "A-list" tasks first each day.* Not everything on your personal to-do list is of equal value. Try giving every item on the list a priority of A, B, or C, and then take care of all the A-items first each day.
- *Write in my success journal each evening.* It's easy to get caught up in failures and shortcomings, but every day has successes in it. Start a success journal where you write each day only those things you enjoyed, felt good about accomplishing, or for which you received recognition.
- *Exercise 3 times per week.* If you find that regular exercise provides you more energy, it may be just as important to effective job-seeking as a good résumé.
- *Get 8 hours of sleep every night.* Depriving yourself of sleep is not good time management and will backfire quickly. Not everyone needs eight hours, so substitute the best number for your needs.
- *Meditate for 1/2 hour per day.* Meditation, drawing or painting, listening to music, gardening, and needlework are just a few examples of the many activities that allow for relaxation and quiet reflection. Just plain wool gathering is fine, too. The idea is simply to give your overworked brain a rest.

Factoring in the Rest Cycle

After nearly twenty years of never being out of work, I voluntarily left an executive position ready to make a change. I wasn't sure what I was going to do next, but I was excited about the possibilities. Little did I know what was ahead.

I focused like a laser on what I needed to do to find the right opportunities. I worked at it day and night, sometimes for hours on end. At times I think I was obsessed with how much I could do in a day or week. After about a month at this feverish pace, I was running out of gas. I became tired, bored, and frustrated. Some days I felt like I needed a forklift to carry me from the bedroom to my home office.

It was at this point that I decided to do something about taking care of myself. A few months earlier, I had purchased a road bike. I wanted to give road cycling a try because I had done some mountain biking. I wasn't convinced that I would really care for riding on the road, but I gave it a try anyway. I had no idea that it was the answer to my job search problems.

I made it a point to ride just about every day while I was looking for a job. I increased my mileage each week and really got hooked on it. I was feeling good about getting in shape and I had a renewed outlook on my job search. My energy came back and I had built up the endurance to withstand the hours I needed to put into my search. As a result, my attitude changed and I started getting more opportunities that turned into interviews.

I found that scheduling in the fun stuff actually helped me deal with the stress associated with finding a job. And there were some good side-effects too. I hooked up with a former boss of mine and we did some riding together.

He had just landed a vice president of sales position at a large telecommunications company. Then he needed a sales director to run one of his regions. Guess who got the job?

Frank Traditi
HIGHLANDS RANCH, COLORADO

- ***Schedule a day of fun each week.*** Relaxation takes many forms and you may need some pleasurable activity more than a rest. Scheduling fun time in advance will ensure it happens.
- ***Review my personal finances each week.*** Think of this as a motivational technique. If you know you need to make $500 more this month to make ends meet or improve your lifestyle, it may encourage you to make one more call or write one more letter.
- ***Spend 1/2 hour each day organizing my work space.*** Keeping track of where each contact or opportunity lies during your Job Search Pyramid ascent can be critical to finding a job. Time spent looking for important information that has gone missing is time you don't have available for your job search.
- ***Visualize daily my perfect job.*** This is an established technique for improved achievement. Spend a few minutes each day visualizing yourself succeeding at finding, landing, and ultimately working at your perfect job. You may even want to do this three times a day.

After reading these descriptions you may be tempted to choose more than one Dessert. Yet you do need to leave enough room for the Main Course, so limit yourself to just one. If one of the Desserts on the menu caused you to say, "That would really help me," that's the one to pick. If you have a self-sabotaging habit that none of these Desserts addresses, make up your own to help you start changing that bad habit.

Record your Dessert as the last Daily Action on your Action Worksheet (see "Adding Daily Actions to the Action Worksheet" below).

Time for the Main Course

The Daily Actions in the Main Course section of the menu are activities directly aimed at finding you a job. The Main Course items are grouped into categories that match the stages of the Job Search Pyramid:

- *Knowing what you want*
- *Finding opportunities and contacts*
- *Applying to employers*
- *Getting interviews*
- *Landing the job*

Because the possible activities for *Finding opportunities and contacts* are so varied, that stage is subdivided into four groups, based on the job search approaches each activity uses:

- Networking and Referral-Building
- Contacting Potential Employers and Informational Interviewing
- Employing Recruiters and Agencies
- Searching Specialized Job Listings and Using Help-Wanted Ads

You will be selecting seven or eight Daily Actions from the Main Course menu (or of your own design) to equal a total of ten Daily Actions. The first rule to follow in making your choices is this: don't read the whole list! Look solely at the category that pertains to the Pyramid stage you are working on. If your stage is *Finding opportunities and contacts,* look only at the subgroups relevant to the job search approaches you have chosen.

GET HIRED NOW!™ Action Worksheet

What approaches will you use?

1. NETWORKING & REFERRAL-BUILDING	2. CONTACTING POTENTIAL EMPLOYERS	3. INFORMATIONAL INTERVIEWING	4. EMPLOYING RECRUITERS & AGENCIES	5. SEARCHING SPECIALIZED JOB LISTINGS	6. USING HELP-WANTED ADS
☑	☑	☐	☐	☐	☐

Where are you stuck or lost?

☐ Knowing what you want   ☑ Finding opportunities and contacts

☐ Applying to employers   ☐ Getting interviews   ☐ Landing the job

What is the job you really want? __project manager in the telecommunications industry__

What would that get you? __buy a new car__

What is your goal for this month? __contacts at 10 potential companies__

What will be your reward? __take a long weekend and forget about job hunting__

Success Ingredients	Target Date
1. __Ten-second introduction__	__5/6__
2. __Networking skills (at 75%)__	__5/13__
3. __Target company list (20 companies)__	__5/20__

Daily Actions

1. __Appetizer: Complete 1 item each day from my Success Ingredient project list__

2. __Main Course: Attend 2 networking events each week__

3. __Main Course: Schedule 2 lunch or coffee meetings each week__

4. __Main Course: Meet 3 new people from my target companies each week__

5. __Main Course: Ask for a referral once per day__

6. __Main Course: Volunteer in my industry once per week__

7. __Main Course: Research companies in print or on the Internet 1 hour per day__

8. __Main Course: Review 1 trade publication daily__

9. __Main Course: Write to 1 person at a target company every day__

10. __Dessert: Exercise 3 times per week__

Special Permission __I can stay positive no matter what happens__

Icons that indicate to which of the six job search approaches each activity is related are on the left-hand side of the menu. For a key to the approach icons, refer to Chapter 4. Some actions are only applicable to one approach, while others could relate to several, depending on how they are used.

Here are two different selection methods you might consider:

1. *Just pick 'em.* As you have worked your way through the exercises in this book, you have already done a lot of thinking. You know where you are lost or stuck on the Job Search Pyramid, what job search approaches you plan to use, and which missing ingredients you need to be successful. Maybe you already have enough information to choose from the Daily Actions listed for your Pyramid stage. When you are ready to begin using your selected actions, you can read more about them in the job search recipes in Part Two of the book.

2. *First understand the theory*. Each Daily Action on the list represents an activity that has been proven effective in job-seeking. Sometimes the purpose of an activity will be immediately apparent. It's difficult to mis-understand "apply each day for 2 advertised positions." Yet other activities are subtler. For example, "speak for an industry audience once per week" is listed under *Getting interviews* because this activity will simultaneously increase your visibility and credibility. When a prospective employer either hears you speak or hears about your talk from someone else, it will greatly increase your likelihood of getting in the door.

If you want to understand more about the purpose of the Main Course activities before making your choices, read the specific chapter in Part Two that describes your chosen stage of the Job Search Pyramid. You can skip those sections that relate to job search approaches you chose not to use.

Is one of these methods for selecting Main Course actions more successful than the other? Actually, no—the difference is in you. If you are comfortable shooting from the hip, use the first approach. It's quicker and easier. If you prefer committing to a course of action only when you have thoroughly evaluated your choices, usethe second approach. It will increase your level of commitment to the actions you choose.

How to Make the Best Selections

Here are the questions you should ask yourself to make the best possible choices from the Main Course menu:

- **Where are you lost or stuck?** You already know on which stage of the Pyramid you need to focus, so choose only Main Course items that pertain to that stage. If you can't find seven or eight actions on the list that seem appropriate for your stage, take one or two from the stage just before or after it, but don't skip around. Choosing actions from several different stages will dilute your job search efforts and sabotage the Persistence Effect.
- **Which job search approaches are you using?** The icons shown for each action indicate to which approaches they relate. Look for the actions that match the approaches you chose in Chapter 2. A majority of the Main Course actions support the approaches of Networking and Referral-Building, Contacting Potential Employers, and Informational Interviewing because these are the areas where the Persistence Effect has the most impact. If you want to include more actions to support other approaches, feel free to invent your own. Remember, though, that you may have already chosen Success Ingredients that address those areas as well.
- **What will you actually do?** If cold calling or attending networking events paralyzes you, there is no point in including these actions in your *Get Hired Now!* program. You will simply avoid doing them. You might choose a Success Ingredient to help you improve your future skills in these areas,

but the Daily Actions you select need to be activities you are willing to do this month. Instead of choosing actions you could find immobilizing, ask yourself three questions:

1. *What are you naturally drawn to?* If you are typically outgoing and enjoy talking to people, choose actions that require going to events or spending time on the phone. But if talking to strangers makes you so uncomfortable that you will do anything to avoid it, select actions that will allow you to concentrate on building referrals with people you already know or writing terrific letters and proposals. If you choose activities you like, or are at least willing to try, you will do them.

2. *How much available time do you have?* If you are unemployed now you may have quite a bit of time available to look for a job. You may be able to spend as much time looking, as you would spend working. But if you're employed, you will have to fit your job search activities into what may be an already full week. Time constraints may require you to conduct more of your search by phone than in person, or during evenings and weekends. Make sure your choices reflect the reality of your situation.

3. *How soon do you need to produce results?* The sooner you need to find work the more aggressive your job search action plan should be. If your situation—financial or emotional—is becoming increasingly desperate, choose actions that are ambitious enough to accelerate your progress.

To make your selections, look at the section of the Main Course menu that corresponds to your Pyramid stage. Place a check mark next to each Daily Action that seems to fit your situation. It's okay to pick one action (but only one) that is easy for you or that you are already doing consistently. You should also choose at least one that is really difficult and will stretch and challenge you.

If the result you have is too many activities, ask yourself which ones would be the most efficient use of your time. What do you think will bring you the most return with the least effort? And remember: it doesn't matter so much *what* you choose as *that* you choose. Everything on the menu works.

When you have selected your seven or eight Main Course actions for a total of ten Daily Actions overall, adjust the quantity and frequency of each to suit you. Then write them on your Action Worksheet.

A Word about Landing the Job

If you are working on the stages of *Knowing what you want* or *Finding opportunities and contacts,* it may have occurred to you to wonder how your Daily Actions are going to help you land a job. After all, the activities on your list are focused on the earlier stages of the Job Search Pyramid.

The key word to understanding the answer is focus. You have chosen to concentrate your effort on a particular stage of the Pyramid because that is where you are feeling lost or stuck. This doesn't mean, however, that you should ignore possibilities while you are doing this that might lead you farther up the Pyramid. If your exploration of the job market turns up a hot lead that seems right for you, follow up on it immediately. If your follow-up suggests you should apply, do so. If your application results in an interview, great! That's what you want!

Your Daily Actions in the program are in no way intended to be a list of everything you must do about job-seeking for the next month. You need to continue pursuing job leads with the same energy you always have (or perhaps a little more because now you have a goal to meet). The intent of the Daily Actions is simply to focus more effort on the area of your job search that needs it the most.

The *Get Hired Now!* program should hold the same place in your job search activities as an exercise program does in your life. You don't quit walking to the bus stop because you are now doing twenty-five sit-ups each morning and, similarly, you don't stop playing ball with the kids because you decide to run a mile three times a week. Routine life goes on while you are exercising; applying and interviewing for jobs can go on while you are improving your performance in the areas of knowing what you want and finding opportunities.

You Have to Market Yourself

I've always approached my job-hunting the same way I do my sales career. I treat my potential employers as if they were potential clients. In one job search, I identified a specific company for which I wanted to work. There was no ad in the newspaper or open position I knew about. I stopped by and dropped off my résumé for the president of the company. I kept stopping in and calling until I got a meeting and interviewed for the job I wanted.

In another job search, there were six brokerage companies that I targeted. I contacted all of them many times and finally got an interview and a job with one of them. I called the hiring manager every day until he finally called me back.

Brock Kane
DENVER, COLORADO

What Is Going to Stop You?

Look at what you have recorded on your Action Worksheet. You have an ambitious goal, Success Ingredients you are going to acquire or create, and a list of ten Daily Actions you are going to perform all in the next twenty-eight days. If looking at this list makes you feel resistant, afraid, or overwhelmed, your reaction is completely normal.

If you have ever before attempted a program (for example, dieting or regular exercise) or taken a motivational seminar or made some New Year's resolutions, you have probably experienced the following familiar scenario: you make new commitments when you are feeling enthusiastic, re-energized, or just plain fed up with the way things are, but then something stops you from following through.

What is that something? Lack of time, and its frequent companion—not enough money—are easy excuses, but the fact is that most of us make choices every day about where to spend our time and money. We choose whether to call a potential employer or chat with a friend; pay the admission price to a networking event or buy a movie ticket. And it's not just choosing between work and play. Suddenly that growing stack of junk mail may seem more important than writing a cover letter, or buying a new cell phone becomes more urgent than paying to have your résumé professionally written.

If you are truly serious about making this time different—about following through on your commitments and getting the results you want—it's time to look at what may get in your way. Are you worried or afraid? If so, of what? Are you resisting something? If so, what is it? Ask yourself, "Is there some special permission that you need in order to be successful with this program?"

Many people, if not most people, are routinely blocked in looking for work by self-sabotaging thinking or behavior. If you thought you were the only one suffering from terminal procrastination or struggling with negative messages from your own inner critic, know you're in good company. Giving yourself permission to alter a long-standing habit can be a powerful step in the direction of lasting change. In the *Get Hired Now!* program, you will be consciously granting yourself a Special Permission every day. Here are some examples:

- I have permission to ask for what I want.
- I am able to do things I fear.
- I deserve to be successful.
- I can look for a new job and still have time for fun.

The best way to design a Special Permission is to ask yourself what you routinely think or do that prevents you from being successful at job-seeking. For

Attitude is Everything

You have to go into interviews with the attitude that you are going to get that job. You know you are. You are the best candidate. Going in with a positive attitude makes all the difference in the world. I have had four full-time jobs in my entire career with only five interviews. The fifth one asked me back to interview with them but I had already accepted another job!

You have to believe in yourself when you are in the interview because it really shows. You have to make the interviewer believe in you. If you don't believe in yourself, how do you expect anyone else to? Attitude is ninety percent of the secret.

Diana L. Sparks
SAN MATEO, CALIFORNIA

example, suppose you never seem to have time to look for a new job because your current job occupies all your time. You know this behavior backfires in the long run because you're unhappy in your current position and you truly desire a change. The permission you might design for yourself is, "It's okay to put my job search first."

Or, suppose that you are stalling in completing your résumé because then you will actually have to show it to someone. And if you did so, someone might find you unqualified for the job you want. Of course you also know that if you fail to show your résumé to anyone, it's unlikely that anyone will hire you. In this case, you might choose this Special Permission: "I believe in my skills and abilities."

Are you wondering what is going to make you believe your Special Permission? After all, you just made it up. What will make it real for you? For one thing, there is simple repetition. Repetition is a primary method of learning. You learned the alphabet by saying or singing it repeatedly. If you look in the mirror each morning and say, "I believe in my skills and abilities," you will begin to internalize this information in the same way that you know "f" comes before "g" without reciting the entire alphabet.

The other reason your Special Permission will be successful is that it will last for only twenty-eight days. Whenever you find yourself questioning the validity of your permission, remind yourself it is merely temporary. You can return to your old way of doing things at the end of the month (if that's still what you want). Just as Samuel T. Coleridge's expression "the willing suspension of disbelief" can be the key to enjoying a novel or play, you too can temporarily allow yourself to believe fully in your Special Permission. If you are skeptical, just try it.

If you already know your Special Permission, write it on the last line of your Action Worksheet. If finding a permission that fits is eluding you, select a random one to start. It's almost a guarantee that some block or obstacle will appear within the first few days of starting the program. Then you can simply design a new Special Permission to address it. If at any point during the twenty-eight days your permission stops working for you, change it.

CHAPTER 6

You're Ready . . . Let's Go!

Putting the System in Action

When action grows unprofitable,
gather information; when information
grows unprofitable, sleep.

— URSULA K. LEGUIN

The Get Hired Now! Tracking Worksheet

Your Action Worksheet is completed—you have chosen your Program Goal, one to three Success Ingredients, ten Daily Actions, and your Special Permission. It's time to put your own personal *Get Hired Now!* program into action.

Your second essential tool for the twenty-eight days of the program is the Tracking Worksheet, which you will use daily to measure your progress through the program. The Tracking Worksheet is quite a magical device. You will be amazed at how much difference this one little piece of paper can make in your job search!

Remember the benefits of goal-setting discussed in Chapter 3? Using the Tracking Worksheet consistently will automatically provide you with focus, evidence, direction, and motivation for your job search. If you arrange to work through the program with a buddy, group, or coach, you will also lock in place accountability, perspective, and support to help you succeed.

Look at Chris Workman's "Partially Completed Tracking Worksheet" on page 100. Each column represents a working day of the program, for which you will make daily entries like these:

Weather Report. On a one-to-ten scale, with one being the lowest and ten the highest, how is your state of mind today? How does your body feel?

This is an intuitive score—put down what you sense is correct. These numbers will go up and down from day to day, as your mood and physical condition fluctuate. This score tells you how much you should expect from yourself on any given day.

Success Ingredients. For each of your one-to-three Success Ingredient projects, what percentage have you completed? If zero percent means you have done nothing thus far and 100 percent means the project is done, how far do you estimate that have you progressed along the range? This too may be an intuitive score, or for some projects you can compute it mathematically. These numbers will go up as projects move forward, but will not go down.

Daily/Weekly Actions. For each of your ten actions, did you do it today (Y) or not (N)? At the bottom of this section, record the total number of actions completed at the end of each day. This number will increase or decrease from day to day as your productivity varies and other activities require your attention. When an action is weekly (or several times per week) rather than daily, you can still score yourself each day based on how well you carry out your plans. For example, if you plan to perform a weekly action on Monday and you do it, you get a Y. If you plan it and don't do it, you get an N. For any day without plans to do a particular weekly action, give yourself a free Y on that line. However, if you get to the end of the week and still haven't taken that action, you must give yourself an N on Friday. Be honest and remember—these scores are for you.

Program Goal. What percentage of your goal have you achieved so far? If your goal for the program is numerical, you will be able to compute this exactly. If not, use an intuitive score. How far along does it seem like you are in achieving your goal? (For example, completing the definition of the job you want or receiving a written job offer?) This number will increase as your goals move forward, but will not decrease.

Special Permission. Do you have your Special Permission today or not? Tell the truth. You will notice how difficult everything is on those days you don't have it.

Partially Completed Tracking Worksheet

GET HIRED NOW!™ Tracking Worksheet

Start Date __4/30/2005__   Name __Chris Workman__

	5/2	5/3	5/4	5/5	5/6	5/9	5/10	5/11	5/12	5/13	5/16	5/17	5/18	5/19	5/20	5/23	5/24	5/25	5/26	5/27
Weather Report (1–10 scale)																				
Mind	10	9	9	9	8															
Body	9	8	9	8	7															
Success Ingredients (% done)																				
1 10-second intro 5/6	5	10	25	50	75															
2 Networking skills—75% 5/13	25	25	35	35	50															
3 Target company list—20 5/20	0	0	0	0	0															
Daily/Weekly Actions (Y/N)																				
1 1 item from S.I. list daily	Y	Y	Y	Y																
2 2 networking events/wk	Y	Y	Y	Y																
3 2 lunch/coffee per wk	Y	Y	Y	Y																
4 3 people from target cos/wk	Y	Y	Y	Y																
5 ask for referral daily	Y	N	Y	Y																
6 volunteer in industry once/wk	Y	N	N	N																
7 research cos 1 hour/day	Y	Y	N	Y																
8 review 1 trade publication daily	Y	N	Y	Y																
9 write to 1 target co/wk	Y	Y	Y	Y																
10 exercise 3 times/wk	Y	Y	Y	Y																
Total (# of 10)	10	7	8	9																
Program Goal (% of target) Contacts at 10 potential cos	0	10	15	20	25															
Special Permission? (Y/N) Stay positive no matter what	Y	N	Y	Y	Y															

On Day One of the program, you will start filling in your own Tracking Worksheet, based on the Action Worksheet you completed at the end of Chapter 5.

The 28-Day Program

For the next twenty-eight days, you will be working steadily on achieving your chosen job search goal. But if you keep your foot on the accelerator the whole time, you will run out of gas!

You should plan ahead which days you will work on your job search and which days you will rest. There are rest days built into the program so you can have time to regroup and recharge. You may choose to spend some of a rest day working on a Success Ingredient project or the exercises in this chapter, but you will be responsible for completing your Daily Actions only on the days you have chosen as working days. In the program outline that follows, your working days are scheduled Monday through Friday, and your rest days are assumed to be back-to-back, on Saturday and Sunday. But if you need to devote weekend time to your job search, you should adjust the program days to fit the schedule you actually plan to follow.

On your program working days, you should set aside in advance time to complete your Daily Actions, especially if you currently have a full-time job. Plan for your job search activities to take place before or after work, on breaks, or during lunch. You may need to experiment to find the best time of day to fit these tasks into your schedule. Don't let having a job already be your excuse for not finding the one you really want. Make your job search program your first priority instead of the last thing you do.

On working and rest days alike, read the entry for each day from the pages that follow. Try to do this as early in the day as possible so that you will keep your job search in mind throughout the course of the day. On each working day, you should also spend a few moments doing a morning review to plan how you will include your Success Ingredients, Daily Actions, and your Special Permission in the day's agenda. At the end of each working day, take another few moments to add up your daily scores on the Tracking Worksheet. There are more details about these activities in the pages that follow.

On some of the rest days there are exercises provided to help you be more effective and productive in your job search. To get the most benefit from the program, be sure to set aside some time to work with each of these, whether or not it is on the day suggested.

DAY 1

Saturday is a great day to begin your *Get Hired Now!* program. Close the door, turn off the phone, and bring out your completed Action Worksheet from Chapter 5. Make an enlarged copy of the blank "Tracking Worksheet" below, or download the worksheet from our web site at www.gethirednow.com. Fill in the dates on the top line and the information in Column One. (See the "Partially Completed Tracking Worksheet" earlier in this chapter.)

On the top line, write the calendar dates of your working days for the next month. If the coming Monday were May 2, for example, you would label the first ten columns on your worksheet 5/2–5/6 and 5/9–5/13, skipping the Saturday and Sunday rest days in between. Next write in Column One the Success Ingredients from your Action Worksheet with your chosen target dates. Then add your ten Daily Actions, Program Goal, and Special Permission.

Award yourself a starting score on each of your Success Ingredients and your Program Goal. Are you starting from zero on your Success Ingredient projects and the goal you set for the month, or have you already made some progress? On Chris Workman's worksheet, he gave himself a starting score of twenty-five percent on "networking skills," believing he was already a quarter of the way there. On his "ten-second introduction," he had done some work, but needed much more, so he scored himself at five percent. For "target company list," Chris had yet to do anything, so he started at zero.

Tracking Worksheet

GET HIRED NOW!™ Tracking Worksheet

Start Date _____

Name _____

Weather Report (1–10 scale)																							
Mind																							
Body																							
Success Ingredients (% done)																							
1																							
2																							
3																							
Daily/Weekly Actions (Y/N)																							
1																							
2																							
3																							
4																							
5																							
6																							
7																							
8																							
9																							
10																							
Total (# of 10)																							
Monthly Goal (% of target)																							
Special Permission? (Y/N)																							

[103]

To give yourself an accurate score now and throughout the program, you may need to quantify your Success Ingredient projects. For Success Ingredients like "networking venues" or "lead and referral sources," consider the question, "How many is enough?" If you're unsure, review the appropriate chapter in Part Two for your chosen stage of the Job Search Pyramid. Write the number you choose on your worksheet, as Chris did for his target company list. If you have chosen a more intangible Success Ingredient, such as "networking skills" or "interviewing skills," score yourself intuitively. If zero equals "scared to network" and 100 percent means "expert networker," where would you rate yourself today? Would you like to be at 100 percent by the completion of the program, or would seventy-five percent satisfy you? If it's the latter, write down "networking skills at 75%" so you know what your aim is.

Now award yourself a starting score on your Program Goal. As described in Chapter 3, this may be a numerical target for contacts, job opportunities, interviews, or another element you can count, *or* it may be a single objective, such as a clear definition of what you want or a job offer. Follow the same guidelines for assigning a starting score as you did for your Success Ingredients.

Be honest with yourself and be specific about what you are measuring. Can you count a job opportunity as part of your score as soon as you hear about it, or only after you apply for it? Does a job offer count if it's not for a job you would be willing to take? Base your score on a way of measuring that will make this goal truly meaningful for you.

Now put the Tracking Worksheet where you will be sure to see it first thing Monday morning. Are you ready to make a commitment to the program that you have designed for yourself?

THOUGHT FOR THE DAY

I am not afraid of storms,
for I am learning how to sail my ship.

— LOUISA MAY ALCOTT

DAY 2

Rest Day. Do something you really enjoy—perhaps an activity you haven't had time for in a while. You're going to be working hard for the next month, so take this opportunity to have some fun. Get plenty of sleep tonight so you'll be fresh and ready to go in the morning.

THOUGHT FOR THE DAY

Tomorrow is a new day; begin it well and serenely and with too high a spirit to be encumbered with your old nonsense.

— RALPH WALDO EMERSON

DAY 3

Are you ready to get hired? It's time to let the Tracking Worksheet start doing its magic. First thing this morning place your Tracking Worksheet in front of you. Each working day of the program, you will be using the worksheet at least twice: once at the beginning and once at the end of the day. To let even more of the worksheet's magic rub off on you, post it where you'll see it all day long.

On this first Monday, begin by doing your first Morning Review. Look over your Success Ingredients and Daily Actions. Which of these tasks do you plan to work on today? Do you need to add them to your daily to-do list or schedule time for them? Check your Special Permission to remind yourself what you need to be successful. Okay, you're ready for the day—go for it!

At day's end, award yourself your first Daily Scores:

Weather Report: Your mind and body on a scale of one to ten.
Success Ingredients: The status of each project from 0-100 percent complete.

Daily/Weekly Actions: Y (for Yes) and N (for No) on each one. Add up the total number of Ys at the bottom.

Program Goal: Progress toward your goal from 0–100 percent accomplished.

Special Permission: Y if you granted yourself your Special Permission today; N if you didn't.

If you have questions about how to score yourself, refer to the description of the Tracking Worksheet at the beginning of this chapter.

You made it through your first working day of the *Get Hired Now!* program— congratulations! Did you accomplish all that you wanted? If you did, great! If not, we'll look at your list again tomorrow to see if you need to make changes. Throughout the remainder of the program, the day-by-day guidelines here will focus on keeping you in action, on track, and motivated. Whenever you have questions about how to implement the Daily Actions or Success Ingredients you chose, refer to the appropriate chapter in Part Two for your stage of the Pyramid to find detailed logistical help.

THOUGHT FOR THE DAY

Someone should tell us, right at the start of our lives, that we are dying. Then we might live life to the limit, every minute of every day. Do it, I say! Whatever you want to do, do it now! There are only so many tomorrows.

— MICHAEL LANDON

DAY 4

Begin the day with your Morning Review. Look at your Success Ingredients, Daily Actions, and Special Permission and plan how you will include each in the day's agenda. You will do this each working day of the program. In today's review, and for all of this first week, pay special attention to the Daily Actions you chose. How did it work for you to add these new activities into your day?

If you scored eight or above on your Daily Actions yesterday, keep them as they are. If you scored lower, but yesterday was unusually busy or chaotic, give yourself another day to see how you do. However, if you're feeling overwhelmed and suspect that your choices may have been too ambitious, you have complete permission to scale back a bit. Rather than eliminating any of the actions you chose, try reducing the level of effort. Is there something you committed to do daily that could happen three times per week instead? Or could you cut down on the number of calls, letters, or meetings you had planned? Now is the time to redesign a list of actions that will work for you within the reality of a normal day.

At the end of the day, compile your Daily Scores. Did you do better today? Terrific! If you're still not satisfied with your scores, don't worry; we will continue to look at ways of making them improve.

THOUGHT FOR THE DAY
Fall seven times, stand up eight.
— JAPANESE PROVERB

DAY 5

Morning Review. Wednesday is the day to look at actions you chose to schedule weekly that have yet to happen. Choose now the day you will do them. If a lunch or meeting is involved, lock it in place by calling to make the appointment or reservation.

Daily Scores. Have you reached a score of eight or higher on your Daily Actions? If so, good work! Try setting up a reward for yourself if you reach a certain score tomorrow. If today's score was six, go for a score of eight; if nine was your score today, make tomorrow's goal a ten.

THOUGHT FOR THE DAY

Don't compromise yourself.
You are all you've got.

— JANIS JOPLIN

DAY 6

Morning Review. What will be your reward if you reach your Daily Actions target today? What do you need to do to make that score possible? Here are three suggested strategies to try:

1. *Do it first.* Avoid doing anything else until your Daily Actions are completed: don't check your e-mail, tidy up the house, or answer the phone. Eliminate every possible distraction until you have reached your target score for today.

2. *Do it now.* You may have some Daily Actions that need to occur later in your day rather than first thing. Every time you think of one of them, do it immediately. Let's say you need to ask for one referral per day. When you are in conversation with someone, just ask for a referral as soon as you think of it—right then, no matter what you are talking about. If you find yourself forgetting, put a rubber band around your wrist and let it remind you each time you notice it.

3. *Block out time.* If your schedule prevents doing all your Daily Actions first, block out time on your calendar. Make a specific appointment with yourself and honor it just as though someone else was expecting you. Use this appointment as an excuse if other people try to detain you. If you're afraid you'll forget or get busy with something else, try setting an alarm.

Daily Scores. Did you earn your reward today? Congratulations! If you're still having trouble, review your Daily Actions list again. If you find it too ambitious, you can scale back your level of effort at any point during the program, as long as you stick to the guidelines for choosing Daily Actions given in Chapter 5. You may decide that you already have the right list, but the problem you need to solve is how to make it happen. Try using again tomorrow the three strategies listed above. It may take you several attempts to successfully change your work habits so that job-seeking becomes a part of your day. Keep at it; the payoff will be worth the effort.

THOUGHT FOR THE DAY

Failure is the opportunity to try again,
this time with intelligence.

— HENRY FORD

DAY 7

Morning Review. It's your last chance to complete any actions scheduled as weekly, so look now at how to fit them in. What Daily Actions score will you go for today?

Daily Scores. How did you do this week? If you got your Daily Actions score up to eight or more, it's time to celebrate your achievement. You are on the path to success in reaching your Program Goal and landing the job you want. If your scores are in the five-to-seven range, you are getting close, but need to make some changes. Revisit the Morning Review for Days Four and Six to see what else you might do. If you are consistently scoring lower than five on Daily Actions, you are not failing; you are learning. There is something in your way, and once you know what it is you can begin to eliminate it. We'll look at some of these potential roadblocks tomorrow.

Complete your week by making a list of your wins over the last seven days. What worked? What went well? What great things did you do, say, receive, and achieve? Here's a sample "wins" list:

- Completed my ten-second introduction and tried it out at a networking event
- Made three good contacts at the Association of Accounting Professionals meeting
- Read two chapters of a book about networking
- Had lunch with my former boss and got some inside info on industry changes
- Found five local companies that might be hiring in this month's issue of *Accounting Pro*
- Heard about a short-term volunteer job for the Helping Hand Foundation

Put your wins list where you can see it, right next to your Tracking Worksheet. Then congratulate yourself—you stuck with the program through Week One.

THOUGHT FOR THE DAY

We are what we repeatedly do. Excellence,
then, is not an act but a habit.

— ARISTOTLE

DAY 8

Rest Day. In the first week of the *Get Hired Now!* program, you may have encountered two of the biggest obstacles to job search success: fear and resistance. If looking at some of the items on your Daily Actions list made your stomach flutter or your throat get tight, that was fear. If you found yourself thinking, "I don't want to . . ." and digging in your heels, that was resistance. Know that you are not alone in these feelings. You may not hear other folks talk about this around the proverbial water cooler, but most people feel afraid, resistant, or both, about certain elements of job-seeking.

Identifying these feelings' source and why you have them is beyond the scope of this book. What you need now is to get past them in order to be successful—and you can! The first step in removing these roadblocks is to recognize they exist; then be specific about their nature. Answer these questions now:

1. *What are you afraid of?* Being rejected? Making a mistake? Failing? Succeeding? Looking silly? Write down as many different fears as you can. If you feel stuck, ask yourself, "What do I think would happen if I . . ," and complete the sentence with whatever Daily Actions are giving you trouble—perhaps ". . . went to a networking event?" or ". . . made a cold call?"

2. *What are you resisting?* Doing the work? Bragging about your abilities? Spending time job-searching despite other priorities? Finish this sentence in your best whining voice, "I don't want to . . ."

Now that these barriers are out in the open, ask yourself if you are going to let them stop you. They don't have to, you know. You can feel afraid yet move forward; you can feel resistant yet still do what you are resisting. The next time you are having trouble, notice what you are feeling and choose whether to let it keep you from taking action. Say to yourself, "Oh, there's the fear again," or "Wow, I'm really feeling resistant right now" and then keep going.

THOUGHT FOR THE DAY

*Everything is so dangerous that nothing
is really very frightening.*

— GERTRUDE STEIN

DAY 9

Rest Day. Reward yourself for a week well done. Spend an entire day not thinking about your job search. Do something relaxing and replenishing.

THOUGHT FOR THE DAY

Life isn't about finding yourself.
Life is about creating yourself.

— GEORGE BERNARD SHAW

DAY 10

Morning Review. Continue planning your day to include all your Daily Actions and try for a daily score of eight or higher. In this second week, we will shift the focus to your Success Ingredient projects. How has your progress been here? You are one-fourth of the way through the program, so you should be twenty-five percent ahead of where you started on your Success Ingredients. If you are working on three simultaneously, each should be progressing at the same rate. If you are doing them in succession, the first should be near completion.

Daily Scores. Were you able to give your Success Ingredients enough attention today? Look now at the rest of your week and see where your schedule might accommodate them. In order to stay on track, you should be halfway through by Friday.

THOUGHT FOR THE DAY

If there is no wind, row.

— CALVIN COOLIDGE

DAY 11

Morning Review. Are you having trouble finding enough time for your Success Ingredients? If you are on or ahead of schedule, good for you! If not, here are some strategies to help:

1. *Give something away.* What else is currently on your to-do list? Is there anything you can hand off to someone else? If you can't unload an entire project, are there some pieces you could ask another person to do? If you are unaccustomed to delegating, you may need to expand your vision of what it looks like. You don't need an administrative assistant in order to delegate; you can delegate to a co-worker, a colleague, a friend, your spouse or partner, your children, your siblings, another committee member, or a paid professional. What are you doing that someone else could do instead? Can you ask someone else? Can you pay someone else? If it enabled you to spend an extra hour a day on your job search, could you afford to pay someone to handle some of your responsibilities?

2. *Put something off.* What on your list can be done later? If you have a habit of planning more things than you can possibly do, you are already putting some things off by default. Why not choose up front what those things will be? Think in terms of your overall priorities. What is more important than your job search? There will certainly be a few things, such as some responsibilities at your current job or spending some time with your family, but it's unlikely that everything on your list is more important than job-seeking right now. Find some tasks that you can defer for the next seventeen days.

3. *Let something go.* If you have had a task on your list for three weeks or more and not gotten it done, does it truly require doing? If you haven't made time for it in that long, how important can it be? Try this: cross it off the list for one week and see if it comes back to haunt you. If you can

forget about it, that's one less thing to do. If you can't let it drop, revisit the first two options above.

Daily Scores. Did you make more headway on Success Ingredients today? What will be your target scores for tomorrow?

THOUGHT FOR THE DAY
Creative minds have always been known to
survive any amount of bad training.
— ANNA FREUD

DAY 12

Morning Review. You have three remaining days to hit the fifty-percent mark on your Success Ingredients. What will it take? If you are having any logistical challenges or how-to questions, read the chapter in Part Two that highlights the stage of the Job Search Pyramid on which you are working.

Daily Scores. Did you hit your target scores? Take a moment to celebrate! Are you still struggling? You may need some additional support. Call your job search buddy or a friend and ask for help in the following specific way:

1. *Set a fixed time to talk.* Whether you meet by phone or in person, set a start and end time for your conversation. This will tighten the focus on solving your problem. Half an hour is enough; an hour is plenty.
2. *Begin by clearing.* Ask your buddy to just listen while you recount what's going on. Your buddy can say things like, "Gee, that's tough," or "How awful!" but should avoid giving advice until you have told the whole story. Talk about not only what is happening but also how it makes you feel. If it sounds like complaining, that probably means you're doing it right. You might be saying something like "I've been trying for two weeks to finish

my résumé but there's just been one emergency after another, and now my mother wants me to help sell her car, and I'm so frustrated! The words I write down just come out wrong, and I don't think it'll ever come together, and I needed it yesterday, and I'm so worried that . . ." You get the idea.

Set a time limit of five to ten minutes for clearing. Then ask your buddy to summarize for you: "I hear how frustrated and worried you are. You seem to have two problems that need to be solved: finding the time to work on your résumé and getting the words to come out right. Are you ready to look at some solutions?"

3. *Brainstorm possible solutions.* Now that your problems are out in the open, you can get some assistance in solving them. Your buddy's job is not to hand you the right answer; it is to help you expand your thinking to come up with some new ideas. Take your problems one at time and together with your buddy make a list of possible solutions. Don't edit the list as you are brainstorming; you will do that later. Anything and everything that comes up should go on the list. A basic principle of brainstorming is that you are not allowed to say, "That won't work," or "I already tried that." Here are the potential results of a brainstorm aimed at getting the right words for your résumé:

- hire a résumé writer
- plagiarize my friend's résumé
- use a thesaurus
- ask my cousin, the writer, to help
- do a résumé with pictures instead of words
- choose not to use a résumé at all
- copy résumés from a book
- take a class in résumé writing
- use existing résumé and stop worrying
- have some colleagues review it

4. **Look for a next step.** You can ask your buddy to help you with this or do it later on your own. If none of the brainstormed ideas seems right, look at each one to see if there's something useful in it. Maybe you can't afford a résumé writer, but you know one you could ask for some free advice. Perhaps a class in résumé writing would take too long, but you could check out a book on it from the library. Find just one thing you can do that will allow you to move forward.

THOUGHT FOR THE DAY

A pessimist sees the difficulty in every opportunity; an optimist sees the opportunity in every difficulty.

— WINSTON CHURCHILL

DAY 13

Morning Review. Set a target for your Success Ingredients score today that is a no-kidding-whatever-it-takes goal. Remember that you said you needed these things to be successful.

Daily Scores. Did you make it? Congratulations! Not quite there? You have one more day to catch up. Take a moment to remind yourself of your Special Permission. Did you have it today? If not, what do you need to do, say, or believe to grant yourself that permission? Now that you have been working with the program for a while, is there any other needed permission you have discovered? It's okay to switch or even have two of them if that serves you in moving forward.

THOUGHT FOR THE DAY

Life is like riding a bicycle. To keep your balance you must keep moving.

— ALBERT EINSTEIN

DAY 14

Morning Review. It's the halfway point in your *Get Hired Now!* program. Where do you want to be at the end of the day?

Daily Scores. You have worked diligently this week so pat yourself on the back. If you achieved your target scores on Daily Actions and Success Ingredients, you are on your way to a successful conclusion by month's end. If you are unhappy with your performance, look at how much more you have accomplished in these two weeks than before you started the program. If you have yet to reach the fifty percent mark with your Success Ingredients, revisit Day Eleven's Morning Review or schedule another call with your buddy to see what else you might do.

Complete your week by making and posting your wins list. Hooray! You made it through Week Two!

THOUGHT FOR THE DAY:

Life begets life, energy creates energy. It is by spending oneself that one becomes rich.

— SARAH BERNHARDT

DAY 15

Rest Day. During Week Two, it's a good bet that you found yourself having at least one conversation with your inner critic. Also known as "the committee" or negative self-talk, this is the self-defeating voice you hear in your head that says: "You're not good enough," "You don't know how," and "They won't like me." The inner critic often has much to say about job-seeking. This is a time in your life when you are putting yourself on the line, often bringing up your concerns with being inadequate. Negative self-talk is one of the biggest obstacles you must overcome to achieve success.

Everyone has an inner critic (yes, everyone!), but some people manage it better than others. It is possible to manage it so well that you hardly notice it. To begin managing your inner critic, here are some suggested steps to follow:

1. *Raise your awareness.* Every time you find yourself fearful, nervous, hesitant, or second-guessing, stop and notice what is happening. You may have a particular behavior pattern that manifests itself when the inner critic is active, such as procrastinating, avoiding people or tasks, or starting and stopping activities. Or there may be a body sensation you can recognize as a warning sign, like a tight throat, sweaty palms, or a sinking feeling in your stomach. When you notice any of these signs of negative self-talk, pause to listen to the conversation. Write down what you hear your inner critic saying to you and keep a list.

2. *Take responsibility.* Once you have a catalog of your inner critic's greatest hits, be aware that you can choose to change the music. Just as with fear and resistance, you don't have to let these negative messages stop you. Begin by constructing a fair and accurate response to each of the messages you typically hear and use your response whenever you notice it. If your negative self-talk threatens, "You should be working," you might respond, "I've worked hard this week and deserve a day off." If your inner critic tells you, "Don't do that—you might make a mistake," a good response is, "Yes, I might, but I'll learn from it and move on." Learning to manage negative self-talk is an attainable skill; the only requirement is that you be willing to try.

3. *Practice self-management.* Learning any new skill takes practice and managing your inner critic is no exception. At first it may be difficult to catch your critic in the act; you may realize only later the origin of the reluctance you were feeling. This is a normal part of learning self-management. Just

use your positive response as soon as you think of it. With practice you will become more skilled at hearing negative messages in "real time" and be better able to immediately respond. If you use this process consistently, the messages will begin to lose their power over you because you no longer believe them.

THOUGHT FOR THE DAY

No one can make you feel inferior without your consent.

— ELEANOR ROOSEVELT

DAY 16

Rest Day. Have fun today! Enjoy an activity you haven't done for a while to make the day feel special. You deserve it!

THOUGHT FOR THE DAY

I am not young enough to know everything.

— OSCAR WILDE

DAY 17

Morning Review. It's the first working day of Week Three, and you're past the halfway mark in the program. Good work! Your target scores for each day this week should continue to be eight or higher on your Daily Actions and fifty to seventy-five percent on your Success Ingredients. The focus this week will be on your Program Goal. At this point in the program you should have reached at least fifty percent of your goal. By the week's end you will need to be at seventy-five percent. Ask yourself this morning, "What will it take to make this happen?"

Daily Scores. Did you see some movement toward your Program Goal today? If you are already at seventy-five percent or above, consider raising the stakes. How much more could you accomplish on your job search by the end of next week? If you're below fifty percent, revisit your Daily Actions. Do you need to boost your level of effort in order to find the job you want? Consider increasing the quantity or frequency of your Daily Actions to make up the gap between you and your goal. Make your weekly actions twice a week; double your target number for calls, letters, or meetings. You've got only two weeks left, so make the most of them.

THOUGHT FOR THE DAY

I can't imagine a person becoming a success who doesn't give the game of life everything he's got.

— WALTER CRONKITE

DAY 18

Morning Review. What can you do to ensure you're pulled toward your Program Goal rather than having to push to accomplish it? Take a moment to reread the first section of your Action Worksheet from Chapter 3. How did you answer "What would that get you?" when you thought about finding the job you really want? Visualize now some of those results. Pick one to be your touchstone for the day and post a word, phrase, or picture somewhere to remind you of it: on your phone, computer, or dashboard.

Daily Scores. Did you feel some pull from your goal today? Try creating an even stronger touchstone for yourself this evening with one of these quick activities:

1. *Write about it.* Write down what it would be like to achieve your goal. What would you have? How would you feel? What could you then do?

2. *Draw it.* Draw a picture of what goal achievement would look like. You don't have to be an artist; even stick figures drawn with markers will do the trick.

3. *Visualize it.* Close your eyes, put on some soothing music, and create your detailed vision of success as you imagine it.

4. *Sing it.* If there's a song that represents achievement or good fortune to you, play it and sing along. Or change the words to any song on the radio to be about you and your success.

THOUGHT FOR THE DAY

If you can't work with love but only with distaste, it is better that you should leave your work and sit at the gate of the temple and take alms of the people who work with joy.

— KAHLIL GIBRAN

DAY 19

Morning Review. Use the touchstone you created yesterday to help motivate you today. Post your essay or picture on the wall, recapture your visualization by briefly closing your eyes, or hum your success song.

Daily Scores. Are you past the fifty percent mark toward your Program Goal? Yes? Keep it up! No? If you are still struggling, revisit "Choosing Where to Focus" in Chapter 2 where you selected the stage of the Job Search Pyramid you would work on this month. Do you think you chose correctly? Has anything changed or shifted since you made your choice? If you're not sure, look at the Daily Actions listed in Chapter 5 for the other stage or stages you are considering. Do any of those actions seem more appropriate for where you are now?

If you've been working at a high level of activity for the last two and a half weeks, it is entirely possible that you have moved forward a stage on the Pyramid. It's also possible that by becoming more active about your job search, you have discovered that your challenges are not what you originally thought they were. If either of these situations exists for you, it's time to re-do your Daily Actions list to better match where you are now.

THOUGHT FOR THE DAY

We must be willing to get rid of the life we've planned, so as to have the life that is waiting for us.

— JOSEPH CAMPBELL

DAY 20

Morning Review. You have two days left to reach a seventy-five percent score on your Program Goal. What sort of game could you design for yourself to play that would make these two days exciting and fun? Could you see how many phone calls you could make in an hour or how many business cards you could collect at a single meeting? Is there a buddy with whom you could play this game and have the winner buy lunch?

Daily Scores. What was it like to be more playful with your job search today? Could you play the same game tomorrow or invent a different game? With what could you reward yourself this weekend if you get to seventy-five percent on your Program Goal by the end of Friday?

THOUGHT FOR THE DAY

Life is what we make it. Always has been, always will be.

— GRANDMA MOSES

DAY 21

Morning Review. Set yourself up for an exciting, adventurous day. Take some risks, put yourself out there, and really go for it!

Daily Scores. It's the end of Week Three and you have been steadily applying yourself to your job search for twenty-one days. You definitely deserve some applause. If you are at seventy-five percent or higher on your Program Goal, you are right on target. If you aren't quite there, congratulate yourself anyway on how much you have learned. We'll look tomorrow at whether you need to make any changes.

THOUGHT FOR THE DAY

I do not think there is any other quality so essential to success of any kind as the quality of perseverance. It overcomes almost everything, even nature.

— JOHN D. ROCKEFELLER

DAY 22

Rest Day. So how did Week Three go? Does it look like you'll be able to reach 100 percent of your goal by the end of next week? It's time to revisit your goal one more time and see if it is serving you the way it should. Goals work differently for different people. Some folks like ambitious goals that they can't quite reach because it makes them try harder. Others find that this approach backfires because they always feel as though they're not doing enough; setting a goal that they know they can achieve is much more satisfying. Which type are you?

If ambitious goals excite you and make you want to get up in the morning, and your Program Goal is at seventy-five percent or more right now, raise it. Give yourself a reason to go all out in the final week. If on the other hand it's important to you that you reach every goal you set for yourself, and you're below seventy-five percent right now, lower your target. This is not cheating! If you can't win the game, there will be a piece of you that doesn't want to play any more. Yet by setting a more achievable goal, you will continue to be motivated by it.

THOUGHT FOR THE DAY

*In the face of an obstacle which is impossible
to overcome, stubbornness is stupid.*

— SIMONE DE BEAUVOIR

DAY 23

Rest Day. Did you promise yourself a reward for reaching your Program Goal target this week? Today is the day to keep your promise. If you didn't make your target, what reward do you get for trying?

THOUGHT FOR THE DAY

What the world really needs is more love and less paperwork.

— PEARL BAILEY

DAY 24

Morning Review. You're on the home stretch with only five more days to go. Your target scores for each day this week should be eight or higher on your Daily Actions, and seventy-five to 100 percent on your Success Ingredients and your Program Goal. Picture the reward for achieving your Program Goal that you chose in Chapter 3. If you reach your goal by Friday, the prize will be yours!

The focus of Week Four is learning. As you have been working your way through the *Get Hired Now!* program, you have discovered some significant information about how you handle looking for a job and promoting yourself in general. If you can capture that learning and use it to better manage your career, you will have accomplished an important result this month. Finding out that you never allow enough time to pursue your personal goals is just as valuable to your ultimate success as landing three job interviews.

As you plan your day this morning and complete your Daily Actions through-out the day, notice what you have learned about time management. Are you managing projects, priorities, and your schedule any differently than at the beginning of the program? What is working for you about the way you manage time? What still isn't working well?

Daily Scores. Were you able to balance all the program elements today: Success Ingredients, Daily Actions, Program Goal, and Special Permission? Take a few moments to write down what you have learned about time management over the last twenty-four days.

THOUGHT FOR THE DAY

Destiny is no matter of chance. It is a matter of choice. It is not a thing to be waited for, it is a thing to be achieved.

— WILLIAM JENNINGS BRYAN

DAY 25

Morning Review. Have you designed a job search game to play this week or is there some other way you can keep job-seeking light and fun? Humor and a sense of playfulness are effective antidotes to fear and resistance. Notice throughout today what you are learning about these two tough adversaries.

Daily Scores. What have you learned about fear and resistance? When do fear and resistance surface for you? What does their appearance signal? What strategies have worked for you in handling these saboteurs? Where do you still have trouble?

THOUGHT FOR THE DAY

One must have chaos within to give birth to a dancing star.

— NIETZSCHE

DAY 26

Morning Review. Keep that reward visible; you're almost there! If you have been using a job search buddy, job club, or career/life coach, is there any extra assistance you'd like to ask for in these last three days to help you meet your goal? Consider today what have you learned about support this month.

Daily Scores. How are you doing on your job search game? As of today, your Program Goal should be at ninety percent or more. Ask yourself what you should do in the next two days to reach 100 percent. Is there any support you need to ask for from your family, friends, or colleagues? What kind of support has been most helpful to you in the past month? Have you found yourself willing to ask for support, or do you wait until you are in a crisis? What support structures would be beneficial to maintain after you complete the program?

> **THOUGHT FOR THE DAY**
> *It is amazing what you can accomplish if you do not care who gets the credit.*
> — HARRY TRUMAN

DAY 27

Morning Review. Is there anything that will get in the way of your being successful today? Are you willing to set aside whatever comes up? Notice what you are learning about self-management.

Daily Scores. Only one more day to go. Take a deep breath and smile big! Have you gotten better acquainted with your inner critic during the program? What are the "greatest hits" playing on your negative-self-talk jukebox? Are there some counter-messages you designed that work particularly well? How does your inner critic interfere with your ability to advance your career? What changes have you noticed in your ability to manage this interference?

THOUGHT FOR THE DAY
Restlessness and discontent are the first
necessities for progress.
— THOMAS EDISON

DAY 28

Morning Review. Are you ready to win? Are you planning your victory celebration? Can you taste your reward? You have earned it! Think about the element of motivation today. What really motivates you? How did having a specific goal for the month change your behavior? Does a far-off goal draw you toward it or do you need to be getting more enjoyment in the moment? Do you reward yourself for progress and learning or only if you achieve certain results? Are you satisfied with rewarding yourself or do you want acknowledgment from others? What motivational techniques backfire on you? Which are your favorites?

Daily Scores. You did it! Way to go! If you reached 100 percent or more on your Program Goal, you have achieved complete success in the *Get Hired Now!* program. If your score is lower, you still deserve a huge commendation for sticking with the program. And you probably learned even more than those who did reach 100 percent.

What have you learned about goal-setting, about job search, about promoting yourself? What did you learn if you didn't meet your goal? The fact is that job-seeking is just another skill that you learn by practicing over time, and you have had a lot of practice this month. If you have always tended to reward yourself only for results, remember our advice to acknowledge your effort, regardless of the outcome. You may find this shift in thinking beneficial in more areas than job search!

THOUGHT FOR THE DAY

*I am only one, but still I am one. I cannot do
everything, but I can do something. I will not
refuse to do the something I can do.*

— HELEN KELLER

What's Next for You?

Whew! You've just completed an intensive 28-day program to find the job you want. After you celebrate and catch your breath, you will probably be wondering what's next. If you found the job you were looking for, pause a moment before putting this book back on the shelf. What career-building habits have you learned this month that you might like to integrate into your life on a regular basis? In the Introduction to this book, we pointed out that you might be looking for another job in four years or less. Keeping your résumé current and staying in touch with your network will get your next job search off to a much better start.

If you didn't find a job yet, you'll want to repeat the program right away. The *Get Hired Now!* program is designed so you can use it as many times as necessary to find the job you want. Next month, or whenever you next feel the need for a career change, you can design a new program for yourself and start again.

Whether you are repeating the program immediately or not, review now your notes about what you learned in the program. Look again at each of the areas you examined in Week Four—time management, fear and resistance, support, self-management, and motivation. How can you develop your skills in these areas to better manage your career? What will you do differently in the future based on what you learned throughout the program about goal-setting, job-seeking, networking, and self-promotion?

Look also at your chosen Success Ingredients. Are any of these projects still incomplete? What additional projects back in Chapter 4 did you consider choosing, and is now the time to move forward on any of these?

Save your notes about learning areas and Success Ingredients to help design your next *Get Hired Now!* program. When you are again ready to start, begin by re-diagnosing your job search condition with the Job Search Pyramid in Chapter 2.

If you went through the program by yourself this time, consider repeating it with a buddy, group, or coach to see how much difference the extra accountability, perspective, and support can make to your success. Or perhaps you're aware of another way to make this program more effective for how you think and work. Be creative, find your own unique solution, and above all, have fun!

PART TWO

THE RECIPES

Introduction to Part Two

You may have reached Part Two because you are reading this book from beginning to end before completing the exercises or starting the design of your own *Get Hired Now!* program. The information here about job search approaches, "recipes," and missing ingredients can certainly be used in this way to generate ideas and inspiration at any time.

A better way to make use of this material, however, is to reference it while you are in the process of building or implementing your action plan, for example, while:

- Selecting your Success Ingredients (Chapter 4)
- Choosing from the Action Plan Menu (Chapter 5)
- Putting the system in action (Chapter 6)

This part of the book contains instructions for preparing your chosen Success Ingredients, as well as job search "recipes" to help you apply the approaches specified in your action plan. A chapter for each stage of the Job Search Pyramid is provided so you can quickly locate the ingredients and recipes you need:

- *Knowing what you want* (Chapter 7)
- *Finding opportunities and contacts* (Chapter 8)
- *Applying to employers* (Chapter 9)
- *Getting interviews* (Chapter 10)
- *Landing the job* (Chapter 11)

You need only look at the specific chapter that covers the stage on which you are focusing. Each chapter begins with an overview of the stage and some of the basic Success Ingredients it requires, then gives recipes for how to apply each job search approach during that stage. Only those approaches suitable for the stage are included, usually in this order:

- Networking and Referral-Building
- Contacting Potential Employers
- Informational Interviewing
- Employing Recruiters and Agencies
- Searching Specialized Job Listings
- Using Help-Wanted Ads

You need only study those approaches you are actually planning to use. For each approach, additional Success Ingredients specific to that approach are described within the recipe that most closely relates to them. For example, the ingredient "ten-second introduction" can be found under the recipe for "Attending Events," and the ingredient "model cover letter" is described in the recipe for "How to Apply by Mail or E-mail." The Success Ingredients covered in each section are listed at the beginning for easy finding.

Happy cooking!

CHAPTER 7

Knowing What You Want:

When You Aren't Sure Who to Contact

Vision without action is a daydream.
Action without vision is a nightmare.

— JAPANESE PROVERB

What Do You Want to Be When You Grow Up?

Remember being asked that question when you were young? Knowing the answer was so easy back then. You saw people at work and became fascinated with what they did. Saying you wanted to be a fireman, nurse, doctor, or teacher was easy. You had no idea what it took to become skilled in those professions. If a job looked like fun, that's what you chose to be.

Now that you're a grownup, this question is more difficult to answer. The job market has changed. You've acquired skills through education or the course of your career but you may not be sure what you would like to do with them. Or you may not like the direction your career has been headed and desire a change. The competition for jobs can be overwhelming; you may need to shift your focus to better compete. Or perhaps you've been applying for a wide variety of jobs trying to find the right fit, but nothing seems suitable.

Knowing what you want is the important first stage of the Job Search Pyramid. In Chapter 1, we pointed out that finding a job is all about people, and that you need to find and connect with the right people in order to find the job you want. But if you don't yet know what that job is, it will be almost impossible for you to know who you should be contacting.

What you'll find in this chapter are suggestions for determining what you want using three distinct methods:

1. Getting to know yourself better
2. Gathering more information about industries and jobs
3. Finding out what others think about where you fit

By using inventories, assessments, and vision exercises, you can learn more about where your strengths lie and what you want for yourself. When you gather information about various industries, companies, and positions, you can begin to see which ones match up with your skills and fit into your vision. With informational interviews, you can ask knowledgeable people to help you determine what would be the right job for you.

Helping you choose a career from scratch is beyond the scope of this book, but if you have at least a general idea of the type of work you want to do, the recipes in this chapter will enable you to form a much clearer picture. If you create some or all of the Success Ingredients suggested here and use the approaches of Networking and Referral-Building and/or Informational Interviewing to add to your knowledge and contact base, you will be ready to move on to the next stage and begin seeking out specific job opportunities.

We'd also like to suggest that you consider working with a career counselor, career coach, or job club for at least part of your journey through this stage to receive additional support and guidance. In any stage of the Job Search Pyramid, a group or coach can help you stay focused and motivated. But when trying to sort out your career options, it can be particularly helpful to have professional support to provide an experienced perspective and specific advice.

A career counselor can administer and interpret assessments, help you discover where you fit in the world of work, and offer advice about your career choices. A career coach will ask you incisive questions about your goals and desires, act as a brainstorming partner, and offer feedback and perspective to help you stay true to yourself. A job club or *Get Hired Now!* action group can provide many of the same benefits as working with a coach, especially if the group has a trained facilitator.

To choose the right kind of professional help, think about where you are most likely to get stuck working on your own. Then ask any prospective counselors, coaches, or group leaders not just what they will help you do, but how they will go about helping you. (The terms "counselor" and "coach" are often used interchangeably, so don't make assumptions about what approach someone uses based on the job title.) Look for a match with what you think you need to get unstuck and make clear decisions about the next step in your career.

Ingredients for Knowing What You Want

SUCCESS INGREDIENTS
Industry research
Sample job descriptions
Career vision
Career assessment
Skills inventory
Major accomplishments list

INGREDIENT:
Industry Research

There are two reasons you may need to conduct **industry research.** If you know you want to stay in the same industry but want to change the type of work you have been doing, industry research will tell you what other jobs you are qualified for and likely to get. If you are new to the job market or pretty sure you want to change to a new industry, research will help you learn what an industry is about and whether it could be right for you.

Remember that in this book we are using the word "industry" to refer to either an industrial sector, like health care, or a job field, like accounting. So your research might span different industrial sectors, different job fields, or both.

Three factors to consider in doing any kind of research are quality, quantity, and a focused approach. Try to find the best mix of these factors as you are researching the industries that may be of interest to you. Spending too much time on getting every last detail about one industry can melt away the day. On the other hand, spreading your research efforts across many industries can make it difficult to find enough information about any one.

To help you get focused and determine how much information to gather, start by considering these questions:

- Am I planning to stay in the same industry or am I looking to change?
- What industries currently need my existing skills?
- What industries are likely to grow, or at least remain stable, for the long term?
- What might I need to know to work in these industries?
- What are the three industries that most interest me?
- Which industries are dealing with the kinds of problems I can solve?

Use your answers to these questions to guide you in selecting a finite number of industries to explore for your next career move.

One of the best places to start your research is at your local library. There you'll find extensive collections of reference books, guides, directories, and other sources about most industries. Here are a few career and industry references you might look for:

- *Career Information Center*, Gale Group (MacMillan) [thirteen-volume set]
- Encyclopedia of Careers and Vocational Guidance, Holli Cosgrove, ed. (Ferguson)

- *Jobs Rated Almanac,* Les Krantz (Barricade)
- *Occupational Outlook Handbook,* U.S. Dept. of Labor (Jist Works)
- *Peterson's Job Seekers Almanac* (Peterson's)
- *Standard and Poor's Industry Surveys* [available by subscription at libraries]
- *U.S. Industry And Trade Outlook* www.outlook.gov

These guides provide information about industry trends, including data and opinions about the outlook for employment and continued growth. Compiling facts and figures from sources like this can help you determine possibilities in the industries that seem best suited for you. You can also eliminate those that aren't a good fit for your skills or don't interest you.

You can further expand your industry research through sources like trade journals, professional association newsletters and web sites, business periodicals (e.g. *Business Week* or *Fortune),* company annual reports and web sites, or books written about (or by) industry leaders.

Local and national newspapers are another good source for keeping abreast of industry trends on a real-time basis. Product news, mergers, acquisitions, breakthrough developments, and industry issues are all discussed in these media, and will give you a good sense of conditions in industries you are considering.

Another advantage of using your local library is their access to online databases available only by subscription. These databases provide the same type of information found in print, but are often easier to use and more up to date. Many libraries offer access via their web site twenty-four hours per day. If you have Internet access, you can visit the library's web site and get directions for how to log on to these databases. If you don't, your library will have access on site.

These subscription databases are an excellent source for archived information. You'll find both recently published articles and reports as well as those going back several years. For example, business magazine articles are archived by *Business Source Premier* or you can find newspaper articles from over 100 U.S. and international papers by searching *Newspaper Source.*

Found: The Job from Hell!

After working twenty-five years for blue chip companies, I found myself searching for a job after losing my vice president slot to a family friend of the newly hired CEO. I immediately set out on a search for new employment and soon had in hand two attractive offers—one from a large, local government agency and another from a small startup firm. The government agency offered me a turnaround challenge as their chief information officer working in their corporate offices in Manhattan. The startup offered me a vice president position, leading one of its software product lines through the next stages of growth with offices on Long Island and the potential of more pay than the semi-civil service assignment with the agency.

One problem—I had no information on the startup beyond what was available from its parent companies. What I didn't discover until after accepting the position with the startup was that it had been formed to manage a long string of liabilities in contracts made over the years, liabilities that were not likely to be readily resolved or satisfied.

Lack of information and research on my part led me into a situation that was intolerable from my perspective and that ran counter to my personal values. The price paid for this shortfall in my job search skills has been very high over the past several years.

Michaela Laune
COLORADO SPRINGS, COLORADO

USING THE INTERNET FOR RESEARCH

The Internet is a valuable tool for researching just about any topic on the planet. This vast network of information can be an enormous asset or a huge time waster. With a few keystrokes and the click of a mouse, you can enter into the world of information overload. You may have a mountain of data at your fingertips, but you don't have all the time in the world to sift through it. Also you should scrutinize carefully information you obtain here because anyone at any time can publish data on the Internet.

So the same rules apply for using the Internet as for any other type of industry research. Discover the best mix of quality, quantity, and a focused approach to help you reduce the time it takes to find what you want. If you're new to researching on the web, ask a librarian to help you find what you're looking for, or see "Internet Research Skills" in Chapter 8.

INGREDIENT:
Sample Job Descriptions

A critical component of knowing what type of job you want is learning what it is that companies want. **Sample job descriptions** from the industries you are exploring will help you match your wants, needs, and desires with what's available in the marketplace. When companies post an open position, they describe the specific skills, training, and experience required to be a successful candidate. By examining descriptions of available jobs, you can get a much clearer picture of the job you might want.

SOURCES FOR SAMPLE JOB DESCRIPTIONS

- *O*NET Dictionary of Occupational Titles* (Jist Works or http://online .onetcenter.org)
- *The Complete Guide for Occupational Exploration,* U.S. Department of Labor

- Internet job boards (e.g., www.monster.com or www.careerbuilder.com)
- Career opportunities posted on company web sites
- Want ads in local, regional, and national newspapers
- Jobs advertised through industry association newsletters or web sites
- Trade and business journals for your profession
- University, community, and vocational school career centers
- State, provincial, and county employment offices
- Recruiters and employment agencies
- Your personal network
- Informational interviewing

Sample job descriptions are a good barometer for both what you might like to do in an industry and what would be the best fit for your skills. Here are some things to consider in evaluating job descriptions:

- *Read between the lines.* Assume that the company, and particularly the hiring manager, wants more from the right candidate than what is described. If you have training or experience you believe would contribute to the job as you understand it, you may still be a candidate even if your qualifications don't match the description.
- *Keep your goals in mind.* There will be many jobs that you could do, but the perfect job will also be one that you want to do. Look for what basic job requirements match your background and skill set. Then look at what will interest you in a job. Next consider the typical salary and advancement opportunities available. Follow that by evaluating what unique value you might bring to the position that would be likely to get you hired.
- *Consider related jobs and/or industries.* Expand your sights beyond the jobs you have done and industries you have worked for in the past. For example, if most of your career has been in the accounting field and the health care industry, you could look at jobs outside accounting in health care or at accounting jobs in other industries.
- *Compare and contrast.* Once you have gathered a good sampling of job

descriptions, look for similarities, key differences, special requirements, and what may be missing. Of all the options available, what positions seem like they would be the best combination of what you want, what you need, and what you are qualified to do?

- *Use job descriptions as suggestions, not rules.* You may not find any job descriptions that are an exact fit for what you are seeking. That doesn't mean the right job doesn't exist. What it does mean is that you may need to create a position for yourself or adapt an existing one. (There's more about this under "Selling Yourself with a Proposal" in Chapter 9.) Allow the job descriptions you have gathered to suggest positions that might be close to what you want and help you find where such jobs might exist.

INGREDIENT:
Career Vision

If someone asked you to describe your vision of the most perfect place on earth, what would it look like? A mountaintop with a spectacular view? A tropical island with a warm breeze, soft sand, and tall palm trees? Now suppose someone asked you to describe in similar detail your vision of the perfect career. How do you draw a picture of something you can't yet clearly see?

In developing a **career vision**, you are creating a word picture of where you want to go with your career. If you can visualize your ultimate goals, it will become easier to choose what your next job should be. Even if some portions of your vision are fuzzy, write down what pieces you do know. It's like creating the scenes of a play. Each scene can be written independently to tell part of the story, and eventually all of the scenes add up to a complete production.

WHAT'S IN A CAREER VISION?

First put aside any negative self-talk that might sabotage your thoughts. Allow yourself to dream a bit about what you really want, regardless of whether it seems possible. Don't worry if your vision is missing some key components. While it may seem a bit hazy at first, the more questions you answer about it, the clearer it will come into focus.

To begin creating a picture of what you want in your career, answer the questions below.

1. *Work environment*
    a. How would you describe your ideal company's culture?
    b. What would be the physical setting of your work, and how would you dress?
    c. Do you prefer a structured work environment or one that allows a lot of freedom?
    d. With what sort of people would you like to interact as co-workers or customers?
    e. How would you describe your ideal manager?

2. *Type of work*
    a. What could you do for eight hours every day and still be excited enough to come back for more?
    b. How would you describe an enjoyable day at work?
    c. What do you not want as part of the job?
    d. In which industries (or job fields) can you see yourself working?
    e. Do you prefer to work alone or in a team of co-workers?
    f. Do you most enjoy working with information, with people, or with physical objects?
    g. Is your preference to work on one project at a time or several all at once?
    h. Does managing people or projects interest you, or do you prefer contributing individually?
    i. If you like to manage, for what sort of people or projects would you enjoy having responsibility?
    j. Where do you see your work taking you five or ten years from now?
    k. What types of advancement opportunities are important to you?

3. *Location and lifestyle*
   a. What personal lifestyle would you like to lead—in terms of living space, physical surroundings, leisure activities, or local culture?
   b. If relocation is an option, where else might you find this lifestyle?
   c. How much travel would you consider acceptable for your job?
   d. What work schedule would allow you to live your desired lifestyle? How much overtime are you willing and able to work?

4. *Salary and benefits*
   a. What minimum salary do you need just to meet your current obligations?
   b. What will your salary requirements look like in five or ten years?
   c. What financial goals do you have other than just paying the bills? What sort of salary would those goals require?
   d. How much money per month would you like to be saving toward your retirement, and when would you like that retirement to be?
   e. What types of employee benefits are important to you?

FORMAT FOR YOUR CAREER VISION

Any format that works for you is just fine. You can write it like a story, list bullet points, or create a formal document with illustrations, graphs, and figures. (See "Career vision" example below.) The important part is that you capture what you already know and get clear on what you don't know but need to find out.

Keep in mind when creating your vision that you want to find a balance between dreaming and reality. If you fantasize too much in your vision, you may feel disappointed and say, "I'll never be able to get all that from my career." On the other hand, you don't want to limit your vision so much that you shortchange yourself and decide on a job that doesn't give you what you want. Treat this time in your life as a chance to make things better for yourself, professionally and personally. Writing out your career vision can help you see what is possible.

Career vision

WORK ENVIRONMENT
- Relaxed company culture
- Campus-like setting with lots of open space; some fieldwork
- Casual dress
- Minimal structure; work independently
- Bright, friendly co-workers
- Easygoing boss

TYPE OF WORK
- Geological research
- Combination of mapping, reading, writing, discussion, and fieldwork
- Not on the computer all day
- Work for university, federal or state agency, private research/ consulting firm
- Frequent collaboration with other people
- Fifty-fifty split working with data and people
- Several simultaneous projects
- No supervisory responsibility; project management okay
- Promotion to next level in two-three years
- Eventual promotion to senior scientist

LOCATION/LIFESTYLE
- Near outdoor activities, coastal or mountain region, not far from metro area
- Relocation okay; not sure yet which geographic areas
- Flexible work schedule; some travel okay

SALARY/BENEFITS
- Need minimum $30,000 per year for expenses
- Will need minimum $35,000 per year within five years
- Hope to buy house in five years; will likely need starting salary of $37–38,000 per year to manage saving a down payment
- Retirement far off; yet would like a 401(k) or pension plan
- Require at least two weeks vacation and full medical benefits

INGREDIENT:
Career Assessment

A **career assessment** is a personalized survey of you. Like a survey, an assessment consists of a series of carefully crafted questions spanning a wide range of topics. Its purpose is to produce an appraisal of who you are, what you are good at, and what you want.

There are two parts to a career assessment. In the first part you answer the questions presented. You'll get the most accurate results when you don't try to figure out the "right" answer and just be as honest as possible.

The second part—and the most important—is the interpretation of the results. You can rely on an automated analysis available online or through career centers, or work with a career professional trained in interpreting the assessment of your choice. In some cases you will need to pay to take a career assessment test and receive the subsequent report of your results. An in-depth interpretation of how you answered the questions gives you a framework for describing what you like, how you communicate, your strengths, weaknesses, and where you perform best. Here are some of the topics an assessment covers:

- How you interact with others—are you outgoing or more reserved?
- How you understand the world—does innovation or experience matter most?
- How you make decisions—do you need all the data first or go from the gut?
- How you deal with uncertainty—do you insist on clarity and order or is ambiguity okay?
- Type of work that interests you—data, people, or things; details or big picture; projects or daily tasks?
- How your personality fits into the world of work—team player or Lone Ranger; independent action or lots of direction?
- A list of professions that relate to your personality and work style

From Vision to Reality

I used to work at a very large bank in a job that wasn't the best fit. I was an accountant and finance guy managing a sales call center. The bank was completing a merger and I was getting a new boss every three months. Each boss would come in and say, "I have a finance guy running my call center?" Finally, not to my surprise, one of them said, "I want someone else running my call center." It was time to move on.

I knew I wanted to get back into finance and work for a smaller company, but that was all I knew. I hadn't had to look for a job in seven or eight years. I remembered I learned about informational interviewing in college. To me the gist of that idea is figure out what you want to do by talking to people who do what you want to do, and at the same time you'll probably find a job. That's exactly what I did.

I spent several weeks meeting with many people in the community to get input into the type of job I wanted. I met with a woman who managed a technology transfer organization connected to the university, mainly dealing with high-tech startup companies. When I met with her, our conversation went something like this:

Me: "I think I want to work for a small company."

She: "An existing company or a startup?"

Me: "I don't know."

She: "A service or technology company?"

Me: "I don't know."

After that conversation, I had to do some more investigating. I met with more people in those types of companies. I ended up with a one-page description of the type of job I wanted. It included a general title, the responsibilities, type of company, the company values, number of employees in the company, my base pay, and the amount of equity I wanted in the company.

I took that description to the woman I had met with before and asked her what she thought of it. She thought it was pretty good and that there were probably some jobs out there like that, and then she said, "I know someone who is looking to fill a position like that. I'll give him your name." He called me and it was a perfect fit. I took the job and it was the best job I've ever had.

Jeff Schneider
HIGHLANDS RANCH, COLORADO

WHAT TO DO WITH ALL THIS INFORMATION

Assessments and their personalized interpretations offer you many guideposts to find your way through the career maze. Some assessments suggest actual job titles that might be a good fit for your interests and personality. For example, if you've been a sales manager in the past, an assessment might suggest customer service manager, marketing director, public speaker, or trainer as possible career options.

Assessments can help you identify an industry in which to work. Your personality, interests, and strengths may be well suited for more industries than you realize. If you have been a project manager in manufacturing, your assessment may suggest that your ability to manage many people, projects, and tasks at once could be just as applicable in the construction industry.

An assessment will often tell you more about your communication style. Your ability to communicate effectively is a key component of a successful job search.

You'll need to communicate while networking, when making contact with employers, in interviews, on your résumé, and over the phone. Knowing more about how you interact with others can be very helpful when you need to get your point across and be understood.

ASSESSMENT CHOICES

Many assessments are in use today and new ones appear on a regular basis. Some frequently used assessment tools are:

- Motivational Appraisal of Personal Potential™ (MAPP)
  www.assessment.com
- Myers–Briggs Type Indicator® (MBTI)
  www.myersbriggs.org
- Self-Directed Search® (SDS)
  www.self-directed-search.com
- Strong Interest Inventory® (SII)
  www.cpp.com

A word of caution about assessments—you'll need to stay objective when digesting the information you receive. Not everything you learn will be applicable for your current situation or worthy of taking action. For example, you may see "actor" on a list of career options because you have personality traits that suggest an ability to work in front of audiences. Even if this interests you, it may make no sense at all for you to pursue an acting career now if you have never done it and have a family to feed.

INGREDIENT:
Skills Inventory

In Chapter 1 we described how a successful job search is more like a marketing campaign that reaches out to many potential buyers than it is a "search" for something that already exists. In this marketing campaign, you are the product. If a product has the right features, benefits the customer, can demonstrate value, and is available at the right price, it is considered marketable. In choosing the right job to pursue now, you must consider how marketable your skills are to prospective employers and their hiring managers. Preparing a **skills inventory** will help.

Your marketable skills consist of both functional skills and unique skills. We'll look at each of these and how they define you as a product.

YOUR FUNCTIONAL SKILLS

Every job requires skills that are essential for handling the basic functions of the position and performing adequately. These functional skills are learned through formal training or on-the-job experience. Functional skills can include abilities that aren't necessarily unique to any job title. Here are some examples:

- Bookkeeping
- Carpentry
- Financial analysis
- Graphic design
- Market research
- Project management
- Proposal writing
- Selling
- Software programming
- Technical writing
- Training
- Word processing

MAKING YOUR INVENTORY OF FUNCTIONAL SKILLS

List all the functional skills you have going as far back as you can recall in your education and career. The telemarketing skills you gained eighteen years ago can be just as applicable today as they were back then. You want to consider all the skills you might wish to market when looking for the job you want.

To identify your functional skills, review your résumé and any cover letters you've written and look at any past job descriptions or performance evaluations you have on hand. List skills for which you have taken classes or completed training. Be sure to include any skills you have learned as a volunteer or in leisure activities. Also refer to any job postings you have considered applying for to see what skills are listed there that you believe you possess.

YOUR UNIQUE SKILLS

Unique skills are exceptional abilities that others in your field may not have or haven't perfected as well as you. These are the skills that can make you stand out. When you express your unique skills with descriptive words or short phrases that tell a story, you can demonstrate your special abilities. For instance, one of your unique skills might be "ability to handle customer issues in one call." Behind this phrase lies a story where you were the only customer service rep in a magazine subscription center that could manage ninety percent of all subscription problems on the first phone call.

In taking inventory of your unique skills you get a clearer picture of your valuable qualities as a marketable product. This picture can help you identify those positions for which you might be uniquely qualified and stand out from the competition. Here are some examples of unique skills:

- Able to build highly effective teams
- Able to manage complex customer issues
- Able to see the big picture
- Creative problem-solver
- Develop unique designs
- Excel at sales prospecting
- Expert in dealing with difficult employees

- Fearless public speaker
- Flawlessly handle busy phone lines
- Meticulous researcher
- Speak four languages fluently
- Superior analytical skills

MAKING YOUR INVENTORY OF UNIQUE SKILLS

Your unique skills often show up in peak experiences. Think of four or five significant accomplishments of which you are proud—in your career or elsewhere in life. Ask yourself, "What did I bring to the table in order to succeed?" Recall several times when you faced a crisis and what you did in response. To uncover strengths that others have seen in you, review any reference letters, performance evaluations, or testimonials you have on file.

Also consider what you find yourself naturally doing without thought of compensation. What do your friends, family, and co-workers often ask of you, even when it isn't part of your job?

INGREDIENT:
Major Accomplishments List

Look back in your career and personal life at everything you've done to solve problems or change things for the better. You'll find plenty of accomplishments for which you deserve recognition. Your **major accomplishments list** is a compilation of powerful statements that describe the positive results you have created in the past. Nobody but you can claim these special victories.

Think about a newspaper headline. It draws you in. You decide what to read based on the interest the headline generates; if it's boring, you just keep looking for one that catches your attention. Your major accomplishments list works the same way. People will want to know more about you once they hear or read these headlines.

Built His Dream Job

After my company was part of an acquisition, I was laid off from my information technology job in telecommunications. For a long time, I've had a
dream to work on the business side of woodworking and cabinetry because
of my woodworking hobby. After twelve-plus months out of work and a five-
month contract doing software project management, I ended up working for
a friend of mine from church who owns half of a kitchen-and-bath design
business.

I feel like I'm in my dream job. I'm working in the office doing purchas-
ing, as well as using my IT background to implement a new computer system to streamline the operations and better track customer contacts. I have
established relationships with many of the suppliers of materials and tools
in the Denver area to benefit the business and, as a bonus, enhance my personal hobby.

Though I'm not making the kind of money that I made in corporate IT, I
am happy with what I'm doing, where I'm doing it, and I have faith that it won't
be too long before my earnings are moving back toward where I was. I don't
expect to get back to the level I was at during the crazy times of the technology frenzy, but through my unemployment experience, I have learned to
make better choices financially and to be content with what I already have.

Going through this experience has been painful, requiring much growing
and stretching, but I am currently in a better place than I've been in a very
long time. I have also learned that I am going to spend the rest of my life in
a networking mode—to meet new people, help others to make connections

wherever I can, and be a part of what makes things work. It's no longer just about me, but about how I can enjoy life and be of service to others, whether that means lending an ear or lending a contact.

Ralph Hart
DENVER, COLORADO

Your major accomplishments list can help you know what job you want in several ways. When you are networking, describing one of your accomplishments is a quick way to let new contacts know what your capabilities are. In an informational interview, being able to speak about your accomplishments will help people understand where you might fit in their company or industry. Comparing your accomplishments list to sample job descriptions will help you get a better feel for which jobs are right for you.

Later in your job search, you'll be able to use your accomplishments list in preparing a résumé, cover letters, a portfolio, or a job proposal; as well as during job interviews.

If you're just beginning your professional career, you still have accomplishments you can write about—as a volunteer, in summer or after-school jobs, on sports teams, in a club, or even in your personal life.

WRITING YOUR ACCOMPLISHMENT STATEMENTS

Which one of the following statements would entice you to read further?

1. Proven track record completing projects under budget and within deadline.
2. In one eighteen-month period, managed five complex technology projects,

generating six million dollars in revenue while saving nearly one million in capital expenses.

You can clearly see the difference between these two statements. You have probably seen (or maybe even written) a statement similar to the first on a résumé or cover letter. And that's the problem—generic statements like this one are so common they are often overlooked.

The more you assign your accomplishments an "economic value"—revenue generated, percent of growth, or money saved—the more you will stand out from the crowd. People will be able to see what you are capable of doing, and so will you.

Here are a few more examples that will help you get the idea:

- Developed an Internet marketing campaign for a technology services company that grew their customer base by 125 percent in three months.
- Reached 120 percent of annual sales quota in less than six months.
- Designed a customer service-training program that reduced total problem-resolution time from ten minutes to three minutes per call.
- Reorganized the benefits department filing system, reducing the average time needed to locate files by twenty-five percent.
- Located a new printing vendor for the campus newspaper, reducing the annual budget by fifteen percent.
- Raised $5000 for my Girl Scout troop's ski trip fund by organizing a crafts fair.

Use this simple three-step process for designing your major accomplishment statements:

1. Use action words to describe your role, such as "developed," "implemented," or "created."
2. Write a short descriptive headline for what you did.
3. Illustrate the value of your accomplishments in money, time, or a percentage of change.

You'll discover just how valuable you are when you get your major accomplishments down on paper. As you create these statements and share them with others, possibilities for industries and companies where you would like to work will emerge. Because you were able to make these things happen in the past, you can repeat them in your next job. These headlines will set you apart from the competition and demonstrate you have what it takes to get the job done, no matter what the task.

HINT:
What If You Are in a Hurry?

You may be at a point in your job search when you feel you can't take much time defining the job you want. When you are running out of money or need to change jobs quickly, it may seem like a luxury you can't afford to take assessments or spend time doing research. If that's the case, then it may serve you best to jump ahead to the *Finding opportunities and contacts* stage even if you aren't yet clear about the type of job for which you are looking.

Before you leave this stage behind, we suggest you complete at least the "career vision" ingredient in this chapter. Then choose "ideal job description," discussed in Chapter 8, as your next Success Ingredient.

A word of caution, however—if you don't take the time to determine what you really want, you may find yourself settling on a job that doesn't give you much satisfaction or is only a temporary solution to making a living. You may also find that your job search is not as efficient as it could be. Without a clear focus for your job-seeking efforts, you are more likely to waste time pursuing referrals and opportunities that don't result in interviews and offers.

So if you decide to skip this stage, make sure you are doing so because your need to move forward quickly is truly urgent, and not just because some of the exercises suggested so far in this chapter seem time-consuming or challenging.

APPROACH:
Networking and Referral-Building

> **SUCCESS INGREDIENTS**
> Industry networking venues
> Educational venues

RECIPE:
Networking in the Industry You're Exploring

Meeting people at organized networking events is one of the easiest and most effective ways to learn more about opportunities in any industry. Start by seeking those associations, organizations, or institutions that serve the industry you're exploring. Get on the mailing lists, find out about specific events, and go shake hands with currently employed people. The places where you go to meet people are your **industry networking venues**.

CHOICES FOR INDUSTRY NETWORKING VENUES

* Trade and professional association meetings where people who work in your industry gather
* Meetings of professional groups from other industries where you could meet referral and information sources
* Lectures, conferences, and fundraisers hosted by educational institutions, nonprofit organizations, and affinity groups
* Private social gatherings organized for the purpose of meeting people in an industry

The best venues for networking are those intended to be a place for people to meet. At this type of event, newcomers and job-seekers will be welcome.

Talking to others connected with your industry is a highly effective means of discovering what you want to do, where you might work, and which influential people you might need to meet.

How do you find these groups and events? Start by asking around. Anyone who is working in the industry, a current job-seeker, or an industry consultant or vendor can probably suggest some events they attend.

You can find groups listed in your local *Yellow Pages* under "associations" or "professional organizations." Your library will have print references and online sources that list industry organizations. Your city's Chamber of Commerce may have a list of local business, industry, and community organizations.

To find scheduled events, look in regional and local newspapers for a business calendar or community calendar section. Be sure to check the *Business Times* or *Business Journal* published in your metropolitan area. National or regional trade publications focusing on your industry, profession, or area of special interest will often have event listings. Also look for web sites that list events by doing a keyword search for your city (e.g., "Minneapolis events").

In looking for events to attend, keep in mind that the way to get the most value from a group is to be a member. You will have more success in your networking if you go back to the same groups repeatedly than if you keep going to new groups all the time. Find two or three that seem to have a good mix of knowledgeable and influential people, and keep going back.

WHAT IF YOU DON'T LIKE TALKING TO STRANGERS?

If meeting new people makes you uncomfortable, you may find that groups with a more structured format work better for you than informal mixers and receptions. Many networking events provide time for introductions, when all members get a chance to stand up and tell the whole group what they do. A great way to network that can make talking to strangers easier is to work as a volunteer. At a professional meeting you can check people in at the registration desk or help distribute literature. In the office of an association or institution that serves your industry, you can stuff envelopes, answer phones, or assist with bookkeeping, web design, or any other professional skill you have. By volunteering, you can establish connections with many people in an industry and also have a chance to show them what you can do.

When you meet new people in any setting who might be helpful in your career exploration, plan to follow up with them by way of a phone call, e-mail, lunch, coffee, or an informational interview. Try to get further acquainted in a collegial way, which may mean discovering how to make a relationship between you reciprocal. Ask your new contacts, "What are you up to in your career right now? Is there any way I can help?" Sometimes just offering help to others is enough to make them feel more generous toward you.

Acquiring better networking skills will benefit you in all areas of your job search. You can learn more about networking skills in Chapter 8.

NETWORKING WITHOUT LEAVING HOME

Getting to know new people doesn't necessarily require going to events. You can also network online, by phone, and by mail. If you are relocating to a new area, you may do most of your networking virtually rather than in person. See Chapter 8 for more about using the Internet to meet new people by way of message boards, live chats, and discussion lists.

Keep in mind that you can always reach out to people you would like to know by phone, e-mail, or a personal letter, whether or not you have already met. It's easier to get someone to take your call or answer your e-mail when you have been referred by a mutual acquaintance. Yet you might be surprised by how friendly and helpful many strangers will be when you ask for their help in planning the next step in your career. Just about everyone has been where you are now at some point in the past. If you are respectful of people's time, they will often be willing to give it to you freely.

RECIPE:
Getting More Education

An interesting thing happens when people are out of work for a while or fear they might be. They often take the opportunity to gain more education. Professional associations, training companies, vendors, and educational institutions provide a wide variety of industry-specific educational programs. Some of these programs offer valuable chances for more professional training, while others can be a sales pitch for the provider's services. Either way, participating in these **educational venues** can be helpful to your job search.

As a job-seeker, you get a double bonus by attending classes, seminars, and workshops. First you get smarter about a topic that interests you and that can advance your career. Second—and just as important—you get to meet people in your industry who can help you. Educational events attract people who want to stay connected in their industry. By attending these events, you can meet influential people who can be great contacts, providing you with inside information about the industry, companies, and specific job opportunities.

SUGGESTIONS FOR EDUCATIONAL VENUES

- Trade and professional association meetings and conferences
- Company-sponsored educational events
- Training seminars offered by consultants and vendors
- College courses and university extension classes
- Workshops provided by independent training companies and learning centers
- Chamber of Commerce workshops and seminars
- Public workshops offered at libraries

Limit your attendance at educational programs to those that connect you with people in the industry you are exploring. You could become an "education junkie" and not have much time for anything else related to your job search!

Found a Job at Night School

Early in my career, I was working in a small audit and accounting firm and had decided to move on to one of the (then) "big eight" accounting firms. As I was gearing up to start mailing out my résumé to various human resources departments, I also happened to be taking a night class to meet New York State's requirements to sit for the CPA exam.

During the first class meeting, I struck up a conversation with the man sitting next to me. As we were talking, I told him that I was working in a small firm but looking to make a move. His eyes lit up as he excitedly told me that his office at one of the big eight was looking desperately for new junior people. The following week at class, I gave him my résumé and was almost immediately invited to come in for an interview. Two weeks later, they offered me a job.

Peter Jacobs
SAN FRANCISCO, CALIFORNIA

APPROACH:
Informational Interviewing

SUCCESS INGREDIENT

Industry informational interview plan

RECIPE:
Using Informational Interviews

Informational interviewing is the process of getting information from formal interviews. What's different about this type of interview is that you are the person conducting it. In an informational meeting, you are speaking with a professional in the industry you are exploring and asking questions you need answered to choose the next step for your career. You're going directly to the source for learning what's happening in an industry, what types of jobs are available, and what it's like to work within that industry.

A key benefit to informational interviewing is that you get information that's impossible to find elsewhere. Special challenges, upcoming opportunities, inside trends, hidden job possibilities, and insightful details about company culture are among the many nuggets of information you can acquire when talking directly with a professional. Published information won't give you this level of detail.

To use this tactic successfully you need an **industry informational interview plan**. You must decide with whom you want to meet and the information you seek. With the appropriate preparation for your meetings, you will come across as knowledgeable and organized. Here's what an industry informational interview plan might look like:

Start with research. Learn about the industry you are exploring through some of the resources described under "Industry Research" earlier in this chapter.

To Get People to Talk to You, Just Ask

I have used informational interviews extensively throughout my career. When I was in college and considering law school, I looked up attorneys' names in the telephone book, called them, and asked if they would meet with me to answer questions about the legal profession. Considering that I was quite shy at the time, picking up the phone was a big step. No one turned me down. They gave generously of their time to tell me about their experiences.

Many years later when I was looking for work, I remembered my success with that technique and called people in the public relations field. I had no background or experience in the field, but it sounded interesting to me so I again contacted people I didn't know and asked them for their time. One of my best job leads came out of those informational interviews.

Cindy Rold, JD, ACC
LITTLETON, COLORADO

Make a list of people who might be considered industry leaders, as well as other executives whose names seem to appear in multiple places. Learn the names of officers in your industry's professional association. Association leaders are excellent resources and are often quite open to being interviewed. **Decide whom to interview.** Start with people you already know who are either in the industry, or who you believe might have industry contacts. As you contact them, inquire if they know any of the names you gathered in your research. Add some of those leaders to your interview list, whether or not you can find someone to refer you. Any time you can gain an audience with a top executive in your industry, you get an insider's look at the big picture.

Another valuable group of potential contacts is alumni from your university or training school. You may be able to obtain a directory from your school with hundreds of names in it. Salespeople to the industry can also offer helpful insights.

Make a list of questions. If you aren't prepared with a list of questions to ask in the interview, you may waste your contact's time and fail to obtain needed information. Here are some suggested questions to get you started:

- Tell me about your job. What does a typical day look like?
- How did you find your job?
- What do you like most about your work? How about the least?
- What qualities are important to be successful at this type of work?
- What are the most important issues facing this industry today?
- What trends do you see for the future of this industry?
- What kind of education and experience would I need to succeed?
- Given what you know about me, what type of job can you envision for me?
- What advice do you have for someone who wants to work in this industry?
- Is there anyone else you can recommend with whom I should speak?

Add to your list of questions any specifics about the industry and available jobs that remain unanswered from your research. If you notice any questions that you're not sure your existing contacts can answer, identify who might be able to answer those questions and add them to your interview list. With your completed plan in hand, start scheduling some interviews.

HOW TO APPROACH PEOPLE FOR INTERVIEWS

You'll probably find that getting people to spend a short time with you to talk about what they do is much easier than getting an interview for a job. People will want to help you if you approach them respectfully. Indicate up front that you don't want to interview for a job. Let them know that you would like thirty minutes of their time to talk about the industry and their job because you are trying to make an informed career choice. With local contacts, ask for an in-person interview whenever possible, but phone interviews are fine, too.

You can ask for informational interviews by calling your contact directly or sending a letter or e-mail with your request and telling them you'll follow up. You will get a better response to your request if you include in your communication what led you to contact them. If you were referred, by all means name the person who referred you. If not, try to establish another shared connection. For example, you could say: "We are both members of the American Society for Training and Development" or "I found the article about your company in last week's *Business Journal* quite intriguing."

The "Informational interview request letter" below depicts an example. Try using this format for a letter or as a script when calling to request an informational interview.

Following any interviews, thank your contacts for their help. Then send a handwritten thank-you note the following day to add a personal touch that will be remembered. File your notes from the interview in a binder, file folder, or computer so you can keep track of your interview results until you are ready to make some decisions.

Informational interview request letter

Dear Susana,

Our mutual colleague Teresa Marques was kind enough to pass your name on to me as a successful executive in the local health care market. I'm hoping you have just a few minutes to assist me.

I am currently working on my next career move in the health care industry and I am trying to learn more about my options by speaking directly with people who understand the industry well and can speak to its long-term outlook. You are obviously one of these people. I would greatly appreciate the opportunity to spend just thirty minutes of your time gaining your insights about career opportunities in health care. I am not looking for a job at this point, but rather gathering information to help me choose the right direction.

I would like to treat you to a cup of coffee and ask you a few questions about your career, the marketplace, and any other information you would be willing to share. I'll call your office after you've received this letter to set up a convenient time.

Thank you in advance for your help. Teresa spoke quite highly of you and I would enjoy the opportunity to meet you.

Regards,
Jorge Silva

APPROACH:
Employing Recruiters and Agencies

RECIPE:
How Recruiters and Agencies Can Help

Most recruiters and employment agency workers are significantly knowledge-able about the industries in which they work, so they can be excellent candidates for informational interviews and valuable networking contacts. It's not a good idea, though, to apply to an agency for permanent employment or begin working with a recruiter if you're still uncertain what sort of job you want. Recruiters and agencies work on behalf of the employers they serve, not for job candidates like you. If you apply to them too soon, they may offer you interviews for jobs you look qualified for, but aren't particularly interested in. Or they may simply ignore your application because it isn't targeted enough for them to match you with any of the available opportunities.

However, registering with temporary employment agencies may help you to find positions you can "try on" temporarily to measure the fit. These agencies will place you in temporary positions based on your functional skills, whether or not you know the type of job you desire. Not all temporary positions are administrative; many agencies specialize in placing workers in industries such as hospitality, accounting, or information technology, or in interim management positions.

Be prepared with your skills inventory when you register with an agency. The more sought for skills you can name, the more likely it is they will place you.

 **APPROACH:**
Searching Specialized Job Listings
and Using Help-Wanted Ads

RECIPE:
Using Job Postings for Your Research

While it's not a good idea to start applying for open positions until you're clear on the type of job you want, job postings are an excellent resource for your research. By scanning specialized job listings or the want ads, you can gather sample job descriptions, discover what types of jobs are currently in demand, and learn a great deal about your targeted industry. Be sure to also keep track of the company names you see advertised; these may be places where you will want to identify contacts for informational interviews. (For some possible sources of job listings and want ads, see Chapter 8.)

Keep in mind that looking at job postings at this point in your job search is about gathering information to make good choices rather than applying for advertised positions. If you do see a position advertised that seems ideal to you, go ahead and apply for it. But don't get sidetracked by starting to apply for multiple positions that have nothing to do with each other. An important part of getting hired is to position yourself as the perfect candidate for the job for which you're applying. (For additional information on this topic, see Chapter 9.) You won't be able to accomplish this with a one-size-fits-all résumé and generic cover letter; you'll need to prepare.

HINT:
Knowing When You're Done

So how much research is enough? When are your inventories and assessments sufficiently complete? When have you talked to enough people? The acid test for being sure that you know what you want well enough to proceed is at the beginning of Chapter 8. If you can complete the Success Ingredient "ideal job description," you are ready to leave behind the *Knowing what you want* stage and move forward to *Finding opportunities and contacts.*

CHAPTER 8

Finding Opportunities and Contacts:
When You Don't Know Enough People to Contact

To keep a lamp burning we have to keep
putting oil in it.

— MOTHER TERESA

Where the Jobs Are

Before you opened this book you may have thought that the best way to find a
job was to discover an open position posted somewhere. Now we've told you
that finding a job is all about talking to people. If you already have a wide network of contacts in the industry and geographic area where you are seeking work,
discovering job opportunities may be relatively easy for you. But if you are changing industries, relocating, new to the job market, or just have never been much
of a networker, you will most likely need to make many new contacts in order
to locate opportunities.

When you focus your job search on finding open positions that have already
been advertised, you will only see fifteen percent of the jobs currently available.
But if you meet and talk with a wide range of people about your job search, you
will locate the remaining eighty-five percent of available positions . . . often
referred to as the "hidden job market."

By choosing now to work on the *Finding opportunities* stage of the Job Search
Pyramid, you are acknowledging that seeking out opportunities is where you need
to put the most effort. As you use the job search approaches you selected in Chapter 2 to make contacts and uncover possibilities, you will likely also begin to apply
for positions and go on interviews. Remember our advice in Chapter 5—even

though you are concentrating right now on finding opportunities, if you find one you like, go ahead and apply for it. Don't wait until later to apply just because you picked the *Finding opportunities* stage as your focus.

It's important to recognize that expanding your network with new contacts will be an ongoing process for as long as you are seeking a job. This means that whatever approaches you decide on for increasing your network, you should be willing to keep them up over an extended period of time. When looking for a job, more of the same works much better than a little of everything. Ideally, your activities to expand your network and find unadvertised opportunities should become automatic and habitual. Even when you are pursuing a hot job opportunity or preparing for an interview, you should allow time for networking, informational interviewing, or whatever your chosen approaches are.

It's natural to wonder whether the approaches you have selected for finding opportunities and contacts are the best choices. You may find yourself wanting to switch around just to see if something else might work better. Be patient and don't change your approach during the twenty-eight days of the *Get Hired Now!* program. It simply isn't enough time for you to judge your results accurately. It's okay to try a different recipe — you might change from attending events to lunch meetings, for example. But don't alter your overall approach, from, say, Networking and Referral-Building to Employing Recruiters and Agencies.

The best way to determine how well a particular job search approach is working is to track your results over time. There are three statistics that can be helpful to you in evaluating the approaches you are using:

1. How many contacts, referrals, or leads did each approach generate?
2. How many job interviews came from those contacts, referrals, or leads?
3. How many of those interviews resulted in job offers?

If you carefully note the source of each contact, referral, or lead, you can easily track these statistics for the month of the program. If you keep tracking your results through the duration of your job search, you will have a much more accurate perspective on which job search approaches work best. Then if you decide to make a change, choose just one new approach at a time with which to experiment. And remember to keep tracking.

Ingredients for Finding Opportunities and Contacts

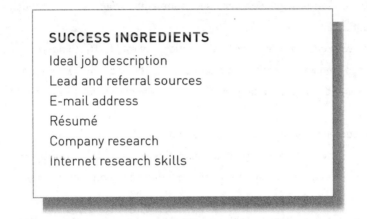

SUCCESS INGREDIENTS

Ideal job description

Lead and referral sources

E-mail address

Résumé

Company research

Internet research skills

INGREDIENT:
Ideal Job Description

In order to begin contacting people about finding the job you want, you need to be as clear as possible about the actual job. Imagine that you asked a friend to go the grocery store and buy you some food. With no further details, your friend might come back with dinner when what you needed was breakfast. If you get a bit more specific and ask for breakfast, your friend might buy you cereal when you were thinking of bacon and eggs.

Creating an **ideal job description** is like handing your friends and other contacts a shopping list. It spells out exactly what type of job you are looking for so they know what opportunities to send your way. It also helps you figure out exactly who you need to be contacting in order to find it. As you begin to share your ideal job description while networking, conducting informational

What Do You Call a Job Like Mine?

My job search efforts have been handicapped by employers, human resources departments, headhunters, employment specialists, and many others with their own mysterious agendas who have made employment searches much more difficult.

I have worked in maintenance for the majority of my life. I fix things, maintain things, and keep records of the same. I am seeking employment managing, training, and supervising people who fix things. Seems like it should be simple.

Now comes the politically correct era and I must find out for which position I am applying: facilities manager, facilities director, facilities supervisor, facilities engineer, facilities technician, building maintenance, building services, building engineer, structural support, operations director, operations manager, operations supervisor, operations engineer, operations technician, and the list goes on.

Each prospective employer uses a different job title and the title has little to do with the actual job responsibilities. A real engineer is someone with a license in electrical engineering, mechanical engineering, or another technical specialty. When employers attach a politically correct imaginary title like this to a position, an outsider has no idea what is meant.

What used to be called the Personnel Department has pretty much settled on becoming Human Resources or HRC. But go to a company's web site and you will have to search under jobs, careers, employment, Human Resources, open positions, and so forth. I have to look for openings in the Facilities Department, Engineering Department, Operations Department, hourly employees, salaried employees, management, mid-level management, and support staff.

It's frustrating, but for a job-seeker to be successful you have to really do your homework to find out what the position you want might be called, and then look for it under as many different categories as possible.

Kenneth C. Wilder
DENVER, COLORADO

interviews, and contacting employers, the people you speak to think of ways they can help you and identify others with whom you might speak. Eventually you can reach enough people with the right connections to discover opportunities hidden from the rest of the world.

CRAFTING YOUR IDEAL JOB DESCRIPTION

The following questions will help you create a description of your ideal job. If you began your journey up the Job Search Pyramid in the *Knowing what you want* stage, refer to some of the Success Ingredients you completed then to help you. (See the "Ideal job description" below for an example of a completed description.)

- What are the most likely job titles for the position you want?
- What would be the main responsibilities of the position?
- In what industry or job field should this position be?
- In what geographic area(s) should the job be located?

Ideal job description

Job title: Major account sales manager or senior manager major accounts
Industry: Telecommunications
Location: First choice — Atlanta, Georgia; second choice — Dallas, Texas
Compensation: Annual salary from $65–$70,000
  • bonus of ten-to-fifteen-percent annual salary
  • full health benefits; two to three weeks vacation
Work environment: Motivated team, high-energy office; boss who rewards top performers
Future growth: Eventually run a full-scale, multi-state, regional sales department. Acquire responsibility for a complete profit center, including sales, marketing, customer service, finance, and operations.
Other considerations: No more than two to three days travel per month

---

• What compensation will you require? (Include salary, bonuses, commissions, and benefits.)
• What type of work environment do you want to be in? (Consider company culture, physical setting, and nature of your co-workers or customers.)
• What opportunities for future growth do you want?
• What other factors are important to you? (Consider reporting relationships, travel involved, level of structure or independence, and other on-the-job conditions.)

Try to keep a balance between your ultimate desires and what you know actually exists when describing your ideal job. Don't limit yourself too much by assuming you can't have what you want. On the other hand, don't make your job search impossible by describing a situation that only exists in a dream world. As you begin sharing your job description with others, listen to how they respond.

When people start pointing you toward opportunities that sound like what you are describing, you'll know you are on the right track.

Your ideal job description may go through some changes over the course of your job search. You may discover that opportunities for your ideal job are scarce, that you don't truly have the appropriate qualifications, or that none of the actual jobs you find seems right for you. When the description no longer fits, it's fine to change it. Just make sure it's a deliberate and well-considered choice to pursue a different target, and not a hasty reaction to some preliminary findings or someone else's opinion.

INGREDIENT:
Lead and Referral Sources

To continually expand your network of contacts and discover new opportunities, you will need a collection of **lead and referral sources**. These are people, institutions, publications, and other resources that provide you with a consistent flow of information about potential job opportunities and ideas for new people to contact. Think of your lead and referral sources as essential nutrition for a healthful job search. To keep climbing the Job Search Pyramid at a steady pace, you need to take along a generous supply of nutritious food. If your job search is undernourished, you won't get very far. If you run out of food completely, you may have to turn back.

Lead and referral sources typically consist of well-connected people you talk to on a regular basis, events you consistently attend, institutions that collect and disperse information, and publications that report on your targeted industry or job field. They are your gateway to discovering where job opportunities are brewing, so you can discover them even though they may not be advertised.

When talking to sources, attending events, or reading publications, look for names of people you can approach for informational interviews or ask about job possibilities. Seek out names of companies you might want to work for as well as news about changes in those companies that could create the need for jobs, such as new product launches, opening new locations, changes in strategic direction, or company-wide initiatives. Listen for industry trends, economic shifts, or new regulations that may create a need for your specialty in many companies. Take note when you hear that a company is hiring people in any category, whether or not your type of position is mentioned.

IDEAS FOR LEAD AND REFERRAL SOURCES

- Managers and executives in your chosen industry or community
- Officers of industry professional associations
- Faculty at universities and training schools for your profession
- Editors of relevant trade publications or local business publications
- Vendors, salespeople, and consultants to your target industry
- Strategic partners and clients of companies where you want to work
- Alumni from your university or training school
- Current and former co-workers
- Friends, family, and neighbors
- Networking groups for your industry or community
- Professional association meetings and conferences
- Chamber of Commerce mixers and events
- Job clubs composed of other job-seekers in your profession or region
- Online chats, message boards, or discussion lists related to your specialty
- Community or neighborhood gatherings
- Classes, workshops, and seminars for your industry
- Professional association newsletters and web sites
- Career centers and bulletin boards at universities and training schools
- Community resource centers (local and online)
- State, provincial, and county employment offices
- Recruiters and employment agencies
- Web sites of companies that interest you
- Business and industry directories

- Trade publications for your industry or field (print and online)
- Local, regional, and national newspapers
- Business periodicals, such as *BusinessWeek, Fortune,* or *Fast Company*
- Internet job boards, such as www.hotjobs.com or www.monster.com
- Want ads in your local paper

As you can see, there is no shortage of possible sources for finding leads and referrals to possible opportunities. The best approach is to choose just a few that seem most helpful in your situation. Sources that are more likely to lead to unadvertised positions will be more effective than those that only let you know about those that are advertised. For more tips about working with people sources, see "Networking and Referral-Building" and "Informational Interviewing" later in this chapter. (For suggestions about working with print and online sources, see the "Company Research" section below.)

INGREDIENT:
E-mail Address

E-mail has become a mainstream method of communication between companies, families, colleagues, and friends. Conversations, negotiations, and business transactions are routinely conducted via e-mail without the parties ever speaking to each other live. In most cases, using e-mail will be an essential part of your communications during your job search.

If the only **e-mail address** you have belongs to your employer or a school from which you will soon graduate, you should get your own address to use while looking for work. Many Internet services—such as *Yahoo!* or *MSN Hotmail*— provide free e-mail addresses.

E-mail can be a highly efficient tool in your job search when used wisely. You have the ability to send your résumé or other material across town or across the country with a simple click of the mouse. You might call someone five times and get no response; then you send an e-mail and receive a reply the same day.

They Never Saw a Résumé Like Mine Before

When transferring from one profession to another you need to be unique and grab attention. I decided to change careers from being a speech and hearing therapist to becoming a sales representative for medical books. I wrote a résumé marketing myself as if I were a pill listed in the *Physician's Desk Reference* .

For the category "Dosage," I wrote "full-time employment." When it came to the category "Contraindications," I wrote, "may be hyper-vigilant about getting the job done."

The interviewer said he was so curious about me that he granted me an interview. I was hired.

Karen Glunz-Bagwell
HOUSTON, TEXAS

SOME INHERENT RISKS IN USING E-MAIL

- *Impersonal.* Some people find that e-mail doesn't reach the human side of their contacts and prevents making a connection.
- *Buried in the stack.* Many managers receive hundreds of e-mails per day, and yours may simply get lost in the pile. Also many of the other e-mails they receive will have a higher priority than yours.
- *Easy to hide.* Some people hide behind e-mail like Venetian blinds on a window. They rarely open them and only peek out when convenient. They may tell you they never got your e-mail, lost it, deleted it, or many other excuses for not responding.

- *Imperfect.* Never assume someone received and read an e-mail you sent. E-mails get lost in transmission or trapped by spam filters, and most people will avoid opening an attached file from someone they do not know.

GETTING THE MOST FROM USING E-MAIL

Put your e-mail address on your business card, cover letters, and on your print and electronic résumés. Post it on your personal web site (if you have one). Use e-mail for networking letters, contacting managers at target companies, and applying for positions. Create virtual connections by using e-mail to subscribe to job-posting lists, industry newsletters, and online discussion lists.

A good habit to get into is combining e-mail with phone calls. Relying on e-mail as your sole mode of communication is unwise. Human contact must play a critical role in all your job search activities.

INGREDIENT:
Résumé

You'll find many books, workshops, professional résumé writers, and even software to help you produce an effective **résumé**. This essential ingredient in job search recipes will be required by just about everyone you speak to while looking for a job. It's important to remember that a résumé alone will not get you a job. Your résumé can help you make contacts, get people to return your phone calls, result in leads and referrals, or even land you an interview, but it won't find you a job all by itself.

Many job seekers fall into the trap of thinking that a great résumé is the guaranteed ticket to getting an interview or a job offer. But your résumé is only one ingredient—not a complete job search recipe. It needs to be used as part of an ongoing process to find opportunities and connect with the people who can hire you.

One way to put your résumé into perspective is to think of it as a brochure.

How many big purchases do you make just by looking at a brochure? Not many, we suspect. Before you buy a car, for example, you typically want to see it in person, perhaps even to test drive it. You may also ask others what they think about that car, as well as compare it to many other cars you could buy for the same price. But a brochure can pique your interest. It may get you to make a phone call, to go see the product, or to find out more information about it in order to make a wise buying decision. This is how a résumé works. It's designed to attract the attention of a potential employer, communicate some basic information about you, and develop enough interest that someone will want to know more.

ELEMENTS OF AN EFFECTIVE RÉSUMÉ

- *Highlight your accomplishments.* Two important questions you must answer in the mind of a potential employer are "What can you do for me?" and "How can you solve my problems?" To answer these questions you must demonstrate how your past accomplishments relate to their current situation.
- *Be explicit, but concise.* Most people don't read résumés; they scan them. This scanning process may take only twenty to thirty seconds. Yours could be one of 200 résumés they are reviewing for one position. Keep your résumé to no more than two pages that describe your experience as concisely as possible. Be sure to include any essential words or phrases that relate to the position you are seeking and its qualifications. These keywords need to jump out at the person (or computer) scanning your résumé, so you get placed in the interview pile, not the reject pile.
- *Customize where possible.* Every job opportunity is different. The exact same position may be called a brokerage clerk, sales assistant, securities clerk, or administrative assistant, depending on the company. One employer may be interested in your ability to handle the registration function for large events smoothly, while another may be more concerned about whether you can promote those events so they are well attended. Don't completely

rewrite your résumé each time you send it out, but do make simple changes like editing your objective or the accomplishments you highlight so they more closely match the opportunity you are pursuing. If a job is not officially advertised, it's especially important that you customize your résumé to more closely address the needs of the organization.

- *Write about you, not a fictitious person.* Be truthful about everything you put on your résumé. False information may turn up in a background check, which more and more companies are engaging in today.

BASIC RÉSUMÉ OUTLINE

The two most popular formats for résumés are chronological and functional. The chronological résumé (see example on pages 184–185) portrays your employment history and job experience in reverse chronological order. This is the for mat that most employers prefer. A functional résumé (see example on pages 186–187) highlights your areas of expertise and special skills. Where and when you gained this experience is listed after these highlights. This format is most frequently used by those changing careers or with a chaotic job history. It calls attention to your transferable skills and minimizes employment gaps or inconsistencies in your experience.

Regardless of the format you use, these are the basic elements that must be included:

- *Contact information.* Name, address, phone number(s), and e-mail address.
- *Objective.* For a management or professional position, this should be a brief statement about how your expertise can solve a specific problem. For other positions, your objective should usually name the position and industry you are targeting. When submitting your résumé for a specific opportunity, this section should be customized.
- *Work history and experience.* List your former employers, job titles, and a brief description of each job you've held. Short, clear statements about your

Chronological résumé

Judy Friedman
123 Success Drive
Nicetown, PA 19000
(610) 555-1234
judy@gethirednow.com

OBJECTIVE

Leadership role in enhancing performance of a marketing team in the health care industry.

LEADERSHIP STRENGTHS

- Accomplished senior manager in public relations, communications planning, and marketing
- Specialist in product and service launches, marketing campaigns, and crisis communications
- Extensive media relations background with a proven track record of story placements
- Expert company spokesperson to local, national, and international media

WORK EXPERIENCE

Marketing and Public Relations Manager

Evergreen General Hospital
Anytown, PA 1996–Present

Served as local and regional spokesperson for hospital and affiliated business lines (skilled nursing facility, women's wellness center, rehabilitation facilities, medical clinics, and physician practices); built numerous long-standing relationships with media outlets.

- Effectively handled media relations for major hospital and community crisis situations.
- Wrote over 100 news releases per year; pitched feature stories to media.
- Crafted strategic communications, public relations, and marketing plans for product lines and affiliated businesses that generated a three-fold increase in new patient registration between 1997 and 1998.

Public Relations Director
Medical Communications and Advertising
Bigtown, PA 1994–96
Developed in-house public relations department, enabling agency to offer full complement of public relations services to strategic clients.
- Wrote comprehensive press kits, news releases, advertisements, and direct-mail copy.
- Developed strategic company Internet plan and wrote web site copy. As a result, thirty percent of all new patients were attributed to web inquiries.

Communications Manager
Classic Health Care Association
Mytown, PA 1991–94
Directed all communications, marketing, and publications for statewide health care professional membership association.
- Completely redesigned and managed web site. Developed, wrote, and upgraded content. New site was credited with bringing in forty-five new members in a three-month period.
- Produced all print communications, including bimonthly glossy magazine, biweekly member newsletter, legislative bulletin, brochures, books, and reports.
- Wrote numerous news and full-feature magazine articles on topics relevant to government employees and legislators.

EDUCATION
Great State University, PA 1990
Bachelor of Arts, Communications

PROFESSIONAL AFFILIATIONS
Public Relations Society of America
Business Marketing Association
Health Care Professionals Association of America

Functional résumé

Paul Vitorelli
123 Happy Lane
Greatplace, IA 52000
(515) 555-1234
paul@gethirednow.com

OBJECTIVE

Human resources specialist applying expertise in recruiting, employee relations, and training.

PROFESSIONAL PROFILE

Results-oriented professional with over nine years experience in human resources administration, training, and management. Expert in selecting highly qualified employees to impact business results favorably. Strong skills in maintaining positive employee relations and staff development. Demonstrated understanding of employment law and its impact on the organization.

Recruiting and Human Resources Administration

- Directed all aspects of the recruiting cycle, including advertising, sourcing, screening, and interviewing candidates. Maintained a 95-percent placement rate of quality candidates.
- Developed and wrote more effective job requirements, resulting in a significant improvement in hiring and training procedures.
- Earned company's top award by generating $23,000 in recruiting fees in a single month.

Training and Development

- Designed and implemented employee training on operations and customer service procedures resulting in a 100-percent improvement in problem resolution.
- Conducted technical systems training for new database applications to ensure consistent customer service.

Supervision and Employee Relations

- Developed employee communications, benefits, and training programs that decreased turnover by twenty-six percent.
- Employed workforce morale and communication programs to motivate and retain an all-volunteer employee base.

Customer Service and Interpersonal Skills
- Strong written and verbal communications ability, resulting in positive customer service experiences.
- Expert mediation skills, including listening to identify problems and analyzing situations to determine creative solutions.
- Ability to work independently and within a team, bridging gaps between members and resolving conflict.

PROFESSIONAL EXPERIENCE
Personnel Associates, Des Moines, IA
Technical Recruiter 2000–Present
Oversaw the full life cycle of the recruiting process, including account manager consultation, candidate sourcing, screening, interviewing, and reference checking.
Research Assistant 1998–2000
Provided research and sourcing support for the information technology recruiting team, increasing the level of applicant flow and maintaining accurate job database files and records.

Big Gym, Greatplace, IA
Operations Manager 1994–1998
Directed all sales, front office, operations, and human resource functions for an 800-member health club, with focus on increasing membership revenues and staff development.

OTHER WORK EXPERIENCE
Vacationland, Inc., Happyplace, FL 1987 – 1994
Multiple positions including: restaurant host, travel consultant, bell captain, registration host, fast-food host

EDUCATION and TRAINING
University of Great Learning, Iowa City, IA
Bachelor of Science in Business Administration in Hotel and Restaurant Management, 1986
E-recruitment Strategies Seminar, 2001
Power Recruiting on the Internet Seminar, 2000
Computer Network Administration Course, 2000
How to Manage and Market your Fitness Center Seminar, 1996
Travel Industry Training Course, 1989

major responsibilities work better than detailed accounts of every function you performed. As a general rule, report the last ten years of your work experience in detail. When you have earlier job experience, you can leave it off completely or group it together under a single heading.

- **Accomplishments and special skills.** These are brief, powerful statements that describe situations in which you excelled. The more specific you can be about facts and figures, the more impact they will have on the reader. These amplify your problem-solving abilities and demonstrate your potential value as an employee. They can either be included under work experience or presented in a separate section. (For sample statements and suggested ideas for composing them, see the "Major Accomplishments List" section in Chapter 7.)

- **Education.** List universities, colleges, and training schools you have attended and any degrees or certificates you've earned. If you have attended college or a training school, including your high school is unnecessary. Also include any specialized training taken through your employer or independently that is relevant to the position you are seeking.

- **Miscellaneous.** You may also include awards you've received, association memberships, publications, and volunteer activities. Present only those items that are relevant to your target and showcase your capabilities.

- **References.** There's no need to include a list of references or even a statement such as, "Available upon request." It is assumed you will be able to produce references when asked.

Review the chronological and functional résumé examples on pages 184–187. Note how they are written for a specific industry and type of job. The accomplishments and work experience position the job-seeker for the exact opportunity he or she is targeting. For additional samples of effective résumés and assistance in writing one, visit your local bookstore or library, or consult with a professional résumé writer.

INGREDIENT:
Company Research

One of the best ways to discover and pursue hidden job opportunities is to identify and research companies for which you may be interested in working. Companies may have many open positions that are never advertised, but when you contact the company directly you can easily discover these openings. In-depth knowledge about a company can also give you an edge on your job-seeking competition in several ways: you can learn what changes a company is planning that may indicate new job openings: uncover challenges a company has for which you can propose a solution; or make contacts who will let you know in advance when positions may be available.

Keep in mind that the term "company" in this book represents any organization for which you might work. It could be a corporation, small business, private firm, nonprofit organization, educational institution, or government agency. No matter what kind of organization your potential employers are, you can identify who they might be and learn more about them from readily available sources.

Your **company research** will probably take three forms. First you will identify companies that are likely to have positions like the one for which you are looking. Second you will find out more about those companies to determine what job opportunities exist now and what might exist in the near future. And third you will learn which people working in those companies are in a position to hire you.

SOURCES FOR COMPANY RESEARCH
- Business directories at your library, such as *Dun and Bradstreet* or *Standard and Poor's*
- Online company directories, such as www.hoovers.com or www.business.com
- "Best companies" lists published by *Forbes, Fortune, Industry Week,* and others
- *Book of Lists* published by your local *Business Times* or *Business Journal*
- Trade journals for your industry
- Professional association newsletters and web sites

Have You Thought About Hiring Someone Like Me?

I was flying to a job interview and read an article in the airline magazine about an insurance executive. It described his interest in the health insurance arena and how successful his various business units were under his leadership.

My background was in building HMO health plans, but the article said his company offered only PPO and traditional health insurance plans. I could have decided his company wasn't a good fit for me, but instead I wrote to him to find out if he would consider hiring someone with my background and experience to build an HMO division for them.

Two weeks after I sent the letter, I received a phone call for an interview and accepted a job offer from him three weeks later.

Michael Carr
DALLAS, TEXAS

- Local and regional newspapers
- Company web sites
- Company publications, such as newsletters, annual reports, and brochures
- Literature available in the company's lobby or retail location
- Online message boards or discussion lists for the company or its products
- Contacting companies and their employees directly
- Your local Chamber of Commerce
- Attending industry events
- Your personal network

WHAT DO YOU DO WITH ALL THIS INFORMATION?

Just collecting data on a company without relating it to your job search is a waste of your time. It's easy to gather data. The important part is to do something with it. The purpose of your research is to identify which companies you may want to work for and decide how best to approach them. If you need more help to do that, see the "Identifying Your Target Companies" section later in this chapter.

INGREDIENT:
Internet Research Skills

There are several places in this book where we suggest using the Internet to find more information. To do this effectively during your job search, you may need to improve your **Internet research skills**.

Search engines and directories such as www.google.com, www.yahoo.com, and www.msn.com will give you access to a massive index of links to web pages and other documents containing chosen words and phrases. Different combinations of keywords will produce a multitude of results, many of which have no relationship to what you are seeking. If you type the word "interview" into a search engine looking for tips on how to interview better, the results will be overwhelming; literally millions of links will be listed. In addition to web sites containing interview tips, you'll see links to interviews with celebrities, news interviews, and books that have the word "interview" in the title that probably have nothing to do with job search. But if you type more specific phrases, such as "job interview tips" or "job interview questions," you'll quickly find more useful information. To learn how to conduct Internet searches more efficiently, look for a "help" or "advanced search" option on the search engine web sites, read a book or article on Internet research, or ask a librarian to help you.

Before you rely on information you find in a search, it's a good idea to verify its accuracy and timeliness:

- When is the last time the page was updated?
- Is the information from a reputable source?
- Are you able to contact the author and verify the data?
- Is there another way to know if the information is valid?

Be careful to limit the amount of time you spend using the Internet to conduct research. The abundance of information available can consume many hours of your precious time. Yet use it wisely, and you'll find a wealth of information that can save you time, rather than waste it.

APPROACH:
Networking and Referral-Building

> **SUCCESS INGREDIENTS**
>
> Company networking venues
> Ten-second introduction
> Business cards
> Networking skills
> Model networking letter

RECIPE:
Building Your Network

In pursuit of a job there are two broad categories of people you ultimately want to get to know: those who are in a position to hire you and those who can lead you to job opportunities by sharing information. Both categories can provide you with all-important access to unadvertised job opportunities. In using the approach of Networking and Referral-Building, you are reaching out to people who you believe can introduce you to hiring managers or give you inside information. This is quite different from contacting an employer directly and pitching them on your capabilities, as you will see.

Think of networking as the process of building a pool of contacts from which you can draw ideas, leads, referrals, and specific information. Remember that the best networking relationships are reciprocal. If you ask how you can help your networking contacts with their personal goals, you will find them much more willing to help you.

The three methods you will typically use in building your job search network are calling, mailing (which includes e-mail), and meeting people in person. You may use each of these methods independently or in combination. You might talk to a referral source on the phone without ever meeting in person. Or you might place a call, send a follow up e-mail, make another phone call, and set a time to meet for lunch. Regardless of the method, your goal is the same: connect with people who have vital information about the hidden job market. Let's look at how each of these methods work:

- *Calling.* Making phone calls is an excellent way to connect personally with large numbers of new contacts, leads, and referral sources. The best approach to begin phone calls is to use your ten-second introduction (there's more about that later in this chapter), then mention how you got the person's name and ask if he or she has time to talk. For example, "Our mutual friend Karl Jablonski tells me you are pretty well-connected in the nonprofit sector. Do you have a few minutes for me to ask you some questions?"

  Be prepared with two or three questions that will tell you immediately whether the person with whom you are speaking would be a good contact for you. If that's the case, ask for a meeting on the spot, or if it's better to meet by phone, try to ask all your questions right then. Don't stall by offering to send your résumé. You may never again get the opportunity to directly speak to this person. Only if your contact declines to speak with you should you offer to send your résumé first.

A Proactive Networker

During the heyday of the Internet boom, I was working for one of the world's largest web-hosting companies. At first it was a wonderful place to work and as a salesperson I was doing extremely well. But the company spent money like there was no tomorrow and it kept getting bigger and bigger. It didn't take long before I saw that what was once a great customer service company had now lost track of its customers and only cared about making its investors happy.

During my time there, I was very proactive about networking in as many organizations as I could. I also found and cultivated a good number of referral partners. One was a ten-person web development and hosting company in Denver. They had been in business for four years and had a client roster that read like a who's who in Colorado list. I got to know the owner of the company and was impressed by how he ran his company on a shoestring budget and never let the draw of easy investment money lure him in.

One day I invited him and the chief operating officer of the company to lunch. I had just come off a year of sales training and used all of my newly learned selling techniques to convince them to invest in me as their newest account representative. I also told them the kind of money and opportunities they would need to offer me to convince me to leave such a prestigious company as my current employer.

It worked. Two weeks later I was working for them after receiving an extremely appealing offer. I've prospered there, and am still happily employed with an amazing company that has an incredible future ahead.

Ken Sabey
DENVER, COLORADO

- *Mailing.* The best mail to send potential contacts is a personal letter. "Personal" means addressed to the person by name and mentioning some situation that makes a connection between the two of you, such as who referred you, an organization you both belong to, or an article that person wrote. These connections give your letter a personal touch and increase the likelihood of getting a response.

- *Meeting people in person.* Getting out of your home or office can be a welcome break from calling and mailing. Keep in mind that you don't have to go to a business-related event to meet people helpful to your job search. You meet new people all the time at community or neighborhood events, grocery stores, coffee shops, health clubs, restaurants, and even at the doctor's office.

  Get in the habit of carrying your business cards everywhere you go (there's more about business cards later in this chapter). Whenever you meet someone, introduce yourself, offer your business card, and ask for one in return. This may feel a bit awkward at first, but it will soon become natural. Never underestimate where you can meet people who can help your job search. The guy on the next exercise machine or the woman ahead of you in line for coffee might turn out to be your next boss.

RECIPE:
Attending Events

We can't emphasize enough that Networking and Referral-Building is the most effective job search approach available. One of the best ways to discover job opportunities and meet people who can help you in your job search is to attend events where the people who work for your target companies gather. We're calling these your **company networking venues** to distinguish them from the more general industry networking venues you may have participated in earlier in your job search. As you get clearer about exactly where you want to work, you can begin to identify places where you can meet the people who work for those companies.

Your Industry Needs You—Volunteer Today!

My success in finding jobs has been through networking as a volunteer. When I was looking for a job in public relations, I volunteered to do public relations for a well-known and well-regarded non-profit organization. In a short time, I proved my skills and ability to people in many industries, and made numerous contacts that were beneficial to helping me find a job.

That was fifteen years ago. This is still an effective way to make contacts today. Last year because of economics I had lost my job and was working for myself. Through an organization I was involved with as a board member, I came to meet the vice president of marketing for a big Chicago firm. At an event where I was handling media and public relations, he approached me to say that he wanted to create a position for me within his company.

Andrew Arden Hayes
CHICAGO, ILLINOIS

Good choices for company networking venues are all the places listed for the Success Ingredients "industry networking venues" and "educational venues" in Chapter 7, plus company-sponsored open houses or public relations events, such as a new product launch. Also consider high-profile community events, such as local award ceremonies or commemorative celebrations. Executives who don't frequent networking meetings often attend such functions.

Come prepared to present yourself professionally with a ten-second introduction and bring plenty of business cards. If a specific company or group of companies is sponsoring the event, take the time to research them ahead of time. You may be able to make a memorable impression that could get you an interview with a hiring manager. You can't get this close to an opportunity by look-ing at the want ads.

You can increase your networking visibility through volunteering. When you volunteer your time at events, or your services to industry groups, you get to work alongside key people. These persons are often movers and shakers in the community or your industry. Letting them see you at work as a volunteer can pay off handsomely once they get to know you.

INTRODUCING YOURSELF IN TEN SECONDS

Your **ten-second introduction** is what you say when you shake someone's hand, call someone on the phone, or stand up in front of a group. It describes who you are, what you do, and what you are looking for in a clear and mem-orable way. One effective format is the benefits-oriented introduction, where you state a key benefit that you offer your potential employers before giving your occupation or job title. Here are some examples:

- "I'm Wendy Chang. I help high-tech companies close sales with customers who need complex technical solutions. I'm a technical sales rep looking for a new position in the Houston area."
- "My name is Ian McDermott. I develop leadership skills in management teams. I'm a corporate training director exploring career opportunities in the financial services industry."

The advantage of this format is that it positions you in the mind of the lis-tener before they have a chance to form their own opinions about what you do. If you introduce yourself as a project manager, for example, your listener has no way to know what a project manager does or what kind of projects you man-age. An introduction that begins, "I manage new software installations for cor-porate clients," is specific enough to be understood and remembered.

Notice that all these introductions use plain language rather then industry jar-gon. Unless you know exactly who your listeners are, use terms a twelve-year-old would understand.

MAY I HAVE YOUR CARD?

To begin the process of building relationships, you should have personal **business cards**. Unless you are looking for work with your current employer's knowledge (as often happens during a layoff), you shouldn't use your employee business cards for job search networking.

The purpose of a business card is to facilitate communication, not to give a complete description of your work history. Place just enough information on your card for people to remember what you do, but don't turn it into a résumé. You want to have a reason to follow up later on.

Include your name, mailing address, phone, e-mail address, plus fax number, and personal web site, if you have them. Don't clutter up your card with a list of additional phone numbers or e-mail addresses. You can put these on your voice mail or elsewhere if you think they are essential.

A question many job-seekers ask is, "Should I put a title on my card?" If you have defined the type of position you are seeking, it's a good idea to include it. It's one more way to remind people what you are looking for and suggest opportunities they can refer you to.

Unless you are a graphic designer wanting to showcase your skills, the look and feel of your card doesn't have to be fancy. Plain, white business card stock with one color of ink will work fine. If you have a computer with a good printer you can produce them yourself. You can also order them from an office superstore, have them custom-made at a print shop, or buy them online.

FOLLOWING UP WITH YOUR CONTACTS

If you don't follow up with the people you meet, you are wasting your time in meeting them. It is simply untrue that someone will call when they have a lead for you. The truth is that if they have only met you once, they probably don't remember you, and it's even less likely they will remember where they put your card. Marketing yourself as a job-seeker means telling the right people what type of job you are seeking, over and over.

Find ways to continue building a relationship with the people you meet by asking them to coffee or lunch, setting up an informational interview, inviting them to an event you are attending, or sharing with them a helpful resource you have discovered.

RECIPE:
Learning How to Network

Without a network, it would be next to impossible to gain access to the hidden job market. Recall all the jobs you've ever had. How did you become aware of the opportunity? Most likely it was through someone you knew. Talk to anyone who has landed a job recently and you'll hear the same thing. They found it through a friend or colleague at a company or some other people connection. This is why learning good **networking skills** is so important.

All too often networking is thought of as a process of bouncing around the room and meeting everyone you can in record time. Unfortunately this negative image has discouraged people who need to develop a network in order to succeed. You may encounter people who try to network like this. They haven't learned the core principle that makes it work: networking is about giving, not getting. This simple principle is the secret to building and maintaining a world-class network.

You may fear networking because it feels uncomfortable, you don't know what to say, or you really don't like meeting new people. You're not alone; many people in your situation feel the same way. Adopt the "giving, not getting" principle in your networking and notice what a difference it makes.

Networking works because it's natural human behavior. People like to help other people. When they hear of something happening where they could offer assistance, their natural reaction is to help. Most of us at one time got a helping hand or some sound advice from someone else about our career. Now when someone asks for our help we feel the need to reciprocate. Does this work every time? Of course not—nothing is perfect. But you can significantly improve your chances to build relationships that can lead to a job if you keep this in mind. If you can help others, they will help you. Before you go to your next networking event, commit to this goal: "I will help five people tonight." That takes all the pressure off you.

YOUR NETWORKING TOOL KIT

Here are the key items you need to become a masterful networker:

- *Business communication tools.* Your ten-second introduction, business cards, and a pen.
- *Resources to share.* Compile a list of helpful information, events, web sites, books, networking contacts, and anything else you can offer as a helping hand to people you meet in your industry. Be a good listener and suggest ideas on the spot after they have told you about their situation.
- *Conversation pieces.* Be prepared with questions, comments, or opinions you present to get conversations going. For example, "How is your company dealing with the current economic situation?"
- *Positive attitude.* Get and stay in the right frame of mind about networking. Approach it with an enthusiastic attitude and with the assumption that good things will come if you practice the art of giving, not getting, at every turn.

A good way to start is to team up with a job search buddy and attend events together. You can help each other meet new people and you will be less nervous. To learn more about networking, pick up a book, listen to an audio, take a class, or work with a career coach. And keep practicing.

RECIPE:
Networking From Your Home or Office

Networking doesn't require going to events and schmoozing. You can also make new contacts by creating a **model networking letter** to customize and send by postal mail or e-mail. Networking via personal letters is a great way to extend your reach beyond face-to-face meetings. A networking letter contains a brief introduction, a statement to make the connection between you, and a polite request for assistance in your job search, such as information about a company or referrals to people who can help you.

There are usually two sets of people you would send networking letters to: your friends, family, and acquaintances; and people to whom you have been referred or located through your research. Don't rule out any friends or family members because you think they can't help. You may be surprised to discover the number of contacts the people who are close to you have at their fingertips. Acquaintances such as other students you knew at school, former co-workers, members of your social group, and former bosses, clients, and vendors are all ideal targets for networking letters.

People who are referred to you or located through your research are also valuable candidates to contact with a letter. For example, alumni from your university or training school are often easy to find through directories the school provides. Approach these people by telling them you share the same alma mater and you'd enjoy the opportunity to connect with a new colleague.

What are the possibilities of increasing your network by reaching out in this way? Let's do some simple math. If you currently have fifty people in your database that you would classify as your network and only half of these people have a new contact to suggest, you would get twenty-five new contacts. You increased the size of your network by fifty percent just by sending a letter! That's the power of networking.

The following examples depict two networking letters you could use as models to send to your contacts.

NETWORKING ONLINE

In addition to using e-mail to send networking letters and follow up with contacts, you can also meet and get to know people online through discussion lists, chat rooms, and message boards. Look for communities that focus on your indus-

Networking letter to friends, family, and acquaintances

Dear [*friend's name*],

I never realized how much my life would change when I decided to enter the job market. While it can be challenging at times, I've discovered a whole new world. I'm currently exploring opportunities for the next stage in my career. This is why I'm writing—to ask for your advice and assistance during this transition.

As you know, I have worked in the [*your industry*] industry as [*your current/former positions*] for the past [*XX*] years. I'm looking for possibilities in [*a new industry or the same*] as [*your job target*].

I would greatly appreciate it if you would review my résumé (see enclosed) and suggest any companies in the [*your target region*] area where I might explore future opportunities, whether or not they currently have any openings. If you could also suggest a name or two of other people that could help in the same way, I'd be grateful if you could provide those names to me.

Any other advice you could offer would be quite welcome. A big thanks to you in advance for your help. I'll give you a call in few days to see if you have any suggestions for me.

Kind regards,
[*Your name*]

Networking letter to other contacts

Dear [*contact's name*],

Both of us are fortunate to know [*name of referral*]. He/she suggested that you would be a great person from whom to seek advice.

I'm currently exploring new opportunities for the next stage in my career. I want to make sure you know I m not asking you for a job, but for help in directing my search. I'm writing to ask for your advice and assistance during this transition.

Briefly, I have worked in the [*your industry*] industry as [*your current/ former positions*] for the past [*XX*] years. I'm looking for possibilities in [*a new industry or the same*] as [*your job target*]. My résumé is enclosed.

I would greatly appreciate it if you would be willing to meet with me and share any advice you may have for my career transition. Perhaps I could buy you coffee or lunch.

Many thanks to you in advance for your help. I'll give you a call in a few days to see if we might be able to get together.

Kind regards,
[*Your name*]

try, geographic area, or job-seeking and career transition in general. Here are some popular homes for online communities:

- America Online   www.aol.com
- Ecademy   www.ecademy.com
- Fast Company's Company of Friends   www.fastcompany.com/cof
- LinkedIn   www.linkedin.com
- Monster Jobs   www.monster.com
- MSN Groups   http://groups.msn.com
- Ryze Business Networking   www.ryze.com
- Tribe   www.tribe.net
- Yahoo! Groups   www.groups.yahoo.com

HINT:
What about Confidentiality?

The process of networking and referral-building we've described seems to suggest that you should tell anyone and everyone you talk to that you're looking for work. And in fact, that is the best way to find a new job quickly. If you need to find a job without your current employer discovering that you are looking, you will be operating with a handicap. When you speak with people directly, you can tell them that your job search is confidential, but the more people you talk to, the more likely it is that word could get back to your current employer.

You'll need to consider the trade-offs involved in trying to keep your job search a secret and perhaps taking much longer to find a job; or being fairly public about your search and making connections that will lead to a new job more quickly.

What you should avoid in this situation is looking for work on company time or using company resources to do so. Then if your employer does find out you are looking, at least they will not be able to accuse you of taking advantage of your current position.

APPROACH:
Contacting Potential Employers
and Informational Interviewing

SUCCESS INGREDIENTS

Target company list
Company informational interview plan

RECIPE:
Identifying Your Target Companies

We've grouped these two approaches together because many of the activities
you will perform while contacting potential employers or informational interviewing are the same. When first trying to decide what type of job you want,
you may conduct informational interviews with a wide variety of people. But
now that you are trying to locate specific opportunities, you will probably be
limiting your interviews and other contacts to companies you may wish to work
in, or people who can directly connect you to those companies. For this you
need to identify a **target company list**.

Your target companies are the organizations where you might want to work.
Through research, networking, and informational interviewing, you identify
them as the best fit for the job and work environment you want. To make this
list, compare your ideal job description to all the companies you discover in your
chosen industry.

Identify what you need to learn about each company to decide if you want
to work there or find out where in the company you fit. Then make a plan to
gather that additional information through networking, contacting the company directly, or conducting informational interviews. Here are some questions

you may want to answer to determine if a particular company is a good target for you:

- What problems is this company facing?
- What are their goals for the future?
- How fast are they growing?
- What do they need to beat the competition?
- How is the company's financial health?
- Who are their strategic partners in business?
- Could I make a difference for this company?
- What skills or experience do they seem to be missing?
- How related is my experience to what they are seeking?
- Does their culture match what I desire?
- Are they able to pay what I need to earn?
- Would this be a fun and satisfying place to work?
- Do I already have contacts at this company?

Remember you are not limiting yourself by choosing to target certain companies; rather you are launching a job search campaign aimed directly at the companies for which you most want to work. If a company not on your target list shows up on your radar screen, you can still pursue it if it looks like a good opportunity for you.

You may be asking, "How many companies should be on my list?" There is no magic number. Too few companies may not give you enough choices, but too many may spread your focus too thinly. Keep your list to a size that you feel you are capable of working effectively. You can always add or delete companies from the list as you find out more about your prospects at each one.

CONTACTING THE COMPANIES YOU TARGET

Once you have a list of places you might like to work, first make contact with each company to find out what open positions they have listed. Then either call or write someone you have identified as having the authority to hire you, or ask for an informational interview with someone who works at the company. It can help to make these contacts if you ask your existing network if they can introduce you to anyone who works there.

When you have identified either an open position that matches what you want, or a need the company has that you want to fill, you're ready to apply to the company. However, this doesn't necessarily mean filling out an application or applying to the human resources department. See Chapter 9 for all the different forms applying for jobs can take.

RECIPE:
Using Informational Interviews

The purpose of conducting informational interviews at this stage of your job search is to learn about specific opportunities at the companies you are interested in and make contacts who are in a position to hire you. A **company informational interview plan** will help you gather the information you need. Using your target company list, you can reach out to people in these companies who can lead you directly to job opportunities.

Think of this process as peeling back the layers of an onion. The first layer is familiarizing yourself with the company's public image, such as its products, services, and customers. Pull back a layer and discover the company's mission and goals. As you get closer to the core, you begin to learn about the inner workings of the company from people who are on the inside. That's when you'll hear about a specific challenge they're grappling with and where they need help— or better yet, an unadvertised job for which you are a perfect fit.

Start by creating a list of job titles of people you want to talk to. Consider all the roles in the company that you would regularly interact with if you were already working there. Ask the people who hold these positions for an informational interview about the challenges and new developments they are currently experiencing. This intelligence will provide you with the key details you need to uncover job opportunities that fit your expertise.

People you should consider interviewing are company executives, managers of key departments—such as marketing, sales, information technology, finance, and customer service—salespeople, and "worker bees," those who work in the trenches serving customers and doing the front line work of the company.

Remember that informational interviewing is not a job interview. Don't try coercing your contacts into landing you an interview or helping you get a job. You are interviewing for information. Approach each meeting as a learning experience. If you get a lead on a specific opportunity, then that's an extra bonus for you (For more suggestions about Informational Interviewing, refer to Chapter 7.)

APPROACH:
Employing Recruiters and Agencies

> ### SUCCESS INGREDIENTS
> Recruiters and agencies list
> Model recruiter/agency letter

RECIPE:
Working with Recruiters and Agencies

Recruiters and employment agencies can be a good source for finding opportunities that haven't been widely advertised. One reason companies use recruiters and agencies is that they don't want to publicize the opening beyond a select group of people. It's important to understand that companies hire recruiters and agencies to fill a specific employment need. The goal of the agencies is to find the best candidate for the company's position based on their assessment of experience, education, cultural fit, and compensation requirements.

There are some differences between employment agencies and recruiters in how they work. Employment agencies place mostly support staff and low-to-mid—level individual contributors. Executive recruiters, on the other hand, place managers, executives, and other highly skilled professionals. Employment agencies often maintain a broad list of job openings that cater to an equally broad range of companies. Recruiters, however, specialize in a particular industry or job field.

With some employment agencies you can work on a temp-to-permanent basis, meaning the employer tries you out temporarily in a role for which they are considering hiring you. You can also work through agencies as a temporary (a.k.a. "temp") in many positions not offering permanent employment. This can be an excellent way to get your foot in the door at a company, meet people who work there, and find out about positions the company is not advertising.

When a company has a need for a management or professional role with special qualifications, they may seek out the services of an executive recruiter. The recruiter is paid by the company to locate candidates that match that particular skill set. If you can get into a successful recruiter's database, this can be a terrific source for locating opportunities.

To begin working with either recruiters or agencies, you'll need to create a **recruiters and agencies list**.

SOURCES FOR RECRUITERS AND AGENCIES

- *Directories of executive recruiters.* Try *The Directory of Executive Recruiters* (Kennedy Information).
- *Yellow Pages.* Look under employment agencies.
- *Recruiter and agency web sites.* Do a keyword search for your city and/or profession.
- *Newspaper want ads.* Look for ads posted by recruiters or agencies.
- *Library.* Check out the reference section.
- *Trade publications.* Look in the careers section for ads placed by recruiters.
- *Employment office.* Find your state, province, or county branch.
- *Industry directories.* You may find specialized recruiters listed.
- *Your personal network.* Referrals, as always, are best.

Temped Her Way to a Job

Being hired as a temporary employee, either through a recruiter or a friend, led me to my last three jobs. Temping is like working that nervous, unsure first day at work every day! To be successful at temping requires that you ask many questions, take notes about instructions and requests, learn quickly to familiarize yourself with the company's purpose and goals, and discover how to establish reliable informants or contacts.

Whether you are hired as a file clerk, secretary, administrator, or manager, you have ample opportunity to demonstrate your job skills. In each of my temporary assignments that became permanent—at an advertising agency, a bank, and a real estate development company—neither the employer nor I initially felt that we were a good fit. Yet in each case, a few weeks later, the employer was making me an offer I couldn't refuse. But I could and did negotiate the employment agreement from a position of strength because both they and I were now convinced that this was indeed a match.

Temping has offered me the opportunity to work in new industries, acquire new skills, and be trained in a variety of systems. It also allowed me to really see how a company operated, choose whether or not I fit with the other employees and the system, and most importantly to be hired with commitment and enthusiasm by my new bosses. They already loved who they were hiring!

Breeze Carlile
SAN FRANCISCO, CALIFORNIA

Model recruiter/agency letter

Dear Recruiter,

I'm currently seeking a leadership role in new business development for a progressive commercial real estate management group. There are a number of areas in which my unique abilities and personal resources could significantly enhance the bottom line of such a company:

- Exceptional contract negotiation skills for commercial property purchases, office space leases, and renovation projects
- Extensive knowledge of real estate research data including occupancy rates, competitive pricing models, demographics, and industry growth rates
- Powerful network of influential contacts including senior executives and local government officials

I'm available to answer any questions you may have about my background and experience.

I look forward to speaking with you and the possibility of joining your roster of candidates.

Sincerely,
George Hart

Enclosure: Résumé

CONTACTING RECRUITERS AND AGENCIES

To introduce yourself to an employment agency in your local area, you'll typically need to make an appointment by phone and visit them in person. Be prepared to describe your marketable skills when you call. They may ask you to fill out an application and send your résumé before making an appointment with you.

With executive recruiters and with agencies located out of town, create a **model recruiter/agency letter** (see example above) to make the first contact.

Companies hire recruiters and agencies because they want to speed up their search or they don't have the resources to manage the process of locating, screening, and narrowing down the field of candidates to only the most qualified. Recruiters need to work fast and have a solid understanding of the candidates they present for any position. Keep these factors in mind when developing your introduction letter. Your letter needs to portray your unique abilities for taking on challenges and solving problems. If you have been referred to a recruiter by one of your contacts, be sure to mention it. If that person was a successful placement for the recruiter, chances are even better you'll get a response.

APPROACH:
Searching Specialized Job Listings and Using Help-Wanted Ads

SUCCESS INGREDIENTS
Job listing sources

RECIPE:
Finding Specialized Job Listings

There is no shortage of **job listing sources** available in print publications, on the Internet, and in dozens of other locations. Your challenge is to find sources that advertise jobs matching your skills and requirements for which there are not already so many applicants that the competition is overwhelming. Throughout this book, we emphasize the importance of locating the unadvertised opportunities that make up eighty-five percent of the job market. Yet there may be a place in your job search plan for reviewing a few select sources of advertised jobs.

Narrowing down your choices of job listing sources is the secret to getting the best results. There are over 100,000 career-related web sites and more appear every day. Resisting the urge to look at every possible list will reduce your frustration in finding the best sources for advertised jobs. Since you already know what type of job you want, you may be able to locate targeted sources for exactly the type of position you are seeking.

SOURCES FOR SPECIALIZED JOB LISTINGS

- Industry-specific Internet job boards
- Career opportunities posted on company web sites
- Job hotlines and job fairs for specific industries or companies
- Jobs advertised through industry association newsletters or web sites
- Trade and business journals for your profession
- University, community, and vocational school career centers

RECIPE:
How to Use Help-Wanted Ads

Ads in the help-wanted section of your local newspaper are usually not a valuable source for job listings. The biggest problem with these ads is that so many people see them that you may be one of hundreds of applicants for any one job. Applying for positions advertised here can be an uphill battle and very discouraging to your job search.

A better way to use help wanted ads is to view them as a data source for researching companies. By seeing which companies are advertising and the type of positions that seem to be in demand, you can get many ideas about who you might approach for a similar position or of companies that might have other needs they are not advertising.

For example, if your job field was web development, and you noticed that a health care company was advertising for people with web design skills, you might decide to approach other health care companies in your area to see if they needed similar skills in their organization. Or if you noticed that a large law firm was advertising for marketing support staff, you might wonder if they were launching a new marketing initiative and therefore might also need a web designer.

The want ads are rarely a good place to find a job, but these listings can be an accurate barometer of changes that will point you to where the hidden jobs exist.

CHAPTER 9

Applying to Employers:

When You Know Plenty of People But You're Not Contacting Them

If I had to live my life again, I'd make
all the same mistakes—only sooner.

— TALLULAH BANKHEAD

What to Do With What You Find

Approaching employers to apply for the job opportunities you locate may seem
fairly simple. You just note every opportunity you find that fits your requirements, then place a call or send them something, or both. If they don't contact
you for an interview right away, you put them on your calendar to follow up
and do the same thing again. Pretty straightforward, isn't it? So why is it that the
process of applying for jobs can be such a stumbling block? Here are the five
most common reasons:

1. *Prioritization.* It's easy to give other responsibilities a higher priority: your
   current job, time with your family, errands, housework, and keeping up
   with bills and mail. Some job search activities, like browsing for job
   opportunities, may be something you can do at odd moments; a planned
   networking event can be put on your calendar. However, sitting down to
   write a cover letter and get it in the mail requires dedicated time, and
   there's no one to remind you to do it. If you don't set aside a time and
   place to apply for the opportunities you find, you won't do it.
2. *Disorganization.* Business cards, newspaper clippings, and scraps of paper

thrown in a drawer are not an efficient system for managing your opportunities and contacts. Without accurate records of whom you contacted, what you applied for, and when, it will be impossible for you to follow up effectively.

3. *Resistance.* Do you find yourself saying, "Why do I have to do this? I'm good at what I do. Why isn't a great job falling into my lap?" You are sabotaging yourself with this line of thinking. Successful people reach out to make new contacts for their career every day. It's one of the ways they got to be successful. Contacting a company about hiring you doesn't make you seem like a desperate job-seeker; it makes them see you as a motivated individual.

4. *Fear.* "If I follow up on that lead, I might be rejected," reasons the voice in your head. "So I'll avoid the pain by not making the call in the first place." Or conversely you may be thinking, "If I place the call, I might get the job; and then I'll have to do the work, and people will have all these expectations of me." The reality is that if you don't place the calls, you're going to fail even more dramatically than in these two imaginary scenarios.

5. *Lack of connections.* You may have already discovered how difficult it is to get an interview when you blindly send your résumé to human resources or to an anonymous post-office box. When you don't know anyone inside a company, you figure you don't have a chance and don't even bother to apply.

You are already addressing three of these issues simply by using the *Get Hired Now!* system to aid your job search. The structure of the 28-day program will help you set better priorities, overcome resistance, and break through fear. In this chapter, we'll tackle the remaining barriers of disorganization and making connections, as well as how to effectively apply for job opportunities.

Applying to employers extends far beyond filling out applications or sending your résumé to a human resources department. Our definition of applying includes making phone calls, writing letters and e-mails, sending job proposals, and scheduling meetings with people who can influence hiring decisions for advertised and unadvertised positions.

Ingredients for Applying to Employers

SUCCESS INGREDIENTS
Hiring manager names
Contact management system
Career success stories

INGREDIENT:
Hiring Manager Names

At earlier points in your job search, you may have identified specific companies you want to target or open positions for which you wish to apply. But to make your application, you will need the name of someone who works at the company. If the position was advertised, you'll have the contact information given in the ad, but that may not be enough. When you try to follow the rules and apply to human resources, you will be competing with dozens or even hundreds of people applying for the same job. Your qualifications will have to fit the position requirements exactly in order to land an interview. If you are applying for a position that isn't officially listed as open, many human resource departments have a standing policy of ignoring your application completely.

To have a real chance at getting interviewed, it's essential that you identify who in the company has the authority to hire you and contact this person directly.

Sometimes finding **hiring manager names** can be as easy as picking up the phone, calling a company, and asking who manages the department or area that interests you. Instead of saying you are looking for a job (and being referred to

You Can Always Bank on Your Network

When I was still in school, I wanted to get a job as a bank teller because the short, steady hours worked perfectly for my class schedule. But there seemed to be dozens of applicants for every opening, and my previous experience as a waiter wasn't getting me in the door for an interview. My roommate worked for a big bank, but in data processing. Although she wasn't a manager and her job was in the corporate offices, not in a branch with tellers, I asked for her help anyway.

She asked her boss if he could help . . . and he asked his boss . . . and that man made a phone call to someone else's boss in another division . . . and the next thing I knew I had an interview. I started work as a bank teller the following Monday and had steady employment the whole time I was going to school.

Arthur Lindstrom
HOUSTON, TEXAS

human resources again), it often works to simply state that you would like to send that manager some information.

Visit the company's web site and look for pages that might list the names of personnel. Membership directories for industry associations—in print and on the web—may also contain the names of employees at the company. Try to locate articles, interviews, or reports written about or by company executives. Remember also to ask your personal network and informational interviewing subjects whom they know at your target companies. For more help with researching companies, see Chapter 8.

INGREDIENT:
Contact Management System

Following up on your applications and with all of your lead and referral sources should become a regular part of your job search routine. Having some kind of **contact management system** is absolutely necessary to efficient follow up. Your method for keeping track of your job search contacts could be a computer system (usually with some information on paper as well), a three-ring binder, or a card file.

In addition to name, address, phone, fax, and e-mail, you should also note the source of each contact, when you were first in touch, and when you were last in touch. It may also be helpful to categorize your contacts by their industry and/or company. That way you can easily find contacts whom may be able to assist you in making a specific approach.

Each time you interact with a contact, make a note of when it was, what happened, and when you next plan to follow up. With a computer-based system, once you enter the follow-up date, you can run a report or use an auto-reminder feature to see when follow-ups are due. If your system is paper-based, you should put follow-up dates in your calendar so you can keep track.

TAKING ADVANTAGE OF TECHNOLOGY

Once you are managing more than 200 contacts, a computer-based system really becomes necessary. You may be surprised how quickly you can accumulate that many names. A computer-based contact management system will allow you to sort and select contacts by location, source, category, date of last contact, or other helpful information. Other reasons to computerize your list are to automate some of your letter writing and better manage your e-mail.

Programs such as Outlook, ACT!, and GoldMine are specifically designed for contact management. We don't recommend using a word processing or spreadsheet program as a contact manager, because they don't offer the full range of needed capabilities.

INGREDIENT:
Career Success Stories

When making contact with employers and other influential people, a helpful job search tool is a collection of **career success stories**. We all love to hear stories—stories that make us laugh or cry; stories which move us, as well as make us think. We identify with people through the stories they tell.

Career success stories are tales of the defining moments in your career when you overcame significant challenges to succeed. Telling people these stories creates a memorable impression and gives the listener anecdotes about you that they can repeat to others. Your stories can help your contacts make the connection between the problems or opportunities of their industry and a person (you) who has the potential to provide a solution.

Personal anecdotes demonstrate your unique ability to solve problems. When you tell success stories, you illustrate how you went about handling a difficult situation at work. Here's the idea—at some point in your career, you were faced with what seemed to be an insurmountable problem. If the problem continued, there would have been severe consequences. Rather than sit back and watch things fall apart, you took initiative and implemented a plan to solve the problem and bring about a positive end result. (See the "Career success story" example below.)

WHO NEEDS TO HEAR YOUR STORIES?

You'll want to tell your story to anyone who has the power to hire you or who could repeat your story to someone who can. This includes prospective employers, managers who can influence the hiring process, networking contacts, and job search buddies.

Here are three steps to creating your stories:

1. *Define the problem or opportunity.* This is the challenge you were up against. It may have been a special project that you were assigned, a volatile customer issue, or an aggressive objective you had never attempted before. Defining the problem sets up the plot of your story.

Career success story

PROBLEM/OPPORTUNITY

Not too long ago we were dealing with a technically complex customer service problem with one of our largest customers. They spent approximately $200,000 per month with us and were not going to stand for poor customer service. They had been dealing with these issues on and off for a period of four consecutive months. They threatened to cancel a long-term contract if we did not take care of the problem within the next forty-five days.

WHAT I DID

I had just taken over responsibility for the sales and service team that managed this account. First I assessed the problem through an all-hands meeting with everyone who came in contact with the client. Next I assembled several teams to each take responsibility for one of the problems related to a specific technical issue. I asked each team to develop a plan of attack to deal with their problem area. They had twenty-four hours to prepare their plan and report back to the other team members.

This method of handling a very complex and technical problem proved successful. It mobilized individuals who, up to this point, were passive and fearful about correcting the customer problem.

POSITIVE RESULT

The bottom line was that all of the client's issues were fixed within two weeks. Their contract renewal came due sixty days after we fixed the problems. As a result of our fast action and determination, they signed a new contract for an additional $150,000 per month in services over a three-year period.

2. *How did you solve it?* What did you do to handle the challenge? You may have developed plans, assigned tasks, held meetings, written proposals, or implemented an immediate solution. Describe the methods you used to tackle the problem, mapping out the process in detail, all the way through to resolution. With your description you are marketing your ability as a problem-solver.

3. **What was the positive result?** Describe the positive end result. Be specific about the increase, change, or improvement that resulted from your actions. If there was a financial impact of your resolution, give that figure in dollars, percent of growth, or reduction in total costs.

APPROACH:
Networking and Referral-Building, Informational Interviewing, and Contacting Potential Employers

SUCCESS INGREDIENTS
Thirty-second commercial
Model cover letter
Electronic résumé
Job proposal
Model follow-up letters

RECIPE:
Pitching Yourself by Phone

It's time to get personal. The telephone is your most important tool in finding the job you want. Whether you are contacting a potential employer or calling a networking contact, you need to be able to deliver a powerful message in a phone call.

In the *Applying to employers* stage of the Job Search Pyramid, you are typically contacting two groups of people:

1. **Potential employers.** To locate the appropriate hiring manager and explore opportunities or pitch your capabilities.

2. *Networking contacts.* To find the right person to contact at one of your target companies or to ask your contact for an introduction.

We recommend whenever possible that you call a company before applying for a position by mail or e-mail. When you have the hiring manager's name and already believe the company has an opportunity for you, the purpose of your call is to begin establishing a connection with that manager and let him or her know you will be sending more information. When you have a name, but not much other information, find out as much as you can before committing yourself to writing. When you don't have a name, call to get one.

Whether you are calling a contact for the first time or you've previously met, use a **thirty-second commercial** to introduce yourself. When you get voice mail, it is a golden opportunity to deliver your personal marketing message directly into a potential hiring manager's ear. If you are fortunate enough to reach your contact directly, your thirty-second commercial can serve as the basis of an interactive conversation. A thirty-second commercial is also useful in networking groups or other situations where you have a chance to let a gathering of interested people know what you do and what type of job you are seeking.

Another name for a thirty-second commercial is an "elevator speech." You have about thirty seconds, the length of a typical ride on an elevator, to make a memorable impression. Your intent is to give people enough information to become curious and want to hear more.

Begin your commercial with a ten-second introduction (see Chapter 8); then continue with some short statements about your special abilities. Try to describe your abilities as solutions to a potential challenge rather than just a job title or list of skills. Here's an example:

"My name is Therese Charbonneau and I specialize in helping companies get more sales from their web sites. As a web design and online sales expert, I've developed reliable techniques for converting higher percentages of web visitors into customers. I'd like to speak with you about a career opportunity with your company where I can share my unique abilities to expand the effectiveness of

End Run Around the Human Resources Department

Networking is always the key. That's how I got my job. A close friend and colleague referred me to an executive recruiter. The recruiter was psyched; I
was exactly what he was looking for to fill a position at a top consulting firm.
Interestingly, I had already applied there through corporate human resources
via the web. Through the recruiter, I was offered a job at the firm at a thirty
percent higher salary and three times the total earnings opportunity than I
had ever had before. The same day I got my offer letter, I also received a letter from the firm's corporate human resources department responding to
my web job application. It said, "thanks, but no thanks," and they would retain
my résumé for future consideration.

Kent Baril
SEATTLE, WASHINGTON

your web site as a sales tool. I can be reached at (212) 555-1234. Thanks, and
I'm looking forward to hearing from you."

Get in the habit of using your thirty-second commercial on every cold call
you make, whether you reach your contacts live or get voice mail. When you
are calling a stranger, you need to leave a memorable message. If you are calling
warm contacts (people you already know) or someone that's been referred to you,
it's still a good idea to repeat your commercial from time to time as a reminder.

When you speak to someone directly, don't rattle off your whole commercial at once. Begin with your ten-second introduction and open an interactive
conversation. Script out what feels comfortable to you using the example above

as a guideline. Edit your words to avoid sounding contrived. Try to make it simple and conversational so it rolls right off your tongue. (You'll find more suggestions under "Telephone Script" in Chapter 10.) And once you have it written out, practice, practice, practice.

RECIPE:
How to Apply by Mail or E-Mail

Marketing yourself effectively to potential employers will typically include both talking with the right people in person and delivering your message to them in writing, with a cover letter, résumé, job proposal, and/or follow-up letters. Each of your written communications should demonstrate your ability to solve problems and pursue opportunities for your potential employer.

The best method to approach a company in writing, regardless of whether the position you are seeking is advertised, is to send your résumé with a cover letter directly to the hiring manager. Another good choice would be to send your information to someone else you know at the company who might be able to influence the hiring manager or at least hand deliver your materials. Applying only to the human resources department should be your last choice.

For an advertised position, it's fine to apply to human resources as well as to the hiring manager. This can help you in some situations, and in others, it won't hurt. For unadvertised positions, we recommend that you avoid applying to human resources entirely.

WHAT TO SEND WITH YOUR RÉSUMÉ

A cover letter is your vehicle to describe why you are the best person for the job and to set you apart from any other candidate. In some cases it will be the cover letter, not the résumé, that determines why one person gets an interview and another ends up in the rejection pile.

Always send a cover letter with your résumé. You want to make a human connection with the person to whom you are writing. You need to engage the

Model cover letter

Dear Carlos:

Recently I met with a mutual colleague of ours, Dan McDuff, and he mentioned that you might have a need for a public relations expert in your organization. I was excited to hear about the opportunity and would like to explore how I can help fill that need.

I have a proven track record of public relations success gained from nearly ten years in a financial services setting and with an advertising/PR agency. Here are my specific skills that could benefit your team:

- Expertise in creating strategic public relations plans that increase awareness and exposure, ultimately bringing new business to the company.
- Skilled writer of powerful news releases and press materials (media kits, fact sheets, company and product backgrounders and histories, and media briefings).
- Outstanding knowledge of how the news media work; how to negotiate with busy reporters to place stories and gain coverage.
- Strong speaking presence to serve as a keynote and panel speaker at trade shows, business gatherings, and special events.

I would like to discuss this opportunity with you in a personal interview at your convenience. I'll call you next week to discuss a good time for us to meet. You may also reach me via telephone at (213) 555-1234 or by e-mail miki@gethirednow.com. I look forward to speaking with you soon.

Enthusiastically,
Miki Sakamoto

Enclosure: Résumé

recipient's interest enough to speak with you in person. A résumé alone cannot do this.

Instead of writing each cover letter from scratch, it will save time to develop a **model cover letter** (see example above) you can use as a template for most of the letters you write. Begin your letter by mentioning any connection you have with the recipient. If you've previously met or spoken, describe the encounter. If you were referred, name the source.

The main body of the letter should address specific issues relevant to the company and the job you are seeking. If you have learned that the company is struggling to keep customers, address how you can help improve customer service. If the manager to whom you are writing is stretched beyond the limit to manage his direct reports, indicate you have a knack for organizing large groups into highly effective teams. If you are new to the job market or the industry, explain how your transferable skills can make a contribution to the company's goals.

Your letter should end with a call to action. Ask for an interview or a convenient time you can meet in person.

SPECIAL CONSIDERATIONS WHEN APPLYING BY E-MAIL

Applying for a position by e-mail requires some additional considerations. The way your résumé appears on your computer could look completely different on someone else's computer. While it's impossible to design résumés to meet every type of software and computer out there, you can make it more likely to be readable by preparing an **electronic résumé**.

Many large companies have implemented automated résumé screening as an integral part of their hiring process. When your résumé is sent via e-mail or an online form, it may end up in an electronic screening system to search for keywords that match the requirements for the position. If it makes it through the automated screening process, a person reviews it next. So if your résumé isn't readable to the system, even if you are the most qualified person coming through the door, you won't be selected. You may be able to avoid this process altogether

Just Follow the Steps

I'm amazed at the number of job-seekers who don't understand the critical importance of the right kind of cover letter and what to emphasize in their résumé. I've had a nearly seventy-percent hit rate on companies contacting me after I've applied. In fact, I've been told I was one of a handful of people being interviewed when the hiring manager had received 200, 400, or even a thousand résumés.

Why? Because of these simple steps that have made my application package stand out:

1. My résumé always focuses on accomplishments and achievements, with specific results, and quantified, if possible.

2. In my cover letter I always bullet-point or highlight each of the specific requirements of the job, listing exactly how my skills or background addresses each area.

3. My cover letter expresses enthusiasm. I often say something like, "I saw your advertisement and became excited about working for your organization because of . . ."

4. I stay away from the "I" syndrome in my cover letters. Too many people say, "I have," "I can," "I am," and "I will" in a cover letter. In today's job market, it's not about you as the job seeker—it's about what you can do for the company and how you can help meet their needs or resolve their pain.

Follow these steps and I guarantee you will be a lot more successful at getting interviews!

Steve Luther
ARVADA, COLORADO

by sending your résumé directly to a hiring manager. Yet despite your best efforts, your résumé may wind up in the screening system anyway. It's best to comply with the system's requirements to get the best results possible.

Another reason for paying attention to the readability of your résumé is that you want to make it easy for companies to receive your information. Having to send your résumé several times to the same person because they can't read it will frustrate them and can make you appear unprofessional.

OPTIONS FOR DELIVERING YOUR RÉSUMÉ ELECTRONICALLY

- As an attachment to an e-mail—use Microsoft Word format or Adobe Acrobat (PDF).
- Part of the text within an e-mail message—the best option if your recipient doesn't accept attachments to avoid potential viruses. It's preferable to use a text-formatted version rather than an HTML-coded one.
- Pasted into an online application form—requires copying your résumé into the space provided. You'll need a plain-text version for this.
- Posted on the web—if you have a personal web site or a page provided by an online job search service, you might make your résumé available by e-mailing a link to the page rather than sending the entire document.

You should have two versions of your electronic résumé. The first version should be a word-processed document created in Microsoft Word or WordPad. When creating your word-processed résumé, keep in mind that your recipients may see garbage on their screen if you use graphics or non-standard fonts. Refrain from adding special effects or other visual components that may interfere with reading the most important part—the content. If your résumé is heavily formatted or was created in a program other than Word, you can also send it as a PDF document.

The second electronic version should be a plain-text format. Use this version when you need to paste your résumé into an online form or directly into an e-mail message. There are some special attributes of the plain-text format to note:

- Each line of text must end with a "hard carriage return" after sixty to sixty-five characters.
- No additional fonts, bolding, italics, underlining, colors, lines, bullets, numbers, borders, long or double (em and en) dashes, or graphics are available.
- To substitute for bullet points or other special characters, use plain-text characters such as an asterisk (*), lower case "o", or a dash/hyphen (-).

To create a plain-text version of your résumé, you can save a Word document as "text only." Then be sure to close and re-open your document to check its appearance.

When you apply to an employer by e-mail, never assume your e-mail was received unless you get a reply. It may have been rejected by a spam filter or deleted because it was from an unknown sender. Be sure to follow up, preferably by phone.

RECIPE:
Selling Yourself with a Proposal

Sometimes you have to color outside the lines. There will be times during your job search you'll need creativity and intuition to apply for a position when you're not sure it exists—or perhaps even invent one. At first this concept may sound strange. There are times when companies are unclear about their needs or they have yet to design a position that addresses a known problem. Making a strong impression at the right time can put you in line for a great job opportunity.

Sending a **job proposal** (see example on pages 232–233) is a unique way to approach a desirable company. Remembering that up to eighty-five percent of jobs are never advertised, it's a likely chance that your target companies have some hidden needs. With a job proposal you can pitch an influential person at a target company as to how you're qualified to help the company exploit an opportunity to grow their business, solve a complex problem, or implement a new idea.

Imagine that you were already working for the company. Try to visualize the challenges it is facing or to anticipate what its future goals might be. What elements of your experience might convince the company you are the best person to help them, and exactly how might you be of service? Use all the methods of company research at your disposal—networking, informational interviewing, web research, or reading print material—to determine how you might present yourself as a solution to the company's problems.

FORMULA FOR A JOB PROPOSAL

1. Select one of your target companies about which you feel truly enthusiastic.
2. Learn as much as possible about the company—operations, personnel, products, marketplace, technology, economic trends, and so forth.
3. Analyze potential opportunities or challenges facing the company where you can anticipate your expertise may be needed.
4. Imagine that you are already an employee of the company and now you must propose to your boss how to handle the opportunities or challenges you identified.
5. Select the one opportunity or challenge for which the ideal solution best fits your abilities, and then craft a job proposal based on that solution.
6. Describe in detail the process, idea, project, or action plan that would implement your solution.
7. Explain why you are the ideal person to implement this solution. Try to include a relevant career success story.
8. Send your proposal to the hiring manager at the company who your solution would benefit the most.
9. Set a follow-up date to call and discuss your job proposal and ask for a meeting.

WHY A PROPOSAL INSTEAD OF A RÉSUMÉ?

As we have pointed out earlier, a successful job search is more like a marketing campaign than it is a search. You have to show people that what you have to

Job proposal

Dear Mr. Chiu,

I have been researching Awakenings Coffee and have spoken with many of your employees. I am impressed with how the company has created a highly unique coffee shop experience in a fiercely competitive marketplace. I read the recent article in the *Business Journal* about your company opening over 400 new locations in less than six years and I felt highly energized.

I asked myself the following questions:

1. How would I ensure that each new location was operating at 100-percent efficiency within thirty days of opening?
2. What would a company-wide training initiative look like for this massive expansion?
3. How would I manage the diverse training needs for these new managers and staff employees?
4. Finally I wondered if these were issues you and your team were up against.

I believe I can help you train these new employees and ensure the quality of your customer service. I'm interested in joining your company in a role leading or supporting the new employee training initiative for your expansion. During the course of my career I have developed and implemented strategic training programs for many new retail operations. These training programs focused on three critical start-up factors:

offer is exactly what they need. Employers and organizations want to be assured that there is little risk in hiring you. Here are a few reasons that a job proposal may help to convince them:

- You're presenting a solution to a challenge they have yet to solve.
- You're proving to them how well you know their business.
- You're demonstrating that you are a strategic thinker and problem solver.

- Delivering unsurpassed customer service to build a new clientele's loyalty
- Efficient day-to-day operations put in place within the first thirty days of opening
- Consistent management, leadership, and employment principles in place from day one

In 2002, I was responsible for leading the new store training initiative for over 100 new locations of the Tasty Ice Cream Company. This extremely aggressive schedule called for opening one new store every two weeks. I oversaw the start-up operations training program for all new managers and staff. I worked with over 800 new employees getting them up to speed on the inner workings of each shop and training them how to deliver superior customer service. As a result, 100 percent of the stores opened on time, were operating at peak efficiency within thirty days, and subsequently delivered to the company an immediate forty-two-percent revenue increase.

I feel I can do the same, if not more, for your company. You will most likely be facing the same pressing issues as I have throughout my career. My direct experience, coupled with my fast-acting problem-resolution skills, will be a key factor in exceeding your goal of opening over 400 new stores in the six years.

Let's take the opportunity to discuss these challenges, your aggressive goals, and how my expertise can help. I can be reached at (313) 555-1234 and look forward to your call.

Sincerely,
Cynthia Hochman

- You'll probably need little training to begin working in the company.
- They have yet to see other candidates present themselves this way. The unique approach sets you apart.
- Management will see you as a valuable potential team player.
- You provide the desired answers to two crucial hiring questions: "What can you do for us?" and "Do you fit in here?"

No Opening? No Problem!

When I was in college and majoring in geology, I needed a job to stay in school and finish my degree. I had a strong interest in astrogeology—the geology of other planets—and I mentioned to one of my professors that I was look- ing for work. He gave me the name of a senior geologist he knew at the U.S. Geological Survey's astrogeology unit in Menlo Park, which was within com- muting distance from my home. It was a tiny department, and they had no open positions, but I wrote a letter to my professor's contact anyway. I expressed my interest in working for him and described how my prior expe- rience in computer programming and technical writing might benefit his department.

To my surprise, he called me for an interview. It turned out he had a proj- ect in mind for which he would need a researcher with computer skills. He hadn't even defined the position yet. After our interview, he wrote a position description that matched my skills exactly and posted the position as being open, which was a requirement for this federal job.

I was really worried when I heard that a woman with a master's degree had applied for the position he had designed. Why would he pick me now? I hadn't even completed my bachelor's degree. But he rejected her applica- tion and hired me instead. Later when I asked him why he chose me, he said, "It was you who approached me first. I could tell that you really wanted the job."

C. J. Hayden
SAN FRANCISCO, CALIFORNIA

Job proposals are appropriate for advertised positions too. Don't rule out sending one because the position has already been publicized. You can also use a job proposal to follow up with a hiring manager who already has received your résumé. The key here is to show off enough of your expertise to make the company notice you.

RECIPE:
Following Up with Your Contacts

Nearly every meeting or phone call with people during your job search will require some form of follow-up. You'll need to thank your contacts for their time or information, recap what was discussed, and remind them what should happen next. Consistently following up with people during your job search campaign is essential to sustain momentum. If you forget or ignore follow-up activities, the result will be like putting your car in neutral. Not only will you stop moving, you might roll backward.

Your contacts are likely to be very busy people. Pressing business issues, meetings, deadlines, and their own personal lives will all be more important than your situation. Sometimes they will forget what transpired in your meeting or phone call or neglect a promise they made. They may not respond for days or weeks to your calls or notes. If you think this behavior is rude, now is a good time to get over it. You need to accept delays and lack of responses as simply normal business practice in an overloaded world. By doing so your job search will be much less stressful.

Plan on making at least one follow-up call per week on each of your applications and proposals. You will also want to follow up with people with whom you had networking meetings or informational interviews and anyone who promised you information. Gently remind your contacts what you spoke about, what was supposed to happen next, and ask for what you need. When you don't get return phone calls, use e-mail to follow up. You may find that some people don't return phone calls, but send them an e-mail and you'll get a response within the hour.

Model follow-up letter after a personal contact

Joan,

I sincerely appreciate your making some time in your busy schedule yesterday to speak with me. I was encouraged by your comments and opinions about the explosive growth in the industry.

There were a few key points on which I wanted to follow up with you. You mentioned it would be good for me to talk with Linda Sooner in your customer service department. I'd greatly appreciate it if you could send me her phone number and email address. Also, you wanted to see a copy of my résumé, which I've attached.

Again, thanks so much for your help. As soon as I hear from you, I plan to call Linda and mention our discussion. I'll follow up with you after Linda and I talk. If there is anything I can do for you, please don't hesitate to ask.

Thanks again,
Jeffrey Nguyen
(206) 555-1234

To follow up effectively, you will also need some **model follow-up letters** (see examples above and below). Sending letters by either postal mail or e-mail has both advantages and disadvantages. Letters sent by post show a personal touch but are not as efficient. Some people love receiving letters in the mail and read every one; others have an assistant open mail and throw out most of it. With e-mail you can send a message instantly, but some busy people are dealing with hundreds of messages per day. Your message may not get read or may be deleted without a reply. Your best bet may often be to send a message both ways—or to alternate between one and the other—until you know more about your contacts' preferred method of communication.

Model follow-up letter for an application

Luis,

I know how busy you are at Arcadia International. That's why I'm writing you. Last week I sent you some information about how I can help take some pressure off the accounting department.

The cover letter and résumé I sent will give you an idea of what I can do to assist the accounting department in speeding up turnaround time and reducing backlog. I have some unique ideas to help streamline workflow and systematize error-processing on a monthly basis.

I'd like just a few minutes of your time to talk about my ideas and career opportunities at Arcadia. I'll plan to call you on Wednesday, May 15, first thing in the morning. In the meantime, please don't hesitate to call me. I look forward to our first conversation.

Regards,
Shannon Mahoney
(316) 555-1234

FORMAT OF A FOLLOW-UP LETTER

In your first paragraph thank the person for his or her time or assistance. Perhaps mention an interesting point they made in your discussion.

Next briefly recap your interaction and highlight the main points that require action on either part. You can write these in short conversational sentences or list them in bullet form.

Use the third paragraph to define what you would like to happen next. This might be a phone call, a promise or request for additional information, or a suggested meeting time. Keep your follow-up letters and e-mails to a single page.

Searched Out the Perfect Job

After September 11, I was desperate to immediately relocate from New York City to someplace out West. I had chosen Cheyenne, Wyoming as my destination—wide-open plains, big sky, and no tall buildings. I didn't know anyone there, however, so I relied entirely on Internet research to find a job. And because job opportunities in Cheyenne were not easily found on the big Internet job boards, I knew I had to get creative.

So I did a search for "Wyoming + business" and began clicking from site to site. Each time I found what seemed like a possible place to work, I e-mailed my text-only résumé to the best contact listed on the site. I included a brief introduction, explaining my desire to relocate to Cheyenne.

I first e-mailed the president of the Greater Cheyenne Chamber of Commerce, not just for a possible job but also to ask if they knew of other places to look. I e-mailed the executive director of the Old West Museum because it sounded interesting. I also e-mailed the Wyoming Business Council hoping for leads.

Within twenty minutes of e-mailing the Business Council, I received a phone call from a woman in human resources. She said I'd be getting a call within ten minutes from the head of human resources. Although they didn't have the position listed anywhere, they had been trying to fill a marketing manager position for over a year. My résumé—heavy in marketing and public relations experience—was perfect.

After two interviews, I got the job and relocated to Cheyenne. I also found the perfect apartment by searching the Internet—a renovated barn on eighty acres of Wyoming prairie. Searching out possible employers and approaching them directly helped me change my career and my life.

Aliza Sherman
LARAMIE, WYOMING

APPROACH:
Employing Recruiters and Agencies, Searching Specialized Job Listings, and Using Help-Wanted Ads

We've included these approaches in this chapter because perhaps you used them earlier to uncover positions for which you now wish to apply. However, we actually suggest you avoid spending much time using these three strategies if you are working on the *Applying to employers* stage of the Job Search Pyramid. Working with agencies and looking at job postings are not strategies that will get you unstuck in the area of applying to employers. The primary purpose of those strategies is to help you find opportunities for which to apply. So if you're focusing your efforts on this stage of the Pyramid, we're assuming that you've already located plenty of opportunities, but now need assistance in actively pursuing them. If this isn't you, you may need to back up a stage to *Finding opportunities and contacts*.

To apply for advertised positions you find in specialized job listings and the want ads, refer to the earlier parts of this chapter for help with locating the best contact at the company, placing phone calls, and applying by mail or e-mail. Keep in mind that when a position is advertised, your qualifications need to be an excellent match for the job requirements in order for you to be considered.

Remember that it's fine to keep seeking out new opportunities while you are applying for and following up on the ones of which you are already aware. As we discussed in Chapter 5, your Daily Actions are in no way intended to be everything you do regarding job-seeking over the twenty-eight days of the program. The secret to success, though, is focusing most of your efforts on the area where you are feeling lost or stuck. If you picked this stage to work on, you are probably finding opportunities to apply for without much effort; thus, you need not pay much attention to finding more. That will take care of itself.

HINT:
A Word About Fear

The thought of applying to employers and following up with important contacts may be even be more paralyzing than making cold calls. After all, these are people you believe have the power to get you the job you really want. Maybe you've already spoken or sent your résumé. You've invested a great deal of time or made a personal connection, so now if you hear "no," the rejection feels quite personal.

What you have to remember is that rejection is not about you. This is a business relationship. Your job prospects are deciding whether or not to take the time to bring you in for an interview or take the risk of offering you a job. There are many factors that go into a decision like this. When your contact tells you the job was filled with someone who has "more experience," the message is that the company hires only people with strong experience in its own industry. This is not about you. If you are told that the competition "came well recommended," the prospect is choosing to hire a friend or a colleague—again, it's not about you.

The best way to defeat your fear of applying for jobs and following up is to have so many job prospects that any one rejection becomes much less important.

CHAPTER 10

Getting Interviews:

When You're Contacting People but Getting No Interviews

I don't know the key to success, but the key
to failure is trying to please everybody.

— BILL COSBY

What's In the Way?

Once you have arrived at this stage of the Job Search Pyramid you are more than
halfway home. With an ample list of opportunities to apply for, a targeted résumé,
and many contacts in the industry, you are bound to have plenty of interviews,
right? That's usually how it works. Finding the right people to contact, and actually contacting them, will produce results in most cases. But it's sometimes not
quite enough.

When you find yourself applying for many opportunities, but rarely getting
interviews, there's something in the way. Assuming that you have skills and experience that your target companies need, what else might be preventing people
from offering you an interview?

1. *You're not positioning yourself correctly.* When you send a résumé or call
   on the phone, the company doesn't grasp that you are the right person for
   the position.
2. *Your telephone skills aren't up to the task.* You are nervous or unprepared
   when you get on the phone and are unable to engage people in conversation.
3. *The companies you are talking to really can't use you.* They don't have an

immediate need, can't afford to hire you now, or are otherwise not ready to take action.

4. *No one has referred you and your name is unknown.* Hiring managers are hesitant to take their time to speak with you.

5. *Your competition seems to have arrived before you.* No one wants to interview you because they already have plenty of qualified candidates.

This chapter will help you find solutions to these problems. Suggestions for improving your basic tools for getting interviews appear first, followed by some ideas for becoming better connected and for selling yourself.

Ingredients for Getting Interviews

> **SUCCESS INGREDIENTS**
> Telephone script
> Telephone interview skills
> Better résumé format

INGREDIENT:
Telephone Script

One of the quickest fixes to how you are positioning yourself when you approach companies can be to change your words. An effective **telephone script** (see example on page 244) positions you as a potential employee in such a way that hiring managers immediately grasp your value. You have to get their attention right away in order for them to be willing to speak with you. A common mistake is to call a prospective interviewer with the intent of introducing yourself and telling this person the type of job you are seeking. But that's about you. Why should they care?

Try asking about the person you are calling instead: "Do you have a moment to talk about your needs in the area of managing new products?" This is a sample opening question. Or lead with a benefit: "I help salespeople learn how to close large deals faster. How are your salespeople doing with landing large accounts?" Or ask a qualifying question: "How happy are you with the results from your marketing campaigns?"

When a prospective interviewer calls you, resist launching into a description of what you do and where you have been employed. Inquire instead about the interviewer's situation. Engaging interviewers in conversation will both establish rapport and provide you with valuable information. Whenever you can, ask open-ended questions rather than encouraging "yes" or "no" answers. "How does your company plan to deal with the new regulations for retirement plans this year?" elicits a much more useful response than asking, "Are you aware of the new regulations for retirement plans?" Include a series of these questions in your script.

The word "script" is not meant to imply that you are reading prepared material. You don't want to come off as though you are a telemarketer. Design your script as a list of talking points that you refer to as needed during an interactive conversation. That way you feel natural and can present yourself clearly.

Once you feel that you have both established rapport and collected enough information from your contacts, tell them briefly and specifically how you can help their situation, using their own words. If your contact says, "We have too many unfinished projects in our department," you might respond, "I can really help you with those unfinished projects. I designed a unique project-management system for Russell Manufacturing that encouraged every team member to complete projects ahead of schedule."

As soon as you know you've got the person's interest, ask for an interview. Don't wait for your contact to suggest it or back away from asking directly. "It sounds as if my skills might be just what you need. Would you like to get together to discuss it further?"

In addition to using your script to contact hiring managers to ask for an inter-

Telephone script

INTRODUCTION

Hi, my name is Laurel Parinello. Mindy Frank, your benefits manager, suggested that I speak with you. I help financial services companies streamline their customer service departments. I'm currently exploring career opportunities as a customer service manager.

OPENING QUESTION

I understand you've experienced incredible growth in new customers over the past three months. Do you have a moment to talk about your goals in continuing to provide efficient customer service?

COLLECT INFORMATION

How does Rose Financial plan to address the increase in customer service calls from these new customers?

SOLUTION STATEMENTS

They say: We'll probably have to hire an entirely new group of customer service representatives. *Or:* We need to get our people to work more efficiently.

I say: I believe I can help you reduce the number of new representatives you'll need to hire. *Or:* I can get your people to do more in the same amount of time. At Walker Finance, I developed a series of job aids that helped their representatives drastically reduce the time it took to resolve customer issues.

They say: We're going to have to re-train our customer service reps to handle the new questions coming in.

I say: I believe I can help you get your staff re-trained on an accelerated schedule. At Walker Finance, I implemented a new on-the-job training program that kept reps in the office while they learned about the new products.

POSSIBLE OBJECTIONS

They say: We don't have an opening for a customer service manager right now.

I say: Yes, I know. I'm predicting that at your rate of growth you will create the need for a new position in the next ninety days, and I'd like to discuss how I might help you prevent getting overloaded before you decide to hire.

ASK FOR THE INTERVIEW

I'd like to set up an interview with you and talk about what you need and how I could help. When would be a good time for us to get together?

view, you might use it also for networking or informational interviewing. In those cases, your closing question might be to ask for a meeting or to inquire who would be an appropriate person with whom to speak next.

COMPONENTS OF A TELEPHONE SCRIPT

1. *Brief introduction.* Your name, name of the person who referred you, any other shared connection, or something you learned in your research about the company.
2. *Opening question.* Direct question about a specific situation; this is generally a problem you suspect needs resolution or an opportunity the company may wish to pursue.
3. *Establish rapport/collect information.* Open-ended questions that engage your contact in conversation and gather helpful information for positioning your skills as a solution.
4. *Solution statement.* How you can help solve the company's problem or pursue the opportunity at hand.
5. *Ask for the interview.* Make a direct request that your contact meet with you to discuss your potential contribution to the company.

Write out what you plan to say for each of these five steps. Include responses to expected objections or questions. Use any wording you developed for your ten-second introduction or thirty-second commercial. Make sure to focus on only one specific problem or opportunity that you suspect your contact is currently facing. Then practice your script with a job search buddy or colleague. If you have trouble remembering what's in your script, become nervous, or just can't seem to think quickly enough to deliver the best responses, keep practicing until you can use your script with ease.

Your odds of getting an interview increase significantly every time you make a call like this. The more calls you make, the better you get, and any fear and resistance you have begins to subside.

He Just Kept Calling

The second day after I moved to California, I was going for a drive to learn my surroundings and noticed a beautiful hotel not far from my new place. After a little legwork, I discovered that it was not only pretty, but it was the only five-star hotel on the West Coast at the time. Deciding that was where my next job would be was easy. Getting in was the challenge.

I went in with my résumé, but getting the name of the personnel director almost slipped my mind in my nervous desire to be a part of this exciting operation. The next day my follow-up call was easier with a name in hand. I was disappointed when the director told me there were no open positions. The conversation went smoothly as I inquired what she liked about working there and I got to slip in my own job desires.

I continued to call the personnel director every other day for two weeks. I was finally told that if a position came open I would get the first call, but to please stop calling. The next Monday, I found myself interviewing with the executive chef and the food and beverage director for what became my most rewarding job ever as a chef.

It was a great experience that showed me "not yet" might mean something other than "no."

Christopher Irwin
SAN MATEO, CALIFORNIA

INGREDIENT:
Telephone Interview Skills

It's common practice with many companies to conduct a telephone interview before scheduling an in-person meeting. Be prepared for a telephone interview at any time. Your call to a hiring manager may turn into a job interview on the spot.

There are several things you can do to improve your **telephone interview skills**. First compile a list of questions you expect will be asked in any interview. (See Chapter 11 for additional information on this topic.) Then write down your responses in the form of talking points. Ask a job search buddy or colleague to ask you the questions and practice your responses. Listen to yourself speak and ask for honest feedback. Alternatively, tape-record your responses and replay them. These techniques will help you become more comfortable with your responses and reduce the stress of phone interviewing.

Making a personal connection over the phone can be challenging. You may find that it helps you to sound and feel more personable if you look in a mirror and smile while you are talking. To improve your skills further, take a class, listen to an audio, or work with a coach.

INGREDIENT:
Better Résumé Format

Your résumé ultimately has one sole purpose—to generate interviews. No one will ever know how much effort you put into it, nor will they care. Your readers are only concerned about filling their own needs and whether you have the required abilities. If your résumé can successfully demonstrate this, chances are likely you'll get in the door for an interview. If it doesn't, it will wind up in the "keep it on file" pile.

You may need a **better résumé format** to position you well for the specific job for which you are applying. Review the suggestions for composing your résumé in Chapter 8, paying special attention to how well the included experience and accomplishments match the requirements for those jobs you are pursuing. It may be necessary to make minor revisions to your résumé each time you apply for a different position. Even when you have done a good job initially at defining what you want, no two jobs will be exactly alike. You may need to address specific points that will capture the attention of a particular hiring manager.

Both people and computers scan your résumé looking for specific keywords that indicate you meet the requirements of the job. The more keyword matches there are in your résumé, the more likely your résumé will be selected for an opportunity to interview.

JOB-SPECIFIC FACTORS COMPANIES LOOK FOR IN A RÉSUMÉ

- Stated objective that matches the opportunity
- Accomplishments related to the job requirements
- Similar level of responsibilities, such as individual contributor, supervisor, or manager
- Related job titles, projects, or functions
- Experience in the same or similar industry
- Specific education, training, or skills essential to the position

Do your homework on the requirements of the job opportunity and then customize your résumé to include those same factors. Sometimes simple changes, like using the title of the position you are applying for as your résumé objective or listing the required skills in your experience summary, will get the attention of a hiring manager. If you send a generic résumé for a targeted job opportunity, you are wasting the research you did to uncover it and sparking little motivation for anyone to call you for an interview.

APPROACH:
Networking and Referral-Building, Contacting Potential Employers, Informational Interviewing, and Employing Recruiters and Agencies

SUCCESS INGREDIENTS
Personal selling skills
Deeper company research
Higher quality leads and referrals
Public-speaking tools
Article-writing tools

RECIPE:
Following Up on Your Applications

To increase your chances of getting interviewed, it's essential to follow up on all the opportunities you are pursuing. Your potential interviewers are constantly being distracted by other responsibilities, urgent problems, and changing priorities. Don't become discouraged when responses take longer than what was agreed to in your last exchange. It often takes multiple calls or letters to get any kind of response. This is just the way the system works so don't let it drive you crazy.

Refer to Chapter 9 for suggestions on how to keep track of your calls and letters, as well as what to say. Set aside a time each week, or each day, for follow-up and put it in your calendar. Get into a daily follow-up habit as consistent as brushing your teeth.

How often should you follow up? Every two or three days may be appropriate when you're in conversation with a hiring manager about a hot opportunity.

A Smokin' Hot Résumé

The most creative action to get résumé attention that I have seen in my twenty-five years as a hiring manager was by a software engineer named Don. After I ignored his résumé the first time it crossed my desk—a fairly typical résumé among the hundreds I had to choose from at that time—Don went out and learned some things about our chief executive officer. Among other things, he discovered that the CEO smoked very expensive, imported cigars.

Don bought one, wrapped it carefully, and sent it to our CEO with a professional-looking letter. His letter said: "Just as one cannot evaluate the quality of a great cigar by merely scanning the wrapper, one cannot evaluate the potential of a great employee by scanning a résumé." In his letter, he asked for an interview. I subsequently received the letter along with a note forwarded from the CEO, asking that I interview him. I gave Don the interview and ultimately decided to hire him. He was a valuable contributor for many years.

I have never forgotten Don's lesson in the importance of getting attention by standing out from the crowd.

Jerry Straks
FREMONT, CALIFORNIA

When following up on an application, once every seven to ten days is usually adequate. When dealing with recruiters, follow up once every other week at the most. Avoid annoying recruiters by repeatedly asking if they have something for you. Remember, they work for their client companies, not you. Employment agencies may give you guidelines for contacting them, which often include calling at the beginning of the week to let them know you are still available. Be sure to follow these guidelines to have the best chance at getting an agency placement.

RECIPE:
Selling Yourself

The higher you climb on the Job Search Pyramid, the more competent your **personal selling skills** need to be. Whether you are trying to land an interview, get a networking contact to meet with you, or sell a recruiter on your abilities, you will have to persuade people that you are the best person for the job. In learning to sell yourself you gain the power of persuasion.

Your potential interviewers are looking for the solution to their problems. They are essentially seeking the right product to do the job at the right price. You are the solution, the product, and also that product's salesperson.

Although you may not be a salesperson by trade, you probably already possess many of the characteristics of a great salesperson. You just need to know what these are and how you can use them. Using the following list, check off how many of these characteristics you already possess.

CHARACTERISTICS OF A GREAT SALESPERSON
- *Good listening skills*. Every great salesperson is a good listener. Listening not only to the words being said but to the meaning behind them is essential. A good listener knows how to interpret what is heard and assess what the "customer" needs.
- *Naturally curious*. Curiosity illustrates interest in the other person and the situation at hand. Being curious helps to build a collaborative

relationship wherein information and ideas can flow. Asking the right questions draws out the customer and uncovers needs.

- **Recognizes what motivates people.** Everyone has a motivation switch. Some are visible; others invisible. Great salespeople have the ability to uncover what motivates the customer. In any selling situation, the quicker you discern what will motivate someone to make a change, the better the chances are of making a successful sale.

- **Understands the product.** Product knowledge is vital in any sales situation. You must be able to speak intelligently about your features (e.g., training and experience) and benefits (e.g., what you can contribute). Then you can match these with what fits the employer's needs the best.

- **Solves problems.** Great salespeople don't force a product on a customer. Rather they determine the customer's problem, explore the circumstances surrounding it, and develop a solution that is customized to the customer's situation.

- **Able to improvise.** A jazz musician can anticipate the flow of the music and seamlessly improvise so that every note appears carefully planned. A great salesperson works similarly with words.

- **Knows how to build rapport.** Great salespeople can make a connection with just about anyone. The salesperson's humor, sincerity, and friendly attitude will alleviate any tension that develops. The ability to meet others at an equal level is key. This is the approach that leads to the most productive business relationships.

As you can see from this list, being a great salesperson is really about being a good communicator and making a connection with the people you contact. If you can do this, the only missing step may be to specifically ask for what you want. For example, don't assume a manager will suggest an interview. Instead say, "It sounds like I'm a good fit for the position. Would you be willing to interview me?" By asking directly, you find out immediately how strong a candidate you are.

Always make a direct request for a meeting in your calls, letters, and job proposals. If you don't get a response, follow up and ask again. A great salesperson (that's you) asks for the business more than once.

If you feel uncomfortable about selling yourself, you may want to get some sales training. You can read a book or listen to audio programs, but the best ways to improve your selling skills are to practice with others in a workshop or role-play with a friend or coach. One of the biggest obstacles to successful personal selling is lack of confidence—practice will help you build it.

RECIPE:
Finding Out More About Your Target Companies

You may discover the information about your target companies that you have gathered thus far isn't enough to secure an interview. You may have learned who has the power to hire you, but not what this person needs. Or you may have acquired a good knowledge of a company's needs but no personal contacts on the inside.

Deeper company research may lead you to discover new problems you can solve or connect you with insiders who can recommend you for an interview. Through networking and referral-building, contacting companies directly, or informational interviewing, you can uncover hidden problems and make important contacts.

METHODS FOR "GOING DEEP" WITHIN A COMPANY
- All the ideas listed for the Success Ingredients "company research" and "company networking venues" in Chapter 8
- Ask all your existing contacts to refer you to people they know on the inside
- Conduct informational interviews with company employees at any level, vendors who service the company, and veterans of the industry who know the inside scoop

They Said They Didn't Need Her

I made a cold call to a university asking how to apply to teach a writing class. A woman within the fiction-writing program told me that because I was unpublished they would not send me an application.

Realizing that woman was a naysayer, I called another division of the same university—the playwriting program. The woman in charge of hiring, Carla, told me that another local playwright, Jane, was currently teaching at the university. I knew that Jane was an unimaginative writer and unqualified teacher, but I did not want to indulge in bad-mouthing her, especially not while trying to apply for a similar position. Still I knew I was more qualified and I needed a job.

When Carla asked me if I knew Jane, I paused for a long time and then said, "You really need to hire a teacher who's an incredible playwright who has received great reviews." I paused again, and then asked her, "Have you ever read Jane's work?"

Carla laughed. I then offered, "I would be willing to submit my work and my rave reviews to you." Carla set up a meeting with me.

At the meeting she told me that I had perfect timing because she was about to cancel the entire playwriting program due to lack of students, but she was impressed with my Ph.D. "Do you have any proposals that might attract more students?" she asked. On the spot I presented three proposals to her, and she loved the last one—my idea to teach comedy to playwrights, television writers, and screenwriters. The course was approved, and I was hired.

Karen Cronacher
SEATTLE, WASHINGTON

- Contact the company as a customer and ask for product information
- Request a copy of the company's press kit from its public relations department
- Talk to the company's customers—you may find a client list on its web site

The new information or contacts you discover can help you more carefully tailor your cover letter, customize your résumé, follow up directly with the appropriate hiring manager, prepare a job proposal, or have your résumé hand-delivered to someone who is sure to review it.

RECIPE:
Getting Better Names to Contact

Some positions are easier to network your way into than others. To learn about open positions before they are advertised, uncover hidden problems in a company, or get someone to refer you directly to a hiring manager, you need a strong network. Not finding the right people to talk to may be holding you back. **Higher quality leads and referrals** will come from people who are better connected or at a higher level in your target industry.

You need to make connections with the people in your industry who are on a first-name basis with decision-makers. Hiring managers would much rather interview a referred candidate than one who responded to an ad or approached them from out of the blue. So how do you get on this inside track to the interview room? When you have a specific company in mind, try to establish how your target company is organized so you can seek the direct path to the key decision-maker. Here's an example of how this might work:

Let's say you are seeking a market research position at Greencoast Manufacturing. At some point in your research or networking you found the name of one of Greencoast's salespeople. Guessing that she probably reports to the same person who might hire you, you consider what you might be able to offer her. You sift through what you know about the industry, looking for information

Down to Her Last Sixpence

I was living in London and had decided to remain and freelance rather than return to the United States with the company that had moved me abroad. I started looking for work but without great results. I looked in the newspaper and sent out résumés, talked to headhunters, spoke with some of the colleagues, vendors, and other contacts I had from my previous job, even sounded out my old boss about taking me back, as it was the easiest way to get the work permit I needed, but no luck.

So I pulled out all the stops. I started calling everyone, I mean *everyone* I could think of, including people I didn't know well, plus anyone who those people recommended. Faced with having to go home unsuccessful, I figured things couldn't get much worse. One of the people I called was a guy I had met at a conference with whom I had kept in very loose touch. By this point, however, I was nearing the end of my financial reserves.

The guy from the conference gave me the names of a couple of people at his company to contact. I was losing hope, but went through the motions — wrote letters and called each of them, only to receive yet more "no thanks" responses. One of these contacts didn't call me back for quite some time, although his administrative assistant was very nice and encouraging when I followed up. Just as I got to the despairing point of deciding whether to buy a potato for dinner or a newspaper to continue looking for work (I bought the potato and found the newspaper on the tube), I got a call from this elusive man. So I pasted on a smile and went in for an interview, trying not to look as down-at-the-heels as I felt.

Surprise, surprise . . . he gave me a project that day which turned into a four-year, defacto marketing manager position at the best pay I'd ever earned. Boy was I glad I hung in there because those were some of the best years of my life.

Deborah Huisken
MONTAGUE, MASSACHUSETTS

that might be useful. Then you contact the salesperson, introduce yourself, and ask if she would be interested in meeting so you can share some market research data you have collected about buying patterns in Greencoast's industry. In return you would appreciate any insights she might have about the marketing department and their need for market research people. The sales representative indicates she would be happy to share with you whatever information she can discover. When you meet you learn there will soon be an open position in market research. You then ask if she would be willing to give you a personal reference as a candidate to the appropriate hiring manager.

Even when you have no specific company in mind you can get on the inside track by becoming better connected in your target industry. Look for special events sponsored by individual companies and vendors, including those designed to promote their products and services. Watch for articles that mention the names of managers, executives, and other key industry players. Then call or write to compliment them on the article and ask for an informational interview or networking meeting. Follow the advice in the previous section about "deeper company research" to determine the most valuable people to contact.

The bottom line in getting higher-quality leads and referrals is to get as close as possible to your industry's decision-makers. If your current network is only getting you to the company borders, then you need to break through by meeting well-connected people.

RECIPE:
Speaking to Boost Your Career

Public speaking creates positive visibility, boosts your credibility, and establishes you as an expert in your industry. It puts you in direct contact with potential hiring managers, industry vendors, and other centers of influence. You may find yourself landing a job interview before leaving the room. It's a powerful way to get known in your industry and connect with people who can help your job search.

At this point you may be thinking, "Why would anyone want to hear me speak? I don't have any credentials as an expert. And what would I talk about?" You might be surprised to learn that industry and community groups are always looking for ordinary people to speak. If you have experience with a topic of interest to people in your industry or community, you can find an audience waiting to hear you.

A boutique manager could speak to a group of local merchants about window displays. An employee benefits specialist could present to an industry meeting on the topic of producing annual benefit statements. Any job-related project you successfully completed or sticky situation you resolved is an excellent candidate for a case study you could share at a trade association conference.

To pursue speaking opportunities like these, you will need three **public-speaking tools:** a description of your topic, a speaker's bio, and some possible speaking venues.

ABOUT THE FEAR OF SPEAKING IN PUBLIC

With all the benefits public speaking offers, it's unfortunate that surveys show most people are more afraid of speaking in public than they are of dying! If this is true for you, wait a bit before including public speaking on your list of tactics. You won't be able to make a good impression on your audience if you're too nervous. First work on getting some practice. The fact is that the most effective way to reduce the fear of public speaking is to get experience doing it.

Try taking a class at your local community college or from a private training organization such as Dale Carnegie. Join a local Toastmasters group where people meet regularly to practice their speaking and receive feedback on their delivery. Or look for a Speaking Circle® in your area. These are groups led by trained facilitators who assist you in developing a natural and authentic speaking style.

You can work more gradually on becoming a public speaker by participating in a networking group or job club that requires members to introduce themselves at every meeting. Your next step might be volunteering to host part of a program or make announcements on behalf of a committee. After this you might be ready to serve on a panel where it is common to speak while staying seated and referring to notes. Over time you will get more comfortable at being in front of a group and be able to carry off a solo talk without experiencing panic.

When you are ready to get started with public speaking you will need to locate some speaking venues. These are the places, groups, or events where you can give presentations to audiences interested in hearing your topic.

IDEAS FOR SPEAKING VENUES

- Chamber of Commerce networking events and workshops
- Service clubs such as Rotary and Kiwanis
- Trade and professional association meetings and conferences for your industry
- Lectures, workshops, and conferences hosted by educational institutions, community organizations, and affinity groups
- Classes offered by community colleges, resource centers, and independent learning centers, such as the Learning Annex
- Job clubs
- Live chats hosted by online services and web sites

If some of the entries on this list look suspiciously like those on the list of suggested places to network, you have noticed something very important! Public speaking is networking on steroids. You can speak to the same groups you might otherwise just visit, and you can find them using some of the same resources mentioned in Chapter 7 for the Success Ingredient "industry networking venues." But as the speaker, you will be standing in front of the room instead of sitting in the audience.

To approach a group about being a speaker, you will need to develop a topic you would like to present. Your topic should be interesting, educational, and distinctive, and show off your specialized expertise. It should allow you to tell stories about your work and include examples of what you have done for your employers. In this way, you can deliver value to your audience and promote yourself effectively at the same time.

Most networking groups, service clubs, and professional organizations give their guest speakers between twenty and sixty minutes for their talk. Breakout sessions at a conference can run from ninety minutes to three hours. Write a brief description of your topic that will give group organizers enough information to decide if they like it, and can be used to promote your talk once it's scheduled. Give your topic an enticing title that will attract plenty of listeners when printed in a group's newsletter or program.

The third essential tool for getting yourself booked as a speaker is a brief biography to accompany your topic description. You can prepare a bio easily by using some of the job experience or accomplishment statements from your résumé and adding a list of any prior speaking experience you have. If you have never spoken before in public and have no credits to list on your bio, don't let that stop you. If you believe you can do a good job, go for it. You have to give your first talk sometime. (See "Topic description and speaker's bio" example on the next page.)

With your topic description and bio prepared, you are ready to start approach-

Topic description and speaker's bio

**FINANCIAL MANAGEMENT FOR NONPROFITS:
UNDERSTANDING THE BASICS**

Geared toward emerging organizations that are in the process of learning how to manage their finances, this program will help you gain a better understanding of roles and responsibilities for board and staff regarding financial management, as well as basic accounting concepts. Here's some of what you will learn:

- The most important principles for sound financial management
- What effective nonprofit boards do
- How to determine what accounting staff your organization needs
- Significance of the chart of accounts in designing an accounting system
- How to record common financial transactions using the chart of accounts and accounting principles

Michelle Hannahs is vice president of finance and administration, Association of American Colleges and Universities, Washington, DC. She is responsible for financial management, personnel administration, membership, and information technology at the association. Prior to joining the association, Michelle was director of administrative services at the Center for Community Change where she provided training and consultation to numerous community-based organizations throughout the United States. Michelle earned her MBA from George Washington University and an MA from State University of New York at Albany. She has presented programs for the McAuley Institute and the Management Assistance Group.

ing your chosen venues. Don't waste your time blindly sending information to the group's main mailing address; as it will most likely be discarded.

For networking groups, service clubs, and association meetings, typically you will need to contact the program chairperson who is often a volunteer working from home or a different office. You may be able to find the program chair's contact information on the group's web site or request the group's information packet for new prospective members and look for it there. Then directly approach the program chair by phone or e-mail.

With educational institutions, resource and learning centers, and industry conferences, study the current catalog or conference agenda before making contact. If they already offer a program on your topic, try to find a different angle that hasn't been covered. Then contact the department chairperson, program director, or organizing committee to see if the group is interested.

You may be asked to submit a proposal for which the group may or may not have written guidelines. If no guidelines are available, send your topic description and bio with a cover letter explaining why you think this topic will be popular with the group's audience. Try to learn how far ahead the group is scheduling speakers. Then follow up after an appropriate interval to see if you can be added to the program.

RECIPE:
Making Connections by Writing and Publishing

As with public speaking, writing and publishing articles can help you become better known in your industry and open doors to land you more interviews. A published article on a subject of interest to others in your industry will get the attention of hiring managers, demonstrate your expertise, and increase your name recognition. Once your article is published you can use it as a job search tool in a wide variety of ways.

GETTING MILEAGE FROM ARTICLES YOU'VE PUBLISHED

- Include copies of the article when you apply to a company or request an informational interview
- Send copies to your networking contacts and ask if they know anyone else who would like to read it
- Enclose a copy in your follow-up letters
- Send a copy with a "nice-to-meet-you" note to people you meet at networking events
- Leave it behind after an interview

To begin getting your articles published you will need some **article-writing tools:** writing venues and a writing query. Appropriate writing venues are the publications that people in your target industry read. Consider newsletters (print or e-mail), magazines, trade journals, newspapers, and web sites. What publications have you read to stay current in your field? Ask your industry contacts what they subscribe to or regularly read. Notice which periodicals are sitting on their desks and poking out of their briefcases. You can also look up possible venues in directories of periodicals, such as Writer's Market®.

If you are new to getting articles published, start with small publications that require little writing experience. Association newsletters can be an excellent initial target. Other possibilities are employee newsletters for companies where you would like to work, web sites or promotional newsletters that serve your industry, or community newspapers.

When you have a venue in mind, the next step is to check the submission guidelines. Some publications will allow you to submit a completed article while others prefer you to send a query letter. If you're uncertain, contact the appropriate editor and ask. Most print publications list the names of editors and the area each one covers in a box near the table of contents inside the front cover, or for newspapers, in the editorial section.

Speaking Launched His Career Into a New Orbit

I wanted to make a career change from being a NASA research scientist to a public contact position in which I could educate people about the space program. I really wanted to break into public speaking. Yet although I have spent my life in the field and am eminently qualified to talk on that subject, I had no formal public-speaking experience. I didn't know the business world of speaking and there certainly weren't any want ads for public speakers about the space program.

So the first thing I did was read some books on the business of speaking and I found a recurring theme. If you want to be a professional speaker, the first thing you have to do is start giving a lot of speeches—even if they are for free! This seemed simple enough so I decided to do it. I set a goal of giving one speech a month. It took a while to get the hang of cold calling and marketing, but it worked. I also joined the National Speakers Association to start mingling with professional speakers. And I told NASA every time I gave a talk just to let them know I was "helping them out." Eventually a public outreach position came open at NASA and they turned to me. I am now one of the leads for public outreach for NASA's research organization.

So when people ask me how to get a job they really want, I tell them to do what I did. First just do it and make sure people in positions to hire you know you are doing it. Send them an e-mail to say, "I just wanted to let you know I'm giving a talk (or whatever it is you do) next week that you might be interested in hearing about." The key is to have your name and accomplishments come to their attention often enough to get them familiar with who you are and what you do. It's more important to do it and let others know about it than to get paid for it at first. The money will come if you persist. Just get out and show your stuff, and eventually someone will say, "We really need that person on our team. Hire him now!"

Bill Carswell
HUNTSVILLE, ALABAMA

When you contact the appropriate editor be prepared to pitch your article idea. Describe your proposed topic, explain why it is of interest to readers, and tell why you should be the one who writes it. Some publications will give you the assignment based on an informal query by phone or e-mail. Others will ask you to send a formal query letter and include some writing samples.

When a query is requested, don't try to skip a step by sending a completed article and hoping they will print it. The editor won't even look at it, and you will have wasted a great deal of time.

A query letter should begin with a strong lead paragraph written just as though it were the opening paragraph of the actual article. (See the "Writing query" example below.) You want it to capture the editor's interest, introduce your topic, and show that you can write. Continue the letter by describing several key points you intend to make in the article. You can then propose the article itself: "I would like to write a 1,500-word article on . . ."

Conclude the letter with a brief description of your background that indicates why you are qualified to write the article. If you have previously been published, send along two or three sample articles with your letter or include the URLs if published on the Internet. Be sure to send a self-addressed stamped enve-

Writing query

Kristy Bianchi
Moms at Work Magazine
1234 Edison Avenue
Boston, MA 02100
Re: Article query—"Can't You See I'm Working?"

Dear Ms. Bianchi,

For many working mothers, telecommuting or a home business may seem like the answer to their prayers. They want to have more time with their kids and greater flexibility so they install a second phone line, set up a computer in the dining room, and take the leap.

However, the first thing they discover is that working from home includes many unexpected distractions. Children, neighbors, and even the family dog all come and go. The result is loud noises, requests for mom's help, or interruptions for just a quick question—always just long enough to break the working mom's concentration.

The way out of this dilemma is to set clear boundaries on space, time, and responsibilities:

- Establish and enforce firm working hours in the household
- Create a work space that affords privacy
- Evaluate when additional child care makes economic sense
- Communicate with children about new boundaries
- Get help from the spouse or partner and the kids with housework and errands
- Hold your boundaries when they get tested

I would like to write a 1,000-word article, titled "Can't You See I'm Working?" for Moms at Work. This article will describe how work-at-home moms can create enough peace and quiet to get their jobs done.

I am the director of the Happy Days Child Care Center and I hold a degree in early childhood education. For five years I have helped parents find a balance between work responsibilities and quality time with their children. I have written several articles for Pacific Parenting. Reprints of two recent articles are enclosed.

If you are interested in this article, please contact me at shelley@gethirednow.com or (617) 555-1234.

Regards,
Shelley Henning

lope if you are querying by postal mail. Most publications now accept e-mail submissions.

Follow up after thirty days if you have not received a response. Unless you are submitting to a publication that accepts previously published articles, you shouldn't send the same query or article to another editor until you are sure the first publication has declined it.

HINT:
A Word about Resistance

Most of our suggestions regarding how to get interviews involve truly putting yourself out there. This may mean doing some things that feel uncomfortable and strange. Calling people you have never met and asking them to meet with you may cause a cold sweat. The thought of improving your personal selling skills in order to get an interview may make you feel like you need to become a used-car salesman. You may find yourself resisting the idea of calling strangers on the phone, following up on applications, or asking acquaintances to help further your job search.

It's completely normal to feel a bit scared about selling yourself. You have no idea how your approach is going to be received, and if your contacts refuse to speak with you or aren't interested, it's difficult not to take it personally. You may not even realize you are afraid, but somehow, mysteriously, a phone number you urgently need to call will sit on your desk day after day and you just won't get around to picking up the phone.

Try asking yourself, "What is the worst thing that could possibly happen if I made that call?" Would it be hearing someone say, "Don't bother me" or "We're not interested"? Or would it be worse if the person is interested in you and you become tongue-tied and blow it? The thing is, you will most certainly lose the opportunity if you don't place the call, so how bad could making the call truly be?

The fact is that most people are polite in their refusals. They say, "Sorry I can't help you," and then hang up. And when someone is interested in what you have to say, the conversation gets easy rather quickly.

So what do you think—can you pick up the phone? You'll never know what you are missing out on unless you try.

CHAPTER 11

Landing the Job:

When You're Getting Interviews
But No Job Offers

Try not; do. There is no try.
— YODA, JEDI MASTER

The Final Frontier

To make your way to this final stage of the Job Search Pyramid, you've already done a lot of things quite well. You've defined the job you want, identified good opportunities, gotten up the nerve to contact potential employers, and convinced them to interview you. Getting stuck at this point, after investing a great deal of time and effort, can be extremely frustrating.

Understand first that you won't get a job offer from every interview, no matter how well you present yourself. You may have a screening interview with human resources and never get to see the hiring manager. Or you may be called for a second interview, meet with several managers and co-workers, think you have a lock on the job, and then they choose someone else. The vast majority of reasons that an interviewer or hiring manager may turn you down are completely out of your control. If you are well connected, well prepared, and have excellent qualifications, you may only need to interview with two or three companies to get an offer. However, if you're a recent college graduate, a career changer, or looking for work in a highly competitive area, you may need ten to fifteen interviews or more—even if you do everything the right way.

A company may decide against making you an offer because of an inside candidate, specific experience someone else offers, bias on the interviewer's part, or the availability of less expensive workers. All of these are factors you can't control. What you are able to control is how you present and sell yourself. Some suggestions for improvement in these areas follow. First we'll look at your performance in the interview itself, and then move on to specific techniques you can use to better position yourself and improve your credibility.

In reading this chapter, keep in mind that you may have several interviews with any one company for the same job. Our advice for turning these interviews into job offers applies to each level of interview whether with human resources, a hiring manager, or other members of the company who influence who gets hired.

Ingredients for Landing the Job

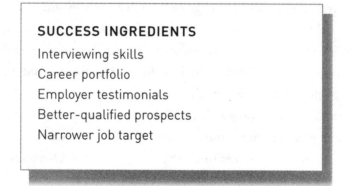

SUCCESS INGREDIENTS
Interviewing skills
Career portfolio
Employer testimonials
Better-qualified prospects
Narrower job target

INGREDIENT:
Interviewing Skills

The interview is the place where you demonstrate your ability to do the job. It can be a nerve-racking experience to have to talk about your skills and experience in this type of setting. If you find yourself getting too nervous in interviews, or don't like the answers you hear yourself giving, you need to spend some time beefing up your **interviewing skills**. To determine where you need to focus your efforts, review the six phases of a typical interview below. For instance, you may not have a problem answering tough questions, but when it comes time for you to ask questions of the interviewer, you freeze up.

While you will encounter most of these phases in a typical interview, they may not occur in this exact order. These six phases apply to an interview with anyone involved in the hiring process. This includes recruiters, employment agency staff, human resources staff, and anyone else with whom you interview before or after the hiring manager.

PHASES OF A TYPICAL INTERVIEW

1. *Getting acquainted.* You'll begin with a handshake, exchange brief introductions, and engage in some small talk. It's safe to talk about something you have in common, such as who brought you together or something you recently read about the company. Even here, the interviewer is already sizing you up. From the first moment, the interviewer will be asking, "Is this the right kind of person for my team?" Take extra care to present yourself in the best possible light at the outset. The interviewer's first impression of you may determine the outcome of the interview process.

2. *Career experience.* The interviewer will often begin by saying, "So tell me a little about yourself." The most effective response is to sell your qualifications to the interviewer by briefly describing your skills, experience, accomplishments, and positive qualities. Express your interest in working for the company and how you can make a significant contribution. Try to make a connection between a challenge or opportunity you believe the company is facing and your relevant skills (see Chapters 7 and 8 for help with describing your skills).

3. *About the company and the position.* The interviewer will give you a synopsis of the company and the position for which you are interviewing. Listen for validation of information you gathered beforehand as well as any new data. Let the interviewer do most of the talking here. Remember that one of the characteristics of a great salesperson is good listening. (See Chapter 10 for more about selling yourself.) While the interviewer is

Learned the Hard Way

When I was a young man my whole job search experience was about fear, frustration, and rejection. I believe I made every mistake in the book. In fact, that was part of the problem. I was willful and stubborn; I never consulted any books or advice columns; I never asked family or friends for input or help. In fact, I became resentful when they offered advice. Let me review my "how-not-to" list of time and energy wasters.

I quit my job and moved back to Philadelphia where I grew up. I never thought it would be a problem finding work. I relied exclusively on newspaper want ads. I would spend a couple of hours with the Sunday paper, circling all the jobs that seemed possible. There were few listings relevant to my background, so I threw my net wider and wider. I started mailing résumés and cover letters to any and all listings that looked even the least bit appropriate.

My father, bless him, kept imploring me, "Just take anything—flip burgers, drive a cab, just to get started." But I was proud and wouldn't deem to stoop to such labors. In time, my money began to run out, and after sending hundreds and hundreds of résumés to employers I had a grand total of two interviews. On both those occasions, I was so desperate to land the job, and I put so much of my hopes into the interview, that I didn't present myself as the qualified, personable man I knew I was . . . and basically blew it both times.

Reflecting in later years, I see now that the interviewer could sense—or maybe even plainly see—my desperation and need. This is fatal to your chances of getting hired. The longer my search took, the more depressed I became, and hence, the less attractive I became as a candidate. Trust me, it shows; no matter what kind of mask you put on.

David Herninko
SAN FRANCISCO, CALIFORNIA

describing the job, the company, and the culture, listen carefully and take notes. You will get clues from the interviewer as to what they are looking for and the type of person that will fit in at this company. These clues will help you answer questions appropriately in the next phase of the interview.

4. *Questions from the interviewer.* This is the meat and potatoes of the interview. It's your chance to convince the interviewer that you have what it takes to do the job. The key to success is being prepared. Before the interview, go over the research you did on the company. Review what you've learned about current challenges in the industry, specific issues at the company, and opportunities for growth.

The questions you get will vary from interview to interview. Typical interview questions fall into one of these four categories:

- *Generic.* Questions asked in most interviews. Popular examples are "Where do you want to be in five years?" and "What are your strengths?"

- *Situational.* Questions posing real-world challenges you might face on the job and how you would deal with them. "How would you handle a project with a tight deadline?" is a good example.

- *Technical.* Questions that uncover your qualifications and experience in specific areas needed for the job. For example, "Tell me about the training you've had in accounting."

- *Experiential.* These questions are about the jobs you've held and your specific responsibilities. A sample question might be, "Describe your job as a project manager at ABC Company."

Be prepared for any of these types of questions. Use your career success stories, as described below, to help you answer these questions.

5. *Questions from you.* Prepare in advance a list of specific questions that will help you find out more about the job, the company, and your future there. Add to these any questions that come up for you during the interview. Remember that the questions you ask are also part of the interview.

The interviewer will be listening for how informed and prepared you are and whether you are carefully evaluating this opportunity or just desperate for a job.

Ask for clarification about the duties of the job, what will be expected of you, the future of the company, what it is like to work there, and where this job might lead you. This is an excellent opportunity to engage in a two-way dialogue with the interviewer. When you ask discerning questions, you find the interview becomes more of a discussion and less of an interrogation. You will learn more and also have more of a chance to show the interviewer who you are.

6. **Next steps.** The interview should conclude with agreement about the next steps in the interview process. If the interviewer doesn't tell you, ask who will be making the decision, if additional interviews will be required, whether other candidates are being considered, and when you should expect to hear from the company. Never leave an interview unless you know what will happen next.

ANSWERING INTERVIEW QUESTIONS

Succeeding at an interview is often more of an art than a science. While your experience, education, and other qualifications play a significant role in the hiring decision, it is still very much based on the personal opinion of the interviewer. He or she will be making a decision about whether to hire you based not only on your qualifications but also on whether your personality will fit in at their company. Often their instinct decides who will get the job offer.

We don't suggest you try to obtain a personality transplant in order to succeed in an interview. If you really won't fit in at a particular company, you don't want to work there. But what you are able to do is be personable and professional. Smile, look the interviewer in the eye, and engage in a two-way conversation. Listen carefully, respond thoughtfully, and don't digress into personal details.

Interviewers need to be convinced that you will be able to fix their problems and help their company achieve its goals. One of the best ways to answer interview questions is to use your career success stories (see Chapter 9 for a complete description). For each question, relate it to a similar situation earlier in your career, talk briefly about how you handled it, and highlight the results. These stories demonstrate to the interviewer that you have specific experience in dealing with similar situations.

For example, let's say you were asked in an interview, "How do you deal with high-pressure situations?"

You could simply answer:

"I'm very good when faced with high-pressure situations. I dealt with them all the time at my last job."

However, this response doesn't do much to convince the interviewer of your abilities. Use a career success story instead:

"I'll give you an example. I was leading a team of national account sales reps and it was the fourth quarter of the year. We were in the running to be the top sales team in the country in our organization. Prior to the fourth quarter, we hadn't even made the top ten. Our sales were good, but we wanted to finish the year as number one.

"I organized and led a sales planning retreat to have my team accomplish three things: First we identified each of our prospects and determined exactly what we could close before the end of the quarter. Second I had each rep—with the assistance of their support team—lay out a tactical plan for winning that business prior to the year's end. Third I asked each rep to make a specific sales commitment with support from their team.

"The bottom line was that we not only surpassed our overall sales plan, we blew away the competition. Every sales rep hit their goal, some topping it by seventy-five to 100 percent. As a result, our sales team production exceeded 250 percent of the target and we were recognized as the top team in the nation. As our award, my team joined the company's top executives on a five-day trip to Paris."

Working with a job search buddy or career coach is a great way to get used

Didn't Know It Was a Job Interview

As my college career was coming to an end, I needed to make some decisions fast. I was three months from graduating with two majors that I had already decided I was not going to use. Spending my last quarter break selling children's books door-to-door turned out to be one of the best choices I could have made.

I was knocking on doors in a neighborhood where my target market of families with children was extremely scarce. After five hours of getting nowhere, I came to a house with multi-colored play objects in the yard. Excitedly I knocked on the door. A woman answered with a newborn in arms and kids running all over the place. Eagerly I showed my products but with no success.

During my presentation, a neighbor with three kids had stopped by so I next went to her house and knocked. Nobody answered. Knowing they were home, I knocked again. Still no one answered, but the man of the house let the dogs in from the back yard. The dogs were barking at the window and leaping at the door like they wanted to eat me. Knowing I never wanted to come to this neighborhood again, I knocked once more, harder and louder so I would never have to come back and follow up.

Finally, a big burly guy swung the door open and shouted, "What do you want?" Knowing at this point I was probably not going to get the sale, I replied only, "It's me, Dave!" He responded, "What religion are you selling?" Dressed like a struggling college student, but remaining calm, I replied, "What—did my shoes give it away?" I got the guy to laugh and relax. Yet Jeff, the vice president of sales for an exponentially growing building company, was definitely not buying. I gave him my best smile and was on my way.

Farther down the street, I was giving yet another presentation to a woman on her porch when a car drove by very slowly and stopped. The woman and I looked at each other with confusion as Jeff walked toward us. He extended his hand with a business card and said, "Give me a call, I want you to come work for me."

A few days later they hired me. I got a job out of a job, and I couldn't be happier. A month ago, I moved from Denver to Allentown. I am in a growing position that will lead me to having my own West Coast branch.

I owe it to persistence, the ability to remain calm even when greeted with hostility, and being able to turn a potentially negative situation into something rewarding.

David Lawrence
ALLENTOWN, PENNSYLVANIA

to answering interview questions with stories. Compile a list of common and not-so-common questions for your buddy or coach and ask this person to play the role of the hiring manager in an interview. Ask your helper to critique your responses. Were you convincing? Did your stories communicate your best qualities and relevant experience?

You may also want to take a workshop, join a job club, or learn more about interviewing from books or audio programs.

DEALING WITH THE SALARY QUESTION

One of the most difficult moments in an interview can occur when you are asked about your salary requirements. The correct answer to this question can be tricky because you could either name a figure too high and end your chances for the job or come in too low and reduce the amount you are eventually offered. With some positions, the available salary range will often be published, which makes your job quite a bit easier.

Before you answer the salary question, make sure you understand the performance expectations for the job. Ask the interviewer about the specific goals of the position; for example, "I'd like to know more about the performance expectations for the position. What are the specific accomplishments you would like to see during the first year?"

Listen carefully to what the interviewer reveals. You may hear requirements about sales quotas, projects to be completed, cases to be handled, or employees to be supervised. As you're listening, take note of how challenging the goals are and formulate a range of what you think the position is worth. Your research on the industry up to this point should help you to make an intelligent guess at what the salary range for this position should be.

Rather than giving the interviewer an exact salary figure, respond with something like, "Based on what you've told me about the job responsibilities and your performance expectations, I see the salary range between $75,000 and $80,000." If you truly have no idea what the position should pay, a safe answer is often to quote a range ten to fifteen percent higher than your last salary. Many companies will not make you an offer higher than that anyway, if they have an idea what you were previously earning.

When you are changing careers and are willing to accept a salary lower than what you were previously earning, it's appropriate to say so. For example, "I understand it may not be possible for you to match my previous salary. I was hoping for a salary in the range of $45,000 to $50,000."

INGREDIENT:
Career Portfolio

Your career accomplishments and expertise are intangible; they can't be seen and touched like a product on a shelf. Consider supporting your career achievements with some visual aids that demonstrate your skills. A **career portfolio** might include samples of your writing, reports you have prepared, project schedules, program outlines, or action photos of you at work. Going through your portfolio with an interviewer, or flipping to a certain page as questions arise, can visibly demonstrate your expertise.

IDEAS FOR YOUR CAREER PORTFOLIO

- Accounting professional—financial reports you produced
- Classroom trainer—photos of you presenting to an attentive audience
- Communications specialist—articles, newsletters, or booklets you wrote
- IT professional—specifications for a system you designed
- Marketing specialist—marketing collateral you produced or a campaign plan you wrote
- Paralegal—index of the research you did for a complex case
- Project manager—project plans you created
- Sales representative—charts of your sales production
- Technical writer—reports or manuals you wrote
- Web designer—screen shots of sites you designed

In addition to helping you present yourself powerfully in interviews, you can use your career portfolio when following up. You can send an excerpt from your portfolio along with your closing letter (discussed later in this chapter).

INGREDIENT:
Employer Testimonials

When you need to hire someone to paint your house or fix your car, you probably ask your friends or family to recommend someone. They will often tell you a story about the good service they received from the person they are recommending. These short stories about their positive experience are testimonials, and they can convince you the person you are considering will do a good job.

You can use this same idea to convince a hiring manager to make you an offer by providing **employer testimonials**.

Employer testimonials are powerful statements written by your former managers or supervisors acknowledging your outstanding work. Instead of a simple reference, which often confirms only your job title and dates of employment, a testimonial brings your work experience to life. (See "Employer testimonial" example on the next page. Notice how it draws a word picture of the capabilities of the person it describes.)

You may already have commendation letters or references you can use for this purpose. If not, identify three or four of your former managers, supervisors, co-workers, customers, professional association colleagues, or people you have worked with as a volunteer. Ask them to write a brief letter about their experience of your work in the style of a testimonial. Give them some examples of how you would like to see it written. You can use these letters as standalones or compile excerpts into a one-page document called, "What Colleagues Say About Me."

INGREDIENT:
Better-Qualified Prospects

It's not always the employer who decides that you're not a good fit for a position. You may be so excited to get an interview that you don't ask enough questions about the job beforehand. During the interview you may realize that the job is not for you. Or perhaps you did some research and on the surface the job looked like a good fit. Yet when you learned more details at the interview, you discovered that the level of responsibility was not what you pictured, the salary range was wrong, or the company culture turned you off. To reduce the number of times this happens to you, you need **better-qualified prospects**.

Some of these situations will be difficult to avoid. However, if you begin to see a pattern of mismatched job opportunities, review the foundation you built

Employer testimonial

Beth Hand, MBA
Hand Associates
3686 King Street, Suite 118
Alexandria, VA 22302

Dear Beth,

We have accomplished so much the past year and a half. Our division is on its way to being a leader in IT investments and acquisitions within the agency and with other agencies. Over one billion dollars a year in services and products is sizable for a division, however, the real measure is in the value we provide our customers and our commitment to increasing that value. You were a key player in this progress by tapping into and drawing out the potential in me in my role as executive director, and in the deputy director. You have collaborated with us as coach, adviser, and friend. I am a better leader for the strategic perspectives you offered, your ability to deliver hard, honest messages with compassion, and your ability to care deeply about what you believe.

I want to thank you too for holding the vision of what our organization could be. You identified the need for strategic planning and the need for the senior leaders to develop strategic thinking skills where goals, measures, and feedback are part of "business as usual." You initiated and followed through on the process that is moving us more quickly than any other actions we could have taken toward fulfilling the vision of who we want to be and how we want to serve our customers.

You and I have spoken often about the challenges in hierarchical, complex organizations and the challenges that accompany senior leadership positions like mine: the political winds, the power plays, and the hidden agendas that everyone seems to have. Throughout this, I always knew that your agenda for me was to be the best, and it inspired and supported me in working toward that goal. Please know how invaluable you have been to us, and especially to me.

John H. Ely
Director, Office of Technical Contract Management
Internal Revenue Service

at the beginning of your search. You may find that you have lost track of your definition of the job you want or strayed far afield from the target companies you originally had in mind. Or perhaps someone in your network referred a job opportunity to you that was off base, and you need to remind your contacts what you are seeking. You may have forgotten that the best opportunities always come from referrals, and began applying for jobs you found in the paper or on the Internet about which you know very little.

Each time you are offered an interview, ask yourself these three questions before you accept:

1. Is this position a good match for my ideal job description?
2. Does what I know about the industry and company make me want to work there?
3. Do I have any personal connections to the people involved in making a decision?

These questions will help you determine what additional work you may need to do in order to assess how suitable the opportunity is. If you choose to go on an interview for a position you haven't investigated, keep in mind that your chances of being hired will be reduced. When you accept an interview for a position that's not what you said you wanted, it may turn out to be a waste of your time.

INGREDIENT:
Narrower Job Target

A roadblock you may be putting in your own way is not getting specific enough about the job that you are seeking. When a hiring manager asks exactly how you can help the company, it can kill your chances when you answer, "I can do pretty much anything. What are you looking for?" It may be absolutely true that you have a broad range of talents, but few hiring managers are looking for a "Jack (or Jill) of all trades." They hire people with particular skills in a specific area that benefits them.

A **narrower job target** will allow hiring managers to grasp exactly what you have to offer and whether they need you in their organization. For example, if a hiring manager identifies you as an expert in e-mail marketing campaigns for the health care industry, rather than just a marketing specialist, you'll be able to convince them you are the best candidate for a job that requires that exact expertise.

Don't stop yourself from getting specific about what you want because you are worried you will limit your options. If you don't target a particular type of job to begin with, you may not have any options at all. Hiring managers and human resources departments will screen you in or out during the interview process based on how well you can meet a specific need. If they perceive you as someone who will take any job that's available, you may not be considered as a serious candidate.

Be prepared to discuss not only the type of job you are currently seeking and your corresponding qualifications, but also your longer-term career goals. Employers want to hire people who they believe will stay in a position because it has a future. When you get specific about the career path you envision for yourself, you can convince an interviewer of your potential as a long-term employee.

HINT:
What If You Are Getting Desperate?

Throughout this book, our suggested methodology has been to first decide what type of job you want and then to systematically set about finding that specific job. Yet we do understand that you may not be able to hold out for your ideal job forever. You may be unemployed and running low on money or urgently need to make a change for other reasons.

If that's the case, we still recommend that you not throw our system out the window and start applying for any job you see. In an ever-more specialized world, changing your job target to "I'll take anything" can actually make your job search

Get a Referral—Get Hired

In the telecommunications industry, networking was always the ideal way to find a job. The industry was large and diverse, but it was rather a small world with regard to people knowing each other's background and experience.

I found both of the last two jobs I had in that industry by networking with my existing contacts. The first job was with a division of a major telecommunications company as the director of sales operations. I first learned of the opportunity from the local newspaper. Then I contacted a former co-worker who worked in that division and asked for a personal referral to the hiring vice president. I was hired a week later.

Several years later the division was downsized. After networking with my contacts, I learned of an open position at another leading telecom company and I asked a co-worker to refer me. It worked again . . . and a week later I was hired.

Greg Bassett
AURORA, COLORADO

more difficult instead of less. It will be much more challenging to position yourself as a satisfactory candidate, and therefore handicap you in applying for unadvertised jobs. You may find yourself relying on Internet job postings and the want ads to locate open positions, which is definitely not the path to help you more quickly find a job.

Instead of abandoning your ideal job description completely, broaden your range of possibilities but stick to one industry or job field. If you have been looking for a position as a payroll manager, begin to consider other positions in accounting. If your ideal job is working as a program director for a nonprofit, look at other possibilities in the nonprofit sector.

By staying focused on a selected industry you will still be able to take advantage of the network you have been building to seek out opportunities in the hidden job market.

APPROACH:
Contacting Potential Employers

SUCCESS INGREDIENTS
- Model closing letter
- Detailed job proposal
- Negotiating skills

RECIPE:
Following Up and Closing the Deal

You can use the time immediately after your interview to considerably increase your chances of getting a job offer. Ask if you can meet with other managers, staff, and departments you would be interacting with on the job. Start to build relationships with people who may become your co-workers and get their perspective on the company, the job, and the hiring manager. Use your research skills to dig up more information about the company's clients, vendors, and strategic partners. See if there is anyone in that group who might put in a good word for you.

If you know which professional associations employees belong to, attend one of their events and look for new contacts who can help you get on the inside track for the job. This is also a great time to call any of your contacts who helped you get the interview. Bring them up to date on where you are in pursuing the opportunity and ask for any assistance they can offer.

Sometimes you may have questions that come up after the interview is over. Don't hesitate to call your interviewer to express gratitude for the opportunity, to share your excitement in becoming part of the team, and to ask any follow-up questions. You can often create an even stronger bond with a hiring manager through this brief contact.

A great salesperson closes the deal by summarizing the benefits of the product and asking for the business. This is the approach you should take to turn your interviews into offers. After you have completed an interview, you should continue the process of convincing the interviewer that you are the best candidate for the job. A **model closing letter** (see example on pages 288–289) will give you a template from which you can draw to send a customized follow-up letter each time you have an interview.

This letter is your chance to step ahead of your competition. Interviewers need to feel confident in their decisions to hire or call people back for second interviews. They may have narrowed the field to two or three candidates for the position, all of whom have equal qualifications. The tough part for them is to single out which person will be the best fit for the job and the company. Your closing letter can give the interviewer the necessary evidence to recognize that you are the best person for the job.

Your closing letter should have three sections:

1. An introductory paragraph thanking the interviewer for the opportunity to discuss the position and re-emphasizing your interest in it.
2. A brief summary of each key point discussed during your interview. For each point, state how your expertise meets the company's specific need.
3. A powerful closing statement that expresses why you are the right person for the job.

Your closing letter should be sent within a day of your interview to sustain the momentum you created in the meeting. Don't be afraid to let your excitement shine through in this letter. If you want this job enough, make your desire known to the person who has the power to hire you.

RECIPE:
When a Letter Isn't Enough

In Chapter 9, we suggested you might use a job proposal when applying to employers. A proposal goes beyond a cover letter by suggesting specific ways in which you can solve problems or achieve goals for the company to which you're applying. Once you have interviewed with the company and know a great deal more about what their needs are, you can create a **detailed job proposal** to close the deal.

Use a detailed job proposal as a unique follow-up tool, ideally sent the day after an interview. Tell the interviewer how you already see yourself working for the company in a capacity that brings considerable value. If a hiring manager can visualize you working with the existing team, your chances of getting a job offer increase dramatically.

During your interviews listen for specific clues that reveal unmet needs. You may hear hints that the interviewer is looking for someone to handle responsibilities not listed in the job description. Or perhaps you may suspect that the company is missing out on a significant opportunity. In your detailed job pro-

Model closing letter

Sharon Adriano, Group Account Director
National Agency
Sunset, NV 98000

Dear Sharon,

As you prepare to select your new account supervisor, I thought it would be helpful to summarize the needs of National Agency and describe how my experience and skills can benefit the company and its major account clients. I also want to restate my strong interest in joining your team and contributing to the success of the company.

Establish strong relationships with (and gain trust of) key contacts at major accounts

- One of my strengths is establishing, maintaining, and growing solid working relationships with key players at all levels within organizations.
- I currently work remotely with diverse teams across North America and always treat them as my own clients.

Maintain and grow the major account client business

- No matter what the project or assignment, I always think creatively to find ways to help clients succeed and grow their own businesses.
- I'm a real stickler for details and believe in immersing myself in the client's business so that I have a thorough understanding of all aspects.
- My industry knowledge and experience would be an asset to understanding your major account clients' needs and would help grow National Agency's relationship with them.

Help secure new business for National

- I am well connected to the local high-tech and marketing communities with strong ties to the most prominent professional and trade associations in the region.
- I enjoy participating in sales and business functions, including giving presentations and promoting the organization for which I work.

Here are a few of the noteworthy attributes I bring with me for this post:

Strategic experience and orientation

Strategic marketing and communications planning is one of my strong suits. I have developed, executed, and measured numerous plans for organizations both large and small, including meticulous research, analysis, and competitive intelligence.

Previous agency experience

I have worked for an agency similar in size to National. I bring with me thorough knowledge and experience in how an agency works, the creative process, and how the account and creative teams work together. I've worked with and managed numerous agency relationships on the client side.

I also have a strong desire to return to an agency role. I am both excited and energized at the prospect of this position and working with your national accounts.

I'll close by letting you know that I bring great initiative and enthusiasm with me. I have a true passion for what I do and it would be a privilege to bring that to National Agency. Thank you again for your consideration for this position, and I look forward to our next meeting.

Regards,
Steve Charles

Owned the Job Before She Got It

My husband was laid off when our second baby was a year old, and I needed to get a job fast. I knew how to type so after a series of depressing interviews for jobs I didn't want and didn't get, I applied for a personal assistant position for an arts entrepreneur.

Bennie's business was buying up old unloved factories and turning them into communities of small units for creative people, often regenerating the area in the process. I loved the concept and was determined that I would work for this man.

Between the first and second interviews, I visited all of the sites I could get to. I sat in the cafés drinking coffee and trying the food, looked around, and spoke to the staff as if I was a potential customer. Then I wrote a report for him, giving him my impressions and constructive feedback on what worked well and what could be improved. When I tried to fax it to him, he was on holiday at a hotel in Scotland so I found the fax number and sent all five pages. I included a letter telling him how much I had enjoyed meeting him, and that I hoped I would make the cut for the second interview the following Thursday.

On Wednesday, I came back from my own holiday confident that I would have a letter inviting me to the interview. There was no letter. Worried that they had tried to call my mobile phone and not succeeded, I called him.

"Glad you've called, Nicola. I have to say that you would make a terrible assistant, particularly working for me," he said. My heart sank with an audible thud. "No, you're management material. Haven't got a vacancy for you, but come in on Monday morning at nine-thirty and I'll have thought of something for you to do, and we can talk money."

> Working for Bennie, I went on to my highest earnings ever, plus performance-related bonuses, and a great deal of personal and professional growth. It was a turning point in my life.
>
> Bennie once said, "Ninety-five percent of people are born employees, nine-to-five types. The biggest challenge for any businessperson is to find employees who act as if they own their job. I always look to employ 'failed' entrepreneurs between businesses because although you only keep them a couple of years, you get ten years worth out of them before they move on."
>
> *Nicola Cairncross*
> WORTHING, WEST SUSSEX, UNITED KINGDOM

posal you can address these needs, opportunities, or additional responsibilities, and then position yourself as both the perfect candidate for the job and a valuable asset for the company.

Let's say you are interviewing for a customer service manager position. The job calls for the candidate to manage a team of ten to fifteen telephone customer-service representatives fielding incoming calls. During the interviews you heard concerns about employee performance in handling customer problems. On average, it took three incoming calls to satisfactorily resolve each problem.

Armed with that knowledge, your detailed job proposal explains to the hiring manager that you have a system for teaching customer service representatives how to handle most customer issues in a single call. You propose to teach this to not only your team, but also every team in the call center, as well as create a job aid that will assist other managers in reinforcing the system. You could add to the impact of your proposal by expressing the potential bottom-line benefits to the call center: "This training program could potentially increase the number of customer problems handled in one call from twenty-five to seventy-five percent. This would provide improved service levels to customers as well as create substantial savings for the company."

Proposing solutions to real problems allows the hiring manager to experience your talents prior to a job offer. This reduces the perceived risk in hiring you and sets you apart from the rest.

Review the guidelines for preparing a job proposal in Chapter 9. Use the same format for your detailed job proposal and insert the specific ideas you now have for the job.

RECIPE:
Negotiating a Job Offer

You may receive a job offer by phone, by postal mail, by e-mail, or at the conclusion of an interview. Before you jump into the arms of the first person willing to hire you, take a step back and evaluate what is being offered. Here are a few questions to consider:

- Is this the job I said I wanted and in the industry I chose?
- If not, can I be satisfied with this job for at least two years?
- Are the working conditions and company culture acceptable?
- On a scale of one to ten, how do I rate the total compensation package?
- Does the salary meet my personal goals?
- Do bonuses or other compensation make up for a lower-than-expected salary?
- Is the benefits package satisfactory?
- What are the advancement opportunities . . . and can I move up at a reasonable pace?

It's quite possible that you like the job, the company, and your future prospects, but the compensation you are being offered is lower than you expected. What

Negotiation Under Fire

One morning upon entering my workplace, my boss said she needed to speak with me in the office of the chief executive officer. It wasn't expected, but my intuition knew what was coming — a layoff. I loved the company I worked for and I couldn't believe what they were about to do.

Initially when the CEO explained it to me, I covered all bases to find out why. Was it my performance as a marketing professional or something else? The CEO assured me it wasn't my performance, just something the company needed to do and they were sorry to let me go.

Okay, so it wasn't my performance. Maybe there was something else I could do for the company. After a moment of quick thinking, I suggested an idea to the CEO. "How about a sales position," I asked. The CEO immediately said no. Desperately I tried to persuade him I could do it. I didn't go without a fight, but I went — directly to the human resources office to sign my final papers and collect my check. Tears swelled as I wondered, "What now?"

As I was signing the papers, the CEO came into the room with a big smile on his face and said, "You have a sales job." I was fired and hired within minutes.

I took the job proudly although I knew they were all making bets I wouldn't last. However, I held that job for six months as a top producer until I found another job elsewhere.

Kristine Kinzli
LAKEWOOD, COLORADO

do you do now? The company's offer is not the final word. You can still negotiate for a higher salary or overall compensation. Other elements of the offer may also be negotiable, including your benefits and job responsibilities.

Some people seem to be born with a natural ability to negotiate. For the rest of us it can be a difficult and scary proposition. The challenge of negotiating may provoke anxiety and discomfort. You may be thinking, "It took me weeks (or months) to get an offer so I'd better take what I can get," "If I try to negotiate, they might get upset with me and withdraw the offer," or "I don't know how to negotiate. Where do I start?"

If thoughts like these cross your mind, you need to work on your **negotiating skills**. One way to begin reducing negative feelings about negotiating is to review the information you've gathered to this point. Research, your network, and informational interviews can help you gain confidence in knowing what you can ask for when it's necessary to negotiate.

Compile all the information you've acquired and use it to make a counter offer. Your counter offer may ask for an increased salary as well as addressing other factors like benefits, bonuses, stock options, vacation, or specific job responsibilities. You can build a case for a higher salary by assuring the hiring manager that you can start the job with little or no training, offering to take on additional responsibilities, or promising to bring in new business. Reiterate the unique value you bring to the position and use that to justify your request.

In most cases you will want to respond to the offer in writing. Put your counter offer into a letter, thanking them for the job offer and explaining how excited you are to start working with them. (See the "Job offer negotiation letter" example on the next page.) If you decide to respond by phone, write down what you plan to say as a script to which you can refer.

If you still fear asking for more than what is being offered, practice negotiating with a job search buddy or coach. You'll find it gets easier each time. Remember, hiring managers like interviewees who have good answers to tough questions.

Job offer negotiation letter

Dear Mr. Chiu,

I'm thrilled to be your top candidate for the position of training manager. I'm very excited to begin working with you and making a contribution to Awakenings Coffee.

After reviewing the job offer in detail, I would like to explore negotiating the offered salary. I feel we are very close and could come to an agreement quickly. Based on my assessment of the position and your performance expectations, I believe the position is worth $75,000 as an annual salary.

I know I will exceed any and all performance expectations in the job. You will not have to be concerned with my coming up to speed quickly as I already know how to perform in this role. Additionally, my ideas for improvement that we discussed in our interviews will more than pay for this small increase in compensation.

Please consider my proposal as a win-win solution. You can count on me becoming one of your best employees and biggest advocates for the company's growth.

I look forward to you speaking with you about this in the next few days.

Best Regards,
Cynthia Hochman

HINT:
A Final Word

Looking for a job may itself be the most difficult job you'll ever have. You have to put yourself on the line every day. Climbing the Job Search Pyramid can be a humbling experience. This may be the first time in your life you have had to market yourself. Whether you chose to take this step or it was chosen for you, at first it can look as insurmountable as Mount Everest.

To be successful at your job search you must face your fears about asking for what you want. Look at this time in your life as a window of opportunity. It could very well be the chance of a lifetime to find the ideal job. If you start your job search off on the right foot, stay organized, and sustain a positive attitude even when things appear bleak, your persistence will pay off.

And never forget your most precious resource in finding the job you want—people.

Index

Other Titles from Bay Tree Publishing

Further information is available at www.baytreepublish.com
Bay Tree Publishing, 721 Creston Road, Berkeley, CA 94708

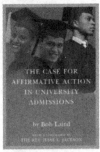

The Case for Affirmative Action in University Admissions
by Bob Laird

Written by the former Director of Admissions at the University of California, Berkeley, this book describes the critical role of affirmative action in creating diverse public institutions, recounts the turbulent debates regarding such programs, and explains the guidelines that will govern affirmative action policies in education in the immediate future.

$26.95 hardcover
ISBN: 0-9720021-4-6

Get Slightly Famous: Become a Celebrity in Your Field and Attract More Business with Less Effort
by Steven Van Yoder

Rooted in his experience as a public relations professional and freelance writer, Van Yoder shows how to tap the business secret everyone knows but few practice: it's easier to attract clients through your reputation than sell someone who has never heard of you.

$16.95 trade pbk,
ISBN: 0-9720021-1-1

Taking the War Out of Our Words: The Art of Powerful Non-Defensive Communication
by Sharon Ellison

Written by an award-winning speaker and internationally recognized consultant, this insightful and moving work provides practical techniques for breaking defensive habits, becoming more open, healing conflicts and building self-esteem.

$15.95 trade pbk,
ISBN: 0-9720021-0-3

Them and Us: Cult Thinking and the Terrorist Threat
by Arthur J. Deikman, M.D.
With a foreword by Doris Lessing

A clinical professor of psychiatry, Deikman makes the connection between classic cult manipulation and milder forms of group pressure that everyone has experienced. Deikman further shows how terrorist psychology represents an extreme along this familiar continuum. A foreword by novelist Doris Lessing discusses the implications of cult thinking for contemporary society.

$17.95 trade pbk,
ISBN: 0-9720021-2-X

C.J. Hayden is a Master Certified Coach and author of the bestselling *Get Clients Now!*™ (AMACOM). Since 1992, she has helped thousands of professionals achieve career success. A recognized leader in the coaching profession, Hayden has taught career skills for Mills College, Chevron, and Federal Express.

Frank Traditi is a career strategist and executive coach with more than 20 years of experience in management, sales, and marketing for Fortune 500 companies, including MCI, Inc. He has taught job search skills for Information Technology Institute, the Universities of Wyoming and Colorado, and the Colorado Department of Labor and Employment.